Meanings
of Work

SUNY Series in the Anthropology of Work
June C. Nash, Editor

Meanings of Work

Considerations for the Twenty-First Century

Edited by
Frederick C. Gamst

STATE UNIVERSITY OF NEW YORK PRESS

Published by
State University of New York Press, Albany

© 1995 State University of New York

All rights reserved

Printed in the United States of America

No part of this book may be used or reproduced
in any manner whatsoever without written permission
except in the case of brief quotations embodied in
critical articles and reviews.

For information, address State University of New York
Press, State University Plaza, Albany, N.Y., 12246

Production by E. Moore
Marketing by Dana E. Yanulavich

Library of Congress Cataloging-in-Publication Data

Meanings of work : considerations for the twenty-first century /
    edited by Frederick C. Gamst.
        p.   cm. — (SUNY series in the anthropology of work)
    Includes bibliographical references and indexes.
    ISBN 0-7914-2413-8. — ISBN 0-7914-2414-6 (pbk.)
    1. Industrial sociology.   2. Industrial relations.   3. Work.
    4. Twenty-first century.   I. Gamst, Frederick C.   II. Series.
HD6955.M38   1995
306.3′6—dc20   94-3370
                                                              CIP

10 9 8 7 6 5 4 3 2 1

For Michael W. Coy

Michael W. Coy, Jr., Anthropologist, A Dedication

This book concerning a theory of work is dedicated to the late Michael W. Coy, Jr., a leading anthropologist of the study of work and of Africa. Mike was my colleague and my collaborator in several projects of research. He discussed with me from its very inception the project "Meanings of Work," which led to this collection of essays. Professionally meeting his classes and other campus commitments to the very end, Mike died of cancer on 30 June, 1991.

Among the many accomplishments in the scholarship of Michael Coy, anthropologist of work, was his extending the craft of ethnological fieldwork into new experiences and perspectives. In so doing, Mike apprenticed himself to a Tugen blacksmith in Kenya. Some of the ideas and data from his several field studies in East Africa are found in his doctoral dissertation, "Social and Economic Relations of Kalenjin-speaking Blacksmiths in the Rift Valley, Kenya" (University of Pittsburgh, 1982); his "Tugen Monopoly: Capitalism and Conflict in the Mountains of Kenya," *Anthropology and Humanism Quarterly* vol. 13, no. 2, pp. 40-47. (1988); and his edited book on apprenticeship, *Apprenticeship: From Theory to Method and Back Again* (SUNY Press, 1989).

In the fall of 1990, Michael Coy, the Africanist anthropologist, organized and chaired a symposium on his campus, St. Mary's College of Maryland, a state school. "Africa . . . for Americans" was participated in by several score of eminent Africanists from sundry disciplines and attended by large, enthusiastic audiences across four, exciting, jam-packed weekends.

Michael Coy is missed and fondly remembered by his colleagues and students in the social sciences and humanities. The death at only thirty-eight years of age of this innovative, prolific scholar, inspiring teacher, and entirely humane person is not just a tragic blow to this family, colleagues, and the campus community he loved so much but also to the world of scholarship. As a living memorial to this scholar-teacher, any books suitable for a university library may be donated in the name of *Michael W. Coy, Jr., anthropologist*, to: The Librarian, Moi University, P. O. Box 3900, Eldoret, Kenya.

Contents

FREDERICK C. GAMST

Introduction

*I don't like work—no man does—but I like what is in work—
the chance to find yourself. Your own reality—for yourself,
not for others—what no man can ever know.*
　　　　　—Joseph Conrad, Heart of Darkness

*After primal man had discovered that it lay in his own
hands, literally, to improve his lot on earth by working,
it cannot have been a matter of indifference whether another
man worked.*
　　　　　　　　　　—Sigmund Freud,
　　　　　　　　Civilization and Its Discontents

　　　Work is so overarching in our daily lives that we tend not
to see or contemplate it. The ways in which we humans organize
our work guide individual fortune, interactions with other persons,
interconnections among groups, and structuring of the wider society.
As we shall see in my opening chapter for this book, *work* has one
of the broadest ranges of meanings of any word in English. Thus
work is diffuse not only in our social relations but in our language
as well.

　　　This collection of essays is a contribution to the ongoing
considerations of the meaning of work in sociocultural anthropology

(ethnology) and the cognate social sciences drawn on by this discipline.[1] The book integrates perspectives on work by ethnologists and sociologists, perspectives both stemming from their common intellectual traditions and overlapping and complementing one another in current scholarship. As will be made abundantly clear to the reader, the essays of the four sociological authors address ethological concerns of work in the manner of this discipline, and the papers of the five ethnologists deal with concerns of work central to the discipline of sociology. This collection, then, offers the reader a truly melded-disciplinary approach to the study of work. After profiting from the cross-disciplinary discussion of the subject of this book, the reader may well wonder why so many joint departments of anthropology and sociology were split apart over the past several decades.

Each of the authors in this book sees work as the central human concern and as what makes us human. All treat work as the central social activity of humans: performed by an individual with reference to and often in cooperation with others, usually for the use of others, and always with regard to collectively carried patterns of culture. Most of them see work in market economies as radically changing with profound consequences for each of us personally, our families, our communities, and our countries.

From the sibling perspectives of anthropology and sociology, *Meanings of Work: Considerations for the Twenty-First Century* examines interconnected social and cultural dimensions of human work including the economic and industrial relational. This collection provides a cross-disciplinary basis for understanding the fast changing patterns of work in a now globally unitary market, increasingly beset with frightening problems such as growth of contingent employment and decline of the Western middle class. In its concentration on considerations of work, the book includes specifically invited essays from Herbert Applebaum, Marietta L. Baba, Ivar Berg, Judith R. Blau, Amitai Etzioni, Walter Goldschmidt, June Nash, and Robert Weiss. Each of these authors have made noteworthy contributions either to the broad multidisciplinary field of industrial and organizational social science or to the still wider rubric of the social science of work.

In ten chapters, the authors of this book discuss the scope, utility, applications, and limitations of historical and contemporary ideas, analyses, and theories of the integration of societies through human work organizations, their occupational and related social statuses, and guiding ideologies. Meanings of work include a range of considerations: the development of ideas about work in Western cultures; work as career in tribal and peasant societies; postindustrialism, post-Fordism, and the crisis in world capitalism; the contingent character of the American middle class; the inequalities in the social relations of work; the constraints of the webs of bureaucratic rules concerning work; and the relations between work and technology in modern society. Included also are the issues of discontent and satisfaction generated by work; the cultural meanings and the myths of work; the exercise of power in work; the decision-making process of work as affected by emotions and values and limited by the ability to deliberate and process information; the social expectations of work and nonwork, including the distinguishing of work from leisure; and the reactions to and processes of retirement from work. In this introduction, themes are reviewed from the considerations of work presented by the chapter authors.

Although the book is published in the SUNY Series in the Anthropology of Work, the volume is intended for a wider market—across the social and managerial sciences, including industrial and human relations. This book treats work both cross-culturally and historically without losing sight of the fact that most college students in the United States and Canada desire to learn about the world of work in which they will spend most of their mature years: the best, and the worst, years of their lives.[2]

ESSAYS ON MEANINGS OF WORK

Considerations of Work

To frame the myriad conceptual strands of the nine following essays, my opening chapter considers a number of broad concerns about work, from how we think about it to pressing issues of contemporary employment or lack of it. The chapter ponders ideas and concepts of work, including linguistic and folk backgrounds. The personal, social, and temporal dimensions of work are considered. Then, a concept of work is constructed, applicable cross-culturally, yet still useful in investigating market-based societies, where most exchange occurs today.

Reviewed next are the central place of work in social scientific research and the long tradition of the community study in North America and its emphasis on work. Contemplated after this are issues of today's work such as employee participation in managerial control of work and the effect of values on the direction of technology.

Finally, the problematic future of work, including the frightening new labor market, is examined. In my opening chapter and in my later interrelated chapter on the web of rules for work relations, a large number of sources are used and cited and are suggestions for further reading on considerations of the meanings of work.

The Concept of Work in Western Thought

To begin, Herbert Applebaum provides this anthology with a historical perspective on the idea of work in Western thought. It is this body of thought that is the basis for social science as it is known today throughout the world. Such thought ranges from the broad conceptions including culture, society, personality, the place of humans in the animal kingdom, and the adaptation of humankind to the environment; to somewhat less broad constructs such as cultural materialism, role sets, normative systems, market exchange, open-system organizations, literary criticism, and social pluralism; to the theories and analyses of the narrower range that overflow from our journals, monographs, reports, and scholarly discourse.

Applebaum covers concepts and views concerning work in the classical world, in medieval Europe, and in the societies of modern Europe including its extension into North America. His analyses of ideas of work are grounded in the sociocultural anthropological perspective of holism, which holds that work is an activity found in all aspects of human life including the family, politics, economics, religion, and so forth. Applebaum reviews the notions from various periods espoused by thinkers who have had an enduring influence on current ideas of work. From Aristotle, to Calvin, to Adam Smith, to Marx, to Arendt, to Gorz, Applebaum examines the salient roots of the social science of work.

He concludes his essay with a discussion evaluating our contemporary changing values concerning work, leisure, and projections for work in the future. Reasons Applebaum, the human condition does compel us to work as a condition of life, and work creates our human-constructed environment. Given this historical framing of this collection of essays, what is "work" in our culture and where are our historically rooted ideas about it taking us? The following essays expand upon these queries.

Work As Career in Premodern Societies

In his essay, Walter Goldschmidt focuses on what careers mean to the character of tribal and agrarian societies. He develops an integrated theory of society and work. In this, the individual is viewed as a motivated actor and not as a passive recipient of central values and role prescriptions, written on his or her mental tabula rasa by the imprint of culture. Goldschmidt's theory treats as the central dynamic in the formulation of institutions the mental process within humans that arouses, maintains, and then directs behavior, that is, motivates, toward career goals. Although accepting cultural definitions, each person adapts to conventions in an individual way. Individual initiative and community restrains relate in a kind of dialectic, fostering change.

Goldschmidt concludes, in striving for careers, humans do not live for bread alone. Their underlying motivation is dual, in the form of both material rewards and social gratifications, including definition of the self. The natures of these rewards and satisfactions are shaped by culture as it operates and changes over time.

A person's pursuit of these two kinds of goals is viewed by Goldschmidt as a career. Because in traditional societies, performances of work tasks are similar, careers are related to the basic economy of production and other ecological circumstances. Careers are shaped by the work tasks required among humans for the necessities of life: provisioning, protection, and reproduction. Careers are thus formed by the kinds of work and collaboration for work needed by the community. Most work cannot be done as individual effort but requires some joint effort. Thus African pastoralists invariably have some kind of age-graded organization to institutionalize cooperation in herding and warfare. But, if the economy of production changes to horticulture, then the age grades become dysfunctional.

The Social Structure and Relations of Work

Ivar Berg examines a number of issues central to a theory of work. He uses as part of his theoretical base an idea he has helped develop, that of the "web of rules" for the social relations of work in any society, from preliterate to industrial. Berg delineates microscopic, messoscopic, and macroscopic structures of work and the social forces related to them.

The three central bodies of actors in the web of rules for work are managers, workers, and concerned government members. The rights and duties of these three actors regarding work are affected, directly and indirectly, by macroscopic forces, including societal and cultural impetuses such as national laws, national customs, and background norms. And the three are thus affected by microscopic forces, comprising the dynamics of organizations, formal and informal groups within these, cliques, and other collectivities. Between these two levels are the messoscopic forces, comprehending those generated by the division of labor in society, social strata, industries, communities, national unions, political parties, and regional labor markets, among other elements.

The utility of Berg's threefold division of interactions in the social structure of work is apparent when we consider the results of the scope of our customary research on work. We conduct microscopic-level studies from observation of work sites and from surveys of individuals in plants and of broad spectra of the actors of work. Studies of these kinds have results in the writings of the human relations school and the psychologically inclined, more recent offshoots of this body of theory. Such studies also resulted in the reports of the adherents of some manner of emphasis on the quality of work life and on worker involvement, or participative management. But, when we read the literature on work conceptualized from a perspective above the micro level, findings indicate fewer, and more complex, options available to employers interested in reducing their employees' dissatisfactions with the job. (For example, in an extreme instance, the forces of the globalized market and the international division of labor might transfer the work of both the manager and the managed in a Michigan plant to a location south of the border with Mexico, in the *maquiladoras*. Here there could be no options for addressing the dissatisfactions of the Michigan workers.)

In his essay, Berg analyzes this kind of disjunction resulting from a researcher's myopic focus on micro analyses of work. He describes a reconceptualization of work according to the perspectives of the micro-, messo-, and macro-levels. With such a reconceptualizing, we can find the true core of the structures and processes of work—involving authority and control relations and including hierarchy and superordinate-subordinate relations.

Work and Technology in Modern Industrial Organizations

Marietta Baba examines the closely interrelated concepts of "human work" and "technology." As she relates, the range of definitions of each of these concepts frequently overlap. Moreover, depending on the discipline and the theorist of work, the concepts could be virtually indistinguishable. Confusion between conceptualizations of work and technology generate several theoretical issues. These include whether work behavior and organization should be considered part of work culture, part of technology, or both. As assumed by sociotechnical systems theory, these issues also include whether work and technology are governed, respectively, by independent sets of laws relating to social and physical phenomena.

Answers to the questions concerning these issues have serious implications for management of organizations and policy for government. This is because these answers indicate whether technological considerations should be primary in the design of the organizations and the technology of work. In her essay, Baba discusses the muddle in the issues related to the intricate construct of work-technology and explores some alternative paths toward clarification of the issues.

Reviewed by Baba are three models of causal relationship between work and technology. These include technological determinism, sociotechnical systems theory, and the cultural (or social) construction of technology. Each of the three, in some way, view work as subordinated to technology. Since the Hawthorne studies, however, fieldwork in industry finds various aspects of work activity not under the total domination of technology and the managers who control it.

Baba, then, examines the situations in which spontaneous and informal work activity have a strong effect on technology and the production flowing from it. Here particular activities of informal work solve problems of production creatively, problems not amenable to solution in the realm of formal technological information. Such work activity constitutes a creative frontier for new technology. This process of work, enhancing and creating technology, she concludes, must be comprehended if production is to achieve standards of quality and efficiency competitive in the globalizing economy.

Work Relations and the Web of Rules

In my own essay, I apply the idea of the "web of rules," or interrelated regulations and prescriptions of all kinds for the relations of work, to ethnological ends. Although the conceptual framework of the web of rules for studying a work force was first developed by Clark Kerr and Abraham Siegel, two scholars outside of anthropology, they specifically said use of their construct enters the preserve of the anthropologist. As an anthropologist of work, I use the idea of the "web" in three ways.

First, I develop an overall ethnological formulation of the framework of the web for application to the entire range of human societies from the technologically simple to the hyperindustrial.

Second, from my own fieldwork, I explore the use of the web construct on traditional, that is, nonmodern, societies—among hunter-gatherers and among peasants of an agrarian state. Third, from my applied studies in industrial and organizational ethnology, I show the utility of the web construct for understanding the work relations of American railroaders. As proper in the use of the web, emphasized is the historical development in American society of various elements of this network of regulations for work relations. In this third purpose, continuity is maintained from an industrial and organizational ethnology originating, along with industrial and organizational sociology and psychology, more than six decades ago in the Hawthorne project.

To examine a single theoretical concept usable heuristically with the aid of the idea of the web of rules and that can be universally used for all of the range of societies, I select that of property rights in work. By this is meant the worker, whatever the relation to the controllers of the toil, has a right or interest regarding value of some kind in his or her work. This examining of a single theoretical concept with the aid of the web is part of my development of an overall ethnological formulation for applying the framework of the web cross-culturally.

In modern times, the process of industrialization has destroyed the traditional property rights to work. Accordingly, much of today's activity in labor-management relations concerning social power and control revolves around attempts by workers at restoration of some kind of strong attachment to livelihood. As one of the oldest industries and by far the oldest with a federal element in the web of rules, the railroads are selected to examine for industrial society the development of property rights to work and of other related economic security of the worker.

Postindustrialism, Post-Fordism, and the Crisis in World Capitalism

June Nash analyzes both the postindustrial models of society by Daniel Bell and by Alain Touraine and the "Fordist" models of corporate welfare policies in society by Michael Aglietta, Alain Lipietz, and others. Based in part on her long-term fieldwork in Pittsfield, Massachusetts, Nash develops an alternative model of contemporary society in its later phases of industrial restructuring. Bell posited a modern economy featuring a decline in manufacturing and other production of goods and an increase in production of services. Ascendant in the social order of this economy are the professional and technological occupations, constituting a new class.

Touraine posited a parallel socioeconomic development in France, with an expanding power and influence of the technocrats—scientists, engineers, and managers. Fordist theories of work, of varying emphases, concern a welfare capitalism. These theories center on the sharing with labor by paternalistic firms of some of the gains from increases in rationalized productivity and on the development of mass markets for standardized, relatively inexpensive consumer goods.

Nash argues insightfully with her alternative model for late industrial society. To begin, the arenas for social change are outside the new technological hierarchies discussed by both the postindustrial and post-Fordist theoreticians of work. Instead, she affirms, these arenas are shifting to the export-producing regions of industrializing countries. And they are shifting to the ranks of both the unemployed and underemployed in the declining older industrial areas, such as that of Pittsfield, and in stagnating economies of the Third World. Such emerging arenas cannot be adequately dealt with by postindustrial or Fordist theories, which are applicable only to a narrow sector of the increasingly global economy.

The Work-Contingent Character of the American Middle Class

In her essay Judith Blau, relates how conventional social scientific wisdom posits that an industrial mode of production will generate a middle class. But, argues Blau, the conditions for development, since our Civil War and especially since World War II, that have supported a large and diffuse middle class in America are now changed in fundamental ways. Middle class values, even espoused by some of the rich, include those relating to working arduously and devotedly and enjoying resultant achievement. A middle-class normative system with such central values has engulfed our entire society.

According to Blau, the American middle class is constructed culturally on an ethos of participatory democracy in which every citizen has a voice and on the central value of the American work ethic—working hard and thereby "making it" economically. But such ideal charters for American society are contradictory to the growing political inequalities, undemocratic organizations of work, and hierarchies of society.

In her examination of the issues she raises, Blau enters the arena of the long-standing debate on whether class is rooted more in the dynamic forces of the political economy or in that socially learned, collectively carried system of information we call culture.

This debate was under way with Marx and Weber, was continued by the Lynds and Lloyd Warner, flared again in the 1960s with the arguments over the validity of Oscar Lewis's culture of poverty, and burns in the 1990s with the interpretations of the roots of poverty in the United States.

Blau holds that the institutional underpinning of the American middle class was contingent upon a unique set of historical conditions. This broad, national class may well be an ephemeral entity. Individual achievement and competition of the able in the marketplace may no longer by "paying off," as it was once thought to do. The current "American middle class" could in significant part constitute a memory culture, reflecting a golden yesteryear that never quite was. And it undoubtedly reflects the short period energized by abundant cheap fuel, 1946-73, a time of relatively stable relations of work between employers and the employed in which most shared in an expanding economic pie.

Processes of Retirement from Work

Robert Weiss bridges work life and the period of retirement beyond it. He reports analyses of his findings from a study of professionals and managers and the ways in which they approach retirement and, then, use these postwork years. Generally, retirement is not a circumstance that his subjects of research actively sought. Accordingly, how do such workers become retired?

Many gradually withdrew from work because of ill health, often as part of the aging process. If unable to perform their jobs, such people were reluctant to continue at work, but such a realization was at first resisted. Some subjects felt in some way misused by their employer. Their reasons varied. Despite this diversity of complaints, a common theme emerged. Each had devoted a part or all of his or her work life to a firm that proved ultimately to be uncaring. Retirement for them was an ending of a bad relationship, with hard feelings as a result, similar to a divorce.

Some respondents were forced out of their employment by handshakes varying from fairly golden to totally leaden. Some were told: retire or be fired. And some were archly asked about their plans for retirement. Often, older workers were marginalized, reassigned to less important and less prestigeful responsibilities. Such an act by management greased the skids for retirement. At times, the worker and those with whom he or she worked withdrew from one another, in a process of social dissociation resulting from an increasingly tense conflict between the parties.

Retirement has as its universal attraction only a negative, freedom from the need to deal with the stresses of work. Just one respondent had a positive postretirement attraction that drew him away from his world of work. Reasonable monetary packages for retirement do not produce this state for workers, but these do make retirement possible. As Weiss concludes, retirement is almost always motivated by a desire for retirement *from* work, a process in which the worker and the organization of work gradually mutually distance themselves until final separation. Retirement is rarely *for* attainment of a postwork goal. Again, work is central in our lives.

The Socioeconomic Perspective for the Study of Work

Amitai Etzioni concludes this collection of essays by examining for the study of work the utility of a unified, socioeconomic perspective, combining views from neoclassical economics with those from the social sciences. In this perspective, it is posited that people not only maximize their satisfaction but also react to their moral values. Utility, then, is twofold, happiness and its facilitating morality. Individual, rational self-interest is balanced against responsibility to the community. Because humans have been highly social, community-bound animals since time immemorial, it is not surprising that self-interested behavior must in some part be explained at the level of a socially learned collective consciousness, or culture. Society is not a confining set of fetters; it is the humanness of the hominid animals. Humans not only have their rational choices skewed by their encompassing normative system but also by their emotions. Furthermore, the individual decision maker's abilities to collect, assess, and process information for rational choices are socially and neurologically limited.

With his essay, Etzioni prepares a systematic overview of human work while applying the new socioeconomic viewpoint. He explores the nature of work and the varied rewards that cause people to so toil. Then, he discusses the shortcomings of the views of neoclassical economists, who hold that money is the sole incentive for work. The inner gratifying characteristics of humans' work must also be taken into account. Work also has a dimension of intrinsic rewards.

In this vein, Etzioni examines the ways in which work is preferred by Americans over leisure. (This is a circumstance discussed also by Weiss in his study of becoming retired.) The human desire for work and its satisfactions indicates that the classic view of work as a "cost," often referred to as "labor," is only partially correct.

Labor, then, is more than one of the major factors of production in which money is paid as compensation for mental and motor exertions; and monetary cost is not the total compensation furnished by a firm for labor. Clearly, it is not valid to treat all persons in all jobs as if they were merely labor and not workers. People work for a variety of motives that are psychic, sociocultural, and economic. Work, therefore, is in part a moral activity. Because different societies place different moral valuations on work, the nature of work is culturally relative.

Finally, Etzioni discusses the modern family, its division of work, and its customary exchanges among unequals (usually between the market-and-credit superior husband and the wife, deficient in these attainments). Not only does one find in the family structured exchanges based on work among those who are social unequals, but also one finds "We" zones of shared interests and identifies. A creative and constantly adjusting tension exists, between competing, acquisitive individuals, on the one hand, and the sharing family group, on the other hand. The familial division of labor, accordingly, is not a stark Hobbesian arena, as depicted by some schools of thought.

NOTES

1. I am grateful to my wife, Marilou Gamst, for her typing and editing of the drafts of my writing in this collection of essays, for her comments on my ideas and data, and for her constant support and assistance. Her able participation was essential for the completion of the book, as it has been for the field and library research either influencing or directly reported in my writing of chapters 1 and 6.

Some aspects of a majority of the essays in this book were presented as papers at a session during the joint annual meetings of the American Anthropological Association and the Society for the Anthropology for Work in New Orleans in November 1990.

2. This book is intended for use in courses on applied anthropology, anthropology of work, economic anthropology, industrial and organizational sociology, sociology of work, industrial and organizational psychology, management science especially organizational studies, economics of labor and work, industrial relations, and human relations.

FREDERICK C. GAMST

1

Considerations of Work

By adding a particular weld to management's fully controlled product, an automobile assembler works so that she can eat, finding expressive outlets and positive affect off the job. A sculptor eats so that he can work, finding expressive outlet and positive affect in his own entirely self-controlled product. A painter creating a still life perhaps to be displayed or a poet a sonnet perhaps to be read is working. This is so even if their work creations are not prepared for sale, at a price, in the market or for reciprocal giving of gifts, of value, at holidays. A forager is working either when hunting to feed only himself or to provision his entire village. What, then, does *work* mean and what is its range of activities? Moreover, why is the study of work important to Americans and Canadians?

Work supports all the other aspects of humans' lifeways. Work, consequently, is the pivotal concern and subject of conversation in all societies. Work relations, accordingly, touch almost all of our social interactions. The place of work, be it a craft person's shop or a plowman's acreage, therefore, is a central locus of the activities people deem important. Because work dominates our psyches and social lives, we must attempt to understand the forces it generates, shaping society and channeling individual behavior. This chapter contributes to such an understanding.[1]

In this chapter, to develop an understanding of work for Americans and Canadians, six topics are discussed. First, we consider *work* as an idea and analytic concept. Here we discuss the Anglo-

Saxon views of work in a cultural context including folk backgrounds and, then, examine several dimensions of work. Second, we analyze exertion not considered to be work. Third, we construct an analytic concept of work, contemplating the individual in the work environment and, then, examining the qualifiers of *purpose* and *gain* in work. Fourth, we examine the place of work in sociocultural theory concerning American and Canadian society, including the centrality of research on work and the tradition of the study of the community and its work. Fifth, we investigate the vital issues of worker participation in the control of modern work, including the quandary of worker participation and the question of who guides technological "progress." And sixth, we ponder some futures of work in American and Canadian societies, including the new nature of work and widespread losses of work.[2]

WORK AS IDEA AND CONCEPT

Because no knowledge exists supra culture, the first task in considering the meanings of work is examining the Anglo-Saxon cultural context shaping our use of this idea. We, then, discuss how work is both intensively personal and socially relational. Relations and organization of work are meaningless without reference to time, explored next.

The Cultural Context of Work

Work is the broadest English word to label both the process of doing something and the state of something done.[3] It is instructive that the English word *work* is derived from the Indo-European root **werg-on*, that is, "to do, to act." Compare also the High German and Low German *werk*, "work, action, performance," and the Greek ἔργον, "work," and ῥέξειν, "to do." It is interesting that in the French roots of the English language and related culture is the word *travail*, meaning, in English, both "exceedingly hard work" and "intense pain and agony." This word, in turn, stems from the Old Latin *tripalium*, or an instrument of torture composed, as the word informs of "three stakes." "Travail" is one central dimension of work for Anglo-Saxons.

Overall we have an ambivalent view of work. It can be a moral necessity, "Satan finds work for idle hands," and the deity's lifelong curse of travail upon humans, "in the sweat of thy face shalt thou eat bread, till thou return unto the ground." In the folk view of work, a dimension of "mind-numbing drudgery" is also found. As far back as 1670 we find recorded the familiar aphorism, "All work and no play, makes Jack a dull boy" (OED 1971:3818). Ideas of some modern intellectuals about the joyous nature of the work of traditional European peasants and craftsmen are most likely unfounded (de Man 1929:146). Herbert Applebaum's following chapter 2 reviews the salient Western thought across the centuries entering the ideas about work of English-speaking peoples.

Despite awareness of our folk views about work, we still trip over the etymological root of English *work*, which approximates all endeavor. Making the problem more vexing, work and technology are closely related and the two logically separate concepts are often conflated by analysts. As Marietta Baba explains in chapter 5, this problem is exacerbated because the interrelations of technology and work change cross-culturally and historically.

What about the analytic utility of the proviso frequently used, that work involves creating goods and services *valued* in society? Valued by whom? It has long been held in ethnology (sociocultural anthropology) that the phenomenon of value for things exchanged, as Melville Herskovits informs, "can only be understood as one part of the wider phenomenon of culture." Furthermore, each system of socioeconomic value "must be analyzed in the light of its peculiar sanctions and its own special social setting" (Herskovits 1952:237). Settings of this kind would include those sub- and subsubsocietal. "Economic value being . . . always relative, so is the work which creates it" (Tilgher 1958[1929]:164-7). The value of work varies, then, even within a single specific, that is, whole autonomous, culture. "Social value" depends on the point of view of the observer.

Creation of social value in one part of a society, for example, that of antebellum plantation owners, could result in loss in another sector, plantation slaves. When the U.S. Army Corps of Engineers builds another pork-barrel project for one of a majority of reciprocally logrolling congressmen, is this work producing valued goods and services for all of the citizens of the United States? Production viewed as having social value, then, is relative to whose ox is being gored, or fed.

Are job actions and even strikes of a labor union of social value? In the United States, they certainly were to auto workers and coal miners and their families and communities, and undoubtedly to the country's development as an industrial democracy. But many business persons do not share the ideology for such a development. As with much functional analysis (cf. Firth 1955:244-5), social-value analysis often views patterns of behavior in terms of either entirely positive or entirely negative relation to society. Almost every social action has a eufunction or value for at least one sector of a society. Despite the relativism of the idea of social value in a concept of work, a useful concept most likely cannot be formulated without it. We, however, should be aware of the relativism.

The Personal Dimension of Work

Work has a personal dimension, in defining one's psyche and creating a self-image. This personal dimension certainly has a strong hold on all persons, in market and in nonmarket societies. In Ethiopia, the Wayto hippopotamus hunter seeks gratifying praise as "a stalwart hunter." There the Qemant plowman seeks rewarding respect as a proficient speaker at a legal proceeding.[4]

In America, this hold on the psyche is true even for those only marginally employable and thus barely sharing in the economic, social, and psychic rewards of work. Summarizing the view of self held by streetcorner men only slightly prepared for participation in the work force in Washington, D.C., Elliot Liebow writes that "the streetcorner man is under continuous assault by his job experiences and job fears. His experiences and fears feed on one another. The kind of job he can get—and frequently only after fighting for it, if then—steadily confirms his fears, depresses his self-confidence and self-esteem until finally, terrified of an opportunity even if one presents itself, he stands defeated by his experiences, his belief in his own self-worth destroyed and his fears a confirmed reality" (1967:71). Work greatly affects the integration of a personality.

The Social Dimension of Work

Work also has a social dimension: it concerns social relations as much as material fabrications. Western scholars recognize the central importance of the social relational aspect of work (see, e.g., König 1958:133-4; Braude 1983:15-32; Bouvier 1989; Spittler 1991). Much of the behavior of work is explainable at the collective level. Individual self-interest is dampened by what could be called the behavioral modalities of work, ranging from norms to etiquette.[5] Such a view long held in economic anthropology is also found in the writings in socioeconomics. For this view in anthropology see Gamst's chapter 6, and for development and assessment of the socioeconomic perspective see Amitai Etzioni's chapter 10.

Cross-culturally compared, not every social relation is work, but work is at least a potential aspect of any social relation. Walter Goldschmidt in chapter 3 analyzes particular social dimensions of work cross-culturally for tribal and agrarian peoples. Work has institutions and patterned social regularities and arrangements that may be considered as its social structures (see Kalleberg and Berg 1987:2-30). These structures are sometimes so large and complex that they are beyond the social relational ken of the average person, but they control his or her work nevertheless. In chapter 4, Ivar Berg discusses at three analytic levels these social structures of work.

In industrial society with its atrophied ties of kinship and community, work provides opportunities for humanly needed socializing. These interactions with coworkers include exchanging positive affect for both work and nonwork experiences, having a "sounding board" for voicing private concerns, releasing tensions before a supportive audience, and having membership in an in-group of intimate persons—a surrogate tribal "us," socially bonded by links of work instead of kinship.

The Temporal Dimension of Work

Through the ages, every human society has been structured around work in its dimensions of time as well as social relations. Accurate minutely divided time reckoning is a hallmark of industrial society. To coordinate and facilitate industrial work including transportation, standard time zones and daylight savings time had to be created. For industrial processes, timing to the microsecond became necessary. Without a precise and invariable reckoning for the fourth dimension, time, the three dimensions of space could not be used efficiently enough for the evolution of the technologically advanced societies of the late nineteenth century.

For effectiveness, work in industrial society must be timed in a variety of modes such as frequency, synchronization, and duration. A needed piece of material must arrive by a particular time; an event must occur in the correct sequence; and a process must be of an exact duration. Without timings of these kinds, work becomes dysfunctionally independent instead of functionally interdependent. Timing is necessary not just for creating goods and services but also for planning them. Without timing of work, terminal dysfunction would undermine industrial society. It is no accident that one of the purposes of public school is to enculturate children to be as regular as clockwork regarding their timed events and tasks. The ridiculing message of the popular rhyme about the "ten o'clock scholar" is not lost upon pupils. The clock, in many ways of work, more than the steam engine, was the serpentine machine in the agrarian garden of preindustrial America.[6]

EXERTION NOT CONSIDERED AS WORK

Much laboring activity is commonly excluded from Anglo-Saxon folk and intellectual thoughts about work. Common denominators of a folk definition are discernable in analysis of such culture-bound ideas of work. Work is recognized as many of the activities directed toward creating goods and services valued in society. Some activities, however, are not commonly considered as work when: the time and exertion for the activities seem sporadic and little planned, the activities are only slightly or not related to an institutional product, and these activities are commonplace in everyday life. Activities thus characterized are thought by the average person not to result in work because they relate to mandatory, universal behaviors in a society (Wadel 1979:379).

Particular kinds of exertion not often viewed by Western scholars as work could be so considered. Does work also include the exertion for nonmaterial ends such as expiation, that is, appeasing members of society or supernatural forces for a past impropriety or infraction of a code of conduct by one person or a group?[7] Inclusion of expiation under the rubric of work allows for human manipulation (or attempts of it) of the physical and sociocultural environments through supernatural, that is, religious, as well as technological methods. We thereby avoid the modern Western prejudice that the processes of work must have a scientifically verifiable effect.

For example, in the realm of the supernatural, the rainmaking ceremonies of the Qemant peasantry of Ethiopia are conducted under the work rules for ritual, created by priests at the command of their great sky god. His priests conduct ceremonies here on earth to counteract the devastating droughts in that country (Gamst 1969). This priestly work is not always effective in producing the desired amounts of rain. We all know this from watching the six o'clock news on television while eating our dinners. But with considerable ritual exertion by the priests, after a few years, the rains have again come in sufficient strength to support the crops. To say that the rain ceremonies of the Qemant priests have no meteorological effect on the environment is to misunderstand the full result of the ceremonies. This includes maintaining the belief that the Qemant control their habitat and their work of cultivation and animal husbandry. Despite their limited technology, nature is not overwhelming, or so they know. Through their priests' effort, the Qemant influence the universe-controlling deity. The Qemant thereby persevere and endure, as they have done in the past, and have faith that they will do in the future. A successfully enduring Qemant agriculture, then, is not just a matter of technological adaptation to the geographic environment; its practice requires a religious adaptation as well.

At times, the highest priest of the Qemant cures with his supernatural rites people having various ailments. The effectiveness of such healing in reality is psychocultural and operating through psychosomatic and purely psychological mechanisms. This effectiveness has long been known (Cannon 1942; Richter 1957; Lex 1974; Hans and Kleinmann 1983; Landy 1990).

Are the rain ceremonies of the Qemants' priests not an attempted work-manipulation of the environment, helping to ensure human ability to survive against its pressures? Is the faith healing of the Qemants' paramount priest not just as much work as similar activity by a psychiatrist (both of whom are compensated for their effort)?[8] What, for one more example out of many, about the shaman who both cures a physically ailing patient and brings solace and well-being to the patient's kinspersons, entirely through her practice of supernatural rites, while she is "possessed" by an officiating spirit? Work of these kinds has exertion in the sociocultural environment of symbolic faith, rather than the geographic environment. Ultimately, work concerns human adaptation to the total environment, that is, both geographical and sociocultural.

CONSTRUCTION OF A CONCEPT OF WORK

For a useful basis in theory, how may a concept of human work be constructed validly both individually and socially, across cultures and down through time, and not overly bound by our contextual language and culture? What considerations of the total environment should enter into this construction of work? Is work purposeful and gainful, and how is it livelihood?

The Individual in the Work Environment

To begin, perhaps it is apt that we contrast a biological *exertion*, involving energetic activity of motor acts and mental processes, with a cultural *work*. It should be noted that a purely mental exertion of work, such as planning a task, can exist in and of itself. But work as solely motor acts probably does not exist isolated from encompassing thought. An example is the "simple" neuro-muscular acts of driving spikes with a heavy hammer, having a long flexible handle, into a wooden crosstie. These acts involve coordination, including perception of the results of the response from the brain's directive to swing the hammer. Information must be processed in the brain in a timely way to keep the acts effective. A spike must be struck squarely on its rounded head with the right amount of force. Even swinging a spike maul, as it is called, takes more than just a strong back and good coordination. Beyond the feedback from perception, hammering spikes has socially learned, informal, technical rules for the effective immediate work of hammering. The task also has learned formal rules for safety at work and for the overall work planned according to some pattern or design. The coordinations and rules are patterns of culture.[9]

Work necessarily takes place in the physical (material) environment. This occurs sometimes directly in nature, in the geographical, that is, natural, environmental part of it. Sometimes work occurs in the artifactual (itself cultural) part of it, such as in or on a building or other artifactual structure, for example, a mine, vehicle, or right-of-way. Often, during work, some element of the geographic environment is modified, often in stages, into a culturally patterned form of product by a cultural manner of procedure. For example, a tree is felled by a logger, trucked by a trucker, made into planks by a sawyer, transported by a railroader, and nailed together by a carpenter, according to the design of an architect and restrictions by the building code of government officials. But such modifications of material are not necessary for exertion to be work. Exertion could be purely mental, as in a new theorem in topology created by a mathematician, or in unrealized organizational planning of all kinds, for example, an oral committee report of academicians.

Because no individual can be self-sufficient, work is necessarily part of the social environment. All human work is social (even when performed in physical isolation from others) because it is patterned by culture. Robinson Crusoe in physical isolation on his island, after all, was still part of a practical, tinkering British society. Socially learned and executed cultural patterns are found in work creations comprising goods and services, for example, a stone hand axe, a performance of a drill team, a cracked cryptographic code, and a trouble shooting and repairing of an inoperable radio. And the patterns are found in the collectively normative social relations of creating and using the goods or services, for example, learning from others how to make and then what to do with a hand axe, practicing with others to create a precision drill performance to meet public expectations for entertainment, receiving support and feedback from within and outside of a group assigned to decipher and report to superiors about codes, and learning about the craft of analysis and repair of defects in electronic equipment to serve client needs.

An individual's work activities usually intertwine with those of others in a role set for creating goods and services. Through coordination or exchange, such a role set interrelates with other sets in a society. Here a work role is a cluster of attributes and expectations for a work status. At the role's core are the behavioral modalities of role rights and duties. A work role is one of many such roles taken by an individual and is formed through learning about and interacting with the same and different roles of others. Even where work is performed in Crusoe-like isolation apart from a role set, it is, nonetheless, enacted regarding behavioral modalities of a reference group for such activity. Thus work is not just a technical action; it is usually directly social relational; and it is always enmeshed in the collective conventions for the patterned symbolic work of a society.

Purpose in Work

Need exertion be purposeful to qualify as work? As many others have, we use this characteristic in a construction of work. Perhaps many of us add *purposeful* because it is part of the common definition reflecting wide folk usage. *Purposeful* denotes not being meaningless, that is directed at a specific culturally defined end. But here purpose overlaps with social value—purpose from the value-oriented perspective of whom? If some thing is meaningless, it is valueless. For example, three Americans each do the exact same exertion in separately felling trees with a chain saw: a lumberjack cutting in a permissible area, a "timber pirate" stealing trees from private woodland, and a vandal maliciously destroying a grove. The first two persons are legally and illegally purposeful in their behavior, the last not so. The purpose is part of the cultural context, in this instance, creating wealth by producing timer; it is not a kind of normatively idiosyncratic quirk, as with the third person. For the Qemant, cutting trees in the sacred groves in which they worship is sacrilegious. No such act could be work among these peasants. But neighboring non-Qemant work at felling such trees, using motor habits, tools, and procedures exactly the same as those of the Qemant in cutting ordinary trees. For the Qemant, the shaman has purpose when she allows herself to become "possessed" in an exertion to cure the afflicted; for the Americans, so does the mathematical topologist, when he calculates a novel solution. Neither the researcher of work nor the worker determines purpose; it exists in the behavioral modalities of a culture.

Cross-culturally constructed, work should not be just about adding material value in a society. It should concern exertion creating things of a class that are material, social relational, ideational, or some combination of these, and that are valued as a class in some part of a specific culture, perhaps in a subsubsubculture. Thus no matter that Van Gogh's impressionist paintings were not salable at first; other paintings in the class were at least mildly so. No matter that paper-wielding bureaucrats are generally unpopular and labeled useless. Members of various sectors of society demand and receive action-encumbering red tape to fetter other sectors. ("There ought to be a law.")

Gain and Livelihood in Work

For an analytic conception of work, we might also refine its construction by adding another qualifying denotative filter. More narrowly considered, work can refer to engaging in *gainful* exertion, including that of a hunter, fisher, gatherer, cultivator, herder, craftsperson, miner, tribal leader, religious practitioner, administrator, teacher, scholar, engineer, transporter, clerk, laborer, soldier, homemaker, entertainer, beggar, artist, or slave.[10] Gainful livelihood may be earned in a nonmarket economy, a market one, or a transitional one in between (see Applebaum 1984a, 1984b). Money, or even exchange with reference to price in the temporary absence of money, is not essential (Gamst 1974:30-34). Gainful work need not be voluntary but may be coerced in some way.

In any society, it might be useful to consider work's attribute of *gainful* as involving compensation that is either an increment or a saving. *Increment* work gains compensation in money, goods, services, or other things of value—including land, human beings, time, incorporeal things, supernaturalisms, positive affect, and so forth—in an exchange that is market, redistributive, or reciprocal in nature.[11] *Saving* work gains a reduction in expenditure of the things of value just enumerated. Work involving increment or saving is on behalf of a worker, embracing family or larger kin group, encompassing organization of work of all kinds, or wider society.

For an individual, statuses and roles regarding gainful work are usually multiple, of varying durations, and the work does not always involve monetary compensation. An American woman may be a full-time, unpaid homemaker (with roles of mother, wife, and community volunteer); full-time, paid administrator with sundry roles in a business office; part-time, unpaid handy Jill-of-all-trades in the home; part-time, unpaid Girl Scout leader; part-time, paid editor of a newsletter for office personnel; part-time, unpaid deacon of a church; part-time administrator of a food co-op, with compensation in produce; and part time member of a reciprocating baby-sitting association, with payment in like service. Each of her work statuses comprises component statuses: the handy woman includes roles of decorator, painter, carpenter, plumber, gardener, and tinkerer.

To avoid a market-bound construction of work, it could be useful to broaden the narrow concept of *livelihood*. From a work status, that is, social position of work usually in a network of social interaction, a total livelihood is gained in the valued things enumerated previously. A livelihood is a means of supporting life, that is subsistence. But by *total livelihood* is meant all the tasks and the social processes encompassing these tasks for supporting both life (biological requisites) and the life way (sociocultural requisites). With reference to the narrowly defined *livelihood*, the concept of work soon gradates into exertion marginal or unrelated to work. But, with reference to the broader *total livelihood*, far more kinds of exertion are encompassed as work.

A Construction of Work

A construction of *work* must be cross-culturally and historically valid, but we should not forget that much of its investigation concerns the today-nearly-universal industrial and industrializing societies. Approaching the twenty-first century, work is increasingly the basis of all elemental concerns about humans. "Work is becoming the key personal, social and political issue of the remaining years of the twentieth century: confusion and ambiguities about its meaning, nature and purpose in our lives are widespread" (Pahl 1988:1). Our eyes must be kept on the industrial ball.[12]

In industrial societies, most families, as we know, are no longer the primary producers of food, tools, or other crafts. As a consequence of the exceedingly minute division of labor, most individuals consume products produced almost entirely by others outside of the family. As part of a consumer-oriented society, continually they gainfully work for increments and savings to improve their standard of living, especially by consuming myriad desired products. They have their personal exertion in work multiplied greatly by machines and electronic devices, with a consequently great human productivity. They are paid for the main work in their lives with a general purpose money, resulting in the independence of individuals from the family. Although money is not essential in our construction of work, in today's market economy it is the touchstone of daily life.

A concept of work with reference to all that has preceded in this chapter is as follows. Human work is exertion, energetic physical or mental activity, having purpose, direction toward a goal with reference to the modalities of behavior of a specific culture or one of its subcultures. More narrowly conceived, work can be gainful when involving compensation that is either an increment or a saving of value in a culture. This construct provides a base line for understanding. It has analytic utility as a foundation of independent variables for analysis, including work skills, work coordination among persons, work design, technological controls on work, work relations between controllers and producers of work, and so forth.

THE PLACE OF WORK IN SOCIOCULTURAL THEORY CONCERNING AMERICAN AND CANADIAN SOCIETIES

Turning our attention more specifically to the industrial United States and, to a large extent, Canada, we now consider how work is central in our lives. Then, to shed further light on the central place of work in our lives, we review the long, formative tradition in anthropology and sociology of the study of the American and Canadian community and its supporting work.

The Centrality of the Study of Work

In the United States and Canada (hereinafter, North America), the workplace has long been the crucible for social scientific conceptualizing. Everett Hughes explains: "In our particular society, work organization looms so large as a separate and specialized system of things, and work experience is so fateful a part of every man's life, that we cannot make much headway as students of society and of social psychology without using work as one of our main laboratories" (1952:426). Regarding the study of modern work and jobs, Joanne Miller introduces her comprehensive review of the subject as follows. "Work relations enter virtually all models of social organization and associated images of man or woman as an actor in and product of structured relationships. Moreover, the workplace per se, as a strategic location in which work arrangements are staged, has been a central laboratory for investigating social order and the dynamics of change" (1988:327).

Even Marx was impressed by the nature of work in the English-speaking countries, which did not foster much of a class consciousness among workers. Marx thought the work provided by the growing capitalist enterprises in Anglo-Saxon lands allowed little opportunity for the development of proletarian unrest to the point of revolution. In 1872, Marx wrote, "We know that the institutions, manners and customs of the various countries must be considered, and we do not deny that there are countries like England and America, . . . where the worker may attain his object by peaceful means" (Kelsen 1948:41). In the work relations of the United States and Canada, then, the workers have, thus far, been buying into the ever-expanding political economy. Until recently, because the size of North America's capitalist pie of reasonable employment had been inexorably increasing, any national reallocations of wealth did not lead to a zero-sum viewpoint by workers, wherein another person's increased slice causes their own decrease. Thus North America was largely spared internal strife over allocating wealth.

The work dominating the life of most North Americans is paid employment. As in other industrial societies, paid, employed work is a central identifier of the self. The characteristic used as a person's overall social identification and evaluation is his or her general occupational status. Upon meeting someone for the first time, after the ritual "How do you do?" we invariably ask as our first meaningful communication, "What do you do?" ("Why, I'm a printer, for thirty years now.")

Work does more than provide our focus of self-identification. It provides our basis of social power and the circumstances of our economic and other welfare. Lose of work, then, is loss of one's power and mooring in society. For the average North American, by far the largest medium of life savings is the family house. With loss of a job, equity in this house is jeopardized; making the necessary house payments is no longer assured. North Americans not only receive pay from their jobs for support of their families and their community organizations such as schools, churches, libraries, recreational facilities, police, firefighters, and hospitals. But also they receive from their jobs paid vacations and holidays, health insurance,

retirement benefits, unemployment insurance, workmen's compensation protection, and sundry other benefits for the work force.

The job delimits the kind of neighborhood (with its amount
of personal safety and property security) available. It delineates the
quality of the dwelling (if any at all) inhabited. It influences the
length and quality of education and life's opportunity for children.
And it restricts territorially who will be friends, neighbors, and fellow
workers. Work provides a temporal order for behavior.[13] It furnishes
a necessary routine in daily life, that is, an expected, regular, largely
prescribed course of activities, reassuring and soothing in face of
all the challenges and anxieties of human existence.

The Study of the Community and Its Work

Work is quintessentially middle-American. On this matter, see
Blau's chapter 8 and Weiss's chapter 9. Since about 1900, the
centrality of work in the United States and Canada has been reflected
in studies of North American communities by ethnologists and
sociologists. Community studies as a method have been extensively
developed and involve intensive firsthand research in relatively small-
scale settlements. Each investigation, reported in a case study having
description and analyses, enables the researcher in the field to reduce
the scope of inquiry to a manageable grouping, a socially well-
bounded, territorial community.[14] Because employment and access
to it support a community, work is almost always a vital interest
of these studies. Among the pioneering community studies in
America, the "Blanktown" investigation of James Williams (1906)
has considerable information on economic activities and work.
Similarly, Wilbert Anderson's "Country Town" (1906), although
concerned in the main with "the great middle class" begins with
"the new industrial order," then transforming America's rural towns.
Class, social stratification, and related work provided the conceptual
framework for the classic community studies. In these studies, it
was the industrial, often factory, towns that attracted the
researchers, although farming towns were also investigated, usually
as part of large-scale agribusiness.[15]

During 1924 and 1925, Robert and Helen Lynd studied
"Middletown," (Muncie, Indiana) as typical of American small towns
attempting to adapt to industrialization while clinging to the
homespun values of an older, rural America (1929). Middletown also
was presented as having great disparities in the wielding of power,
with undue influence in the community by the controlling family
"X" (the Balls of glass jar fame) of industrialists. A restudy of Muncie

in 1935, by Robert Lynd continued its foci on "getting a living" and the power in the community of the Ball family (1937).[16]

The study of community life was a great direction in the development of American sociology, especially with its "Chicago School," using that city as a natural ecological laboratory for field and other research. Typically investigated in these community studies were social problems fostered by industrialization and urban growth (Bulmer 1984). Among the Chicago investigations was Louis Wirth's, of the Jewish ghetto in this city, examined against a background of such communities elsewhere in the world (1928). Harvey Zorbaugh's *The Gold Coast and the Slum* contrasted an elite lake front neighborhood in Chicago with an adjacent "Little Sicily." Here he examined the ways in which geographic and social distance in a community do not necessarily coincide and how those living side by side with divergent interests do not necessarily become neighbors (1929). Related to the Chicago studies was Albert Blumenthal's research in "Mineville," Montana, exploring the networks of interpersonal relations in a small mining town (1932). Apart from the Chicago School, in Utah, beginning in the late 1920s, Lowry Nelson studied the Mormon farming community (1930).

Inspired by the Lynds and encouraged by Clark Wissler, who told her "anthropology is what the anthropologist does," the paragon of field research Hortense Powdermaker was the first ethnologist to study an American community (Powdermaker 1966:133). In 1932 through 1934, she studied Indianola, Mississippi, a community in stark black and white contrasts of race (1939). Among the kinds of workers she encountered in a variety of caste system were black "yard boys" and (hand) laundresses who held positions of great responsibility in the black sector of this polarized community—of those subordinated and those who superordinated themselves, often by violence. Powdermaker, writing experientially from fieldwork about the American dilemma of race relations (1939, 1941), presaged the massive survey study on this subject conducted by economist Gunnar Myrdal and his colleagues (Myrdal 1944; but see Ellison 1964).

The communities studies by W. Lloyd Warner and his colleagues had a focus on stratification and the social order in America—as did many other pioneering community investigations—but continued elements of the industrial research Warner began in the 1930s (Gamst 1990). The Warner group did fieldwork in "Old City," Mississippi (Davis, Gardner, and Gardner 1941); "Jonesville," (Morris, Illinois) (Warner 1949); "Yankee City" (Newburyport, Massachusetts)

(Warner and Lunt 1941; Warner and Low 1943, 1946, 1947); and a black neighborhood of Chicago (Drake and Clayton 1945). The study of Old City, supported in part by the federal Works Progress Administration, included a cogent Marxist analysis of workers and the political economy, noting, among other control mechanisms, white empowerment through lynchings. In the series of Warner's reports on Yankee City, a central interest concerning the relations of work emerged, specifically, in the interdependence of the American social system and industrial organization. Here, in the study of a shoe factory and its community setting, Warner was concerned with the interrelations of stratification and the growing mechanization of shoe manufacturing. A strike in all the shoe factories, Warner labeled as "industrial war" in the community. Incidentally, Jonesville is the "Elmtown" of a community study of adolescents and education by August Hollingshead (1949).

Fred Cottrell's *The Railroader* is a community study of Milford, Utah, the railroad town he "was raised in" and where he "went to work for the railroad" (1940:v).[17] This research that he conducted as participant observer in the manner of "ethnological studies" may be considered to begin in 1918, when he first hired out on the railroad, and to end in 1939, when he wrote the resulting book (1940:v-vii), in which the community structure is overshadowed by the transcontinental industrial plant of the railroad. In a concern for the unemployment and widespread hunger of the Depression, during 1938-39, Frederick Richardson conducted a study based on participant observation in a resettlement community set within an Appalachian coal county having great unemployment. The (Utopian?) community experimented with a return to subsistence farming and with cooperatives, while some persons held at least part-time jobs in the mines or worked in the community sweater factory (Richardson 1941, 1942, 1948).

Study of power and economic control, government acts of commission and omission, and agricultural work relations led to a number of classic community studies by ethnologists. The first of those published by the U.S. Department of Agriculture (DOA) in its series *Rural Life Studies* was by Olen Leonard and Charles Loomis (1941), at a time when the department was still friendly to ethnologists. In 1939, Horace Miner conducted a community study of Hardin County, Iowa, for the DOA. His study had critical implications for controversial New Deal policy (1949). "This report immediately created controversy over the advisability of publication" (Miner 1949:iv). Miner's ethnological insights resulted in his accepted report being "lost" by the DOA and not published until a decade later, by a university.

Perhaps the most widely read study of a farming community, and one not done for the DOA, is "James West's" (pseudonym for Carl Withers) investigation in 1939 through 1941 of "Plainville," an isolated, undeveloped Ozark town. Little involved in the nonagricultural sector of the economy, this hill town was self-characterized as: "We're all just one class of common average working people here" (Withers 1945:viii). Withers attempted to capture the social organization and economic structure of a rural community just before it was integrated into the industrial world by a new highway. Art Gallaher restudied Plainville fifteen years later (1961). In the late 1930s, Horace Miner studied the French-Canadian community of St. Denis, Quebec (1939). He discovered a rural worldview paralleling that of the Anglo-Saxons of North America, one of a limitless frontier of wilderness—only situated to the north instead of the west—into which a growing population could expand and earn a living.

If the DOA received heart murmurs from Miner, Walter Goldschmidt caused it a reactive heart attack, with his ethnological grapes of wrath, *As You Sow* (1947), and a related report to Congress (1946). Goldschmidt's late-Depression study of the communities of Wasco, Dinuba, and Arvin in California's San Joaquin Valley was politically consequential. Among other things, he examined conflicting interests of large factory farms and small family farms and the cleavage between exploited farm-labor families and the dominant families in industrialized agriculture (Goldschmidt 1946, 1947). As a result of his study of agribusiness and the federal participation in it, the DOA then protected itself by deciding never to allow an ethnologist to conduct a study under its sponsorship (Goldschmidt 1978). Such is the power of a community study.

In 1945, among his similar studies (e.g., Lewis 1946), Oscar Lewis conducted research for the DOA focusing on cotton farming in Bell County, Texas. This federal agency never published his report (Lewis 1948a, 1948b). Study of a Hawaiian company town and its agricultural industry was conducted by Edward Norbeck across five years, while a manager of a pineapple plantation, beginning in 1938, and in subsequent fieldwork during the late 1950s (1959). An earlier, 1930s, community study of the Chicago School by Andrew Lind in Hawaii depicted urban industrial life diffuse across an island dominated by the sugar industry (1938).

Working under the guidance of ethnologists, William Foote Whyte during the late 1930s studied "Cornerville," the Italian-American North End of Boston and focused on racketeering, gangs, and social relations in what he depicted as a "slum" (1955[1949]).[18] In a study during 1957 through 1958 of Boston's Italian-American West End, Herbert Gans investigated the lifeway of a low-income, working class subculture and its maintenance of ethnic identify, in what he specifically said was not a slum (1962). ("Che bellezza!") From 1946 through 1947), the superb fieldworker Hortense Powdermaker studied Hollywood with an intense focus on the social relations of making movies and doing lunch (1950). But, even with the help of the ethnologist and motion-picture director Paul Fejos, she was not entirely satisfied with a study that never quite came to grips with this ungraspable community (Powdermaker 1966:210, 229-31).

With fieldwork in the 1950s, Herman Lantz produced an insightful study of "Coal Town," Illinois a one-industry community, dying, with drastic consequences for its citizens, because of the closing of its mines (1958). Arthur Vidich and Joseph Bensman studied the lack of agreement between American ideals and actuality in behaviors in "Springdale," New York, and the functioning of an "invisible government" not accountable to the citizenry (1958). Springdalers complained about the perceived offensive tone of and revealing of personal identities in the penetrating study. These complaints prompted one of the largest discussions ever in social science about the reporting of field data, in the pages of *Human Organization* from 1958 through 1960 and in reviews since then (Vidich, Bensmen, and Stein 1964; Emerson 1981:363-75). Conducting a community study can be a bit like clearing a mine field. To escape from the limitations of studying a single town, the farming and ranching adaptations of the "Jasper" region of Saskatchewan, a dispersed plains community, was studied by John Bennett and reported for the 1960s (1969). The ethnologist of business and work, James O'Toole, did an innovative comparative study of the communities of Watts in Los Angeles and Woodstock in South Africa (1972). Looking beyond work, a retirement community was studied by Jerry Jacobs, in which he showed that few retirees participate in the active "fun" lifestyle (1974).

Vernon Boggs, G. Handel, and S. Fava, using the outlook of the Chicago School, depicted Big Apple life, in the communities within New York City (1983). Terry Buss and F. S. Redburn investigated the unemployment consequences of a one-factory town, Youngstown, Ohio, losing its steel plant (1983). A French-American community of Cajuns, Henderson, Louisiana, was studied by Marjorie Esman, complete with reports on local businesses and on "making a living" (1985). The historical community study of St. Clair, Pennsylvania, by Anthony Wallace was conducted entirely from written sources but displays the strong imprint of the ethnologist. Many threads of the development of the local anthracite industry and its structuring consequences for the town are woven into one of the most masterful of community studies (Wallace 1988). Pittsfield, Massachusetts, is the locus of June Nash's penetrating decades-long study of the effect of the large General Electric plant, and particularly its defense contracts, on the surrounding community. This historically oriented research progresses through an analysis of the current American restructuring of industry as it impacts Pittsfield (Nash 1989). Melvin Williams in a restudy, a decade later, of his microethnography labeled "on the street where I lived" demonstrates the investigative power of the community study, focused here on the trials and joys of everyday life along Lang Avenue in Belmar, a Pittsburgh neighborhood (1992). Continuing in the tradition of Upton Sinclair, Carol Andreas traces the development of the meat-packing company town of Greeley, Colorado into the control of its restructured plants by a megacorporation bent on exploiting its employees (1994).

Across the entire twentieth century, the community studies examine work as the focus of North American society and its social activity, even for those not working. All of the community studies emphasizing stratification of statuses depicted the differential rewards going to North Americans according to their kinds of occupational and other roles. A stratified community is one of socioeconomic inequality these studies repeatedly demonstrated. Although a community is not a microcosm of the encompassing national society, its study does yield profound insights and otherwise unreachable information on work and its relation to the rest of social life. The nine decades of these penetrating community studies also yield a historical comparison of the changing ways of work. As a nonfiction genre with a profound influence on our society, the North American community study, not surprisingly, has spawned a fictional derivative. Peter Davis, the celebrated producer of many documentaries, including the six-part PBS series "Middletown," wrote an acclaimed novel in the style of the community study, *Hometown: A Portrait of an American Community*, complete with factory, trade union, and industrial strike (1982).

WORKER PARTICIPATION IN THE CONTROL OF
MODERN WORK

Continuing with our turn to American and Canadian society, we discuss the issues of employee participation in the managerial control of work in the "new industrial relations" developing for the twenty-first century. We also discuss the control of technology in a democracy, where such control affects everyday life, often more powerfully than by an election change in political parties.

The Quandary of Employee Participation

For Americans and Canadians also necessary for recognition in a conception of work are the crucial issues raised by employers' programs of participation, to varying extents, of employees in the decision making and information gathering of a firm. These programs have various forms and labels, among others: quality of work life, employee involvement, labor-management cooperation, team concept, and quality circles. Are these participation programs a reincarnation of the managerially similar goals of both the scientific management and human relations schools of work relations? Or will the programs eventually lead to increased empowerment of workers under the web of rules for work relations?[19] These issues of work have yet to be settled; so, let us explore them.

Labor-management cooperative programs date back to those of the 1920s, sponsored by John D. Rockefeller, with Standard Oil's "employee representation," by Charles Schwab, in U.S. Steel's "constructive cooperation," and by Daniel Willard, with the Baltimore & Ohio's "cooperative plan." For unionized workers, participation programs by their very existence broaden the nature of customary labor-management relations. (For discussion of these relations see Gamst's chapter 6.) It should be noted at the outset that a participation program—if properly developed and then controlled through bilateral (labor-management) negotiations—*can* result in mutual achievements and benefits for the two parties. Like gunpowder, a cooperative program is not always dangerous, but its uninformed use frequently is explosive for labor. Participation programs have long been fraught with danger for employees in all kinds of industries. Despite all manner of advocacy for a new cooperative model of labor-management relations, as yet, no such broadly workable arrangement has emerged (Sleigh 1993:2).

Participation programs are often founded in a simplistic trendy optimism, naively taking no account of the historically highly consequential exercises of power and opposing goals in the relations of labor and management. For example, the current result of such exercise of power and opposing goals in the American railroad industry is the steadily increasing mileage to be run in earning the basic day's pay for employees in freight service. This increased basic day has neutralized the effect of cost of living and other increases in pay during the 1980s for railroaders in such service. Other current results include outsourcing of mechanical and clerical work, reduction of train crew size, and manning trains through home terminals. Some railroads have shifted part of their facilities to nonrailroad ownership or have spun off lines to remove their employees from their protection under the federal Railway Labor and Interstate Commerce acts. The firms have thus been making repeated end runs around their railroad employees and involved unions. In Canada during 1993, at the time of the near demise of the pro-labor New Democratic Party, current results include railroad and federal governmental attacks on the nature of the rail craft bargaining units existing for over a century. A participation program can be a managerial wolf in cooperative sheep's clothing.

A business firm by definition is an organized managerial entity. As a modern organization it possesses great socioeconomic power, alone and in coordination with similar organizations, united in trade associations and with special access to government (Clegg 1990; Coleman 1982, 1990). Unorganized (nonunion) employees and "disorganized" ones—those in a trade union but not insisting that all matters affecting the wages and conditions of employment be negotiated and agreed under labor law—are at a great disadvantage in the formidable power relations of the labor market. A true employee participation program, having meaningful employee involvement, therefore, "requires that management be willing to relinquish some control over workplace behavior" (Schuster 1984:218). As former president of the United Auto Workers Douglas Fraser instructs: "I am convinced that you cannot have a cooperative, collaborative relationship unless there's equal partners, equal power. Now, without a union you can't have that equal partnership" (Parker and Slaughter 1993a:9). Relinquishing of and sharing power is something most management is not ready to do. That is, management wants organized labor to cooperate solely on managerial terms.

Can dangers occur for employees in cooperative programs established by the employer? On the level of the individual worker, cooperative programs leading to increased productivity might reduce the number of employees needed by a firm and might displace employees from customary desired to new less desired work tasks and work schedules, and even to lower paying assignments. On the level of the group of employees constituting a bargaining unit, the problems are more momentous.

A labor union's fundamental power stems from the solidarity and commitment of its members and from cooperation with other unions. In its traditional adversarial role of countering and undermining a labor organization's power and influence, through cooperative programs management can usurp responsibilities and duties of a union. In other words, management can attempt "union busting" with a new weapon. By cooperative programs, management could appear to be the advocate, protector, and benefactor of employees. The union's lawful role as the exclusive representative chosen by employees is thereby gradually whittled away. Through cooperative programs, change could surreptitiously be made from formal collective bargaining to formal and informal individual bargaining with an employee. In other words, the employer can use cooperative programs to weaken and to circumvent the union rules, policies, and procedures hard-won across the years. This may be done as part of a firm's policy for labor relations, with or without the consent of its labor relations officers, and it may be enacted by local managers with or without the knowledge of higher managers. Employee-involvement programs must not become management's route, in these ways, to its desired union-free environment. The fox cannot be enable to safeguard the hen house.

The market pressure on wages and conditions of employment is inexorably downward. On any level, to attain competitive advantage, management is interested in diminishing the rates of pay and the terms and conditions of employment written into the current labor contracts. Such is the job and the path for career advancement of managers. For example, cooperative activities could be used to change negotiated provisions and customary practices regarding the scheduling of assignments, tasks included in jobs, and handling of grievances. At times, the activities could be used to discover and enlarge differences of opinion and even schisms regarding negotiable issues among members of a bargaining unit. Given managerial involvement in matters at least in part formerly handled by the leaders of a bargaining unit, regarding some employees there could be a lessening of union organizational cohesiveness, weakening of ideals of the labor movement, and reduction of identification with collective goals and values for labor relations.

The National Labor Relations Board ruled on the seething issue of employee participation in a 1992 landmark case, *Electromation, Inc.*, 309 N.L.R.B. 163. Here the board found an ordinary management-organized participation group for employees to be a "labor organization" under the pivotal Section 8(a) (2) of the National Labor Relations Act of 1935 as amended—and therefore unlawful.[20] The Congress has before it proposals from business to rewrite Section 8(a) (2). Such an enactment would make legal again management-sponsored organizations for employees regarding their conditions of employment. The American labor movement is divided over this crucial, intricate issue of rewriting its future (Parker and Slaughter 1993b; 7, 11; Boal 1993: 10; Rivers 1993: 11-12, 14).

Ordinarily, all labor-management disputes are settled in one of three actions (Fisher and Ury 1983): (1) by use of power, with one party forcing its will upon the other; (2) through exercising lawful rights such as in laws, contracts, norms, and established practices; (3) when the two parties attempt to settle differences although protecting their own self-interests. In most instances, the use of power has been management's action of choice (Sexton 1991). Cooperative labor-management programs can only be a part of the third action, bilateral labor-management relations. To have these programs exist in any other context is to court labor-relations disaster for employees.

If, in the United States and Canada, there will be a "new industrial relations," innovative directions in collective representation of workers, and improvements in the quality and security of work life, these must be developed in partnership with organized labor and not dictated in whole or in part to labor by its adversary. Logically, and equitably, the much heralded "end to adversarialism" in labor relations cannot be implemented unilaterally by just one of the two parties. Discussions by unionized employees of issues of quality, efficiency, and competitiveness on the job cannot in logic or labor relations be dealt with apart from the composite whole of the wages and conditions of employment. These last two are correctly handled solely in bilaterally negotiated agreements. Labor-management committees of any kind created or maintained apart from a collective bargaining agreement, therefore, constitute "sharpshooting" at this contract. Such committees in a nonunion workplace can be an impediment to unionization. The central issue, then, is not, should employees have cooperative programs but, why should these programs not be bilateral in their genesis?

Control of Technological "Progress" in a Democratic Society

The sectarian, laissez-faire ideology of technological "progress" and its included value of having persons suffer from the consequences of this progress without any compliant or redress has been a legitimizer of business practice. Despite the paeans to technology sung by Americans and Canadians taught the idealized lyrics of national prosperity through technological development, the worker should always be aware that technology is not a neutral force affecting his life and shaping society, as if by an invisible and impartial hand of advance in the various industries (Westrum 1991). "Progress" is directed by a visible, self-interested hand. Technological change, then, is not blind in its development but is given guidance and goals by private firms, public agencies, and other organizations, including labor unions. Part of the North American national mythologies is an unquestioning belief in both the attainability and efficacy of a technological solution to a country's problems. North Americans must realize, however, that without their reflection and questioning they cannot rely on technology for their salvation. Our cultural fetish of imbibing technological panaceas such as the current "reindustrialization" and "reengineering" is without reflection on the social toxins of raw power and domination within the old technological snake oil in new bottles of this kind. As David Nobel does reflect regarding technological change: "The cultural fetishization of technology . . . has allowed Americans to ignore and forget what is not changing—the basic relations of domination that continue to shape society and technology alike" (1986:x).

On railroads, for example, management ordinarily controls technology, often within a general web of government regulations (for example, those of the National Mediation Board, Interstate Commerce Commission, and Canadian Labour Board). This managerial control of technology, at times, has lead to the impoverishment of work life, the impairment of family life, and even the devastation of communities, such as towns of railroad home terminals.[21] Only rarely does management exercise control over its employees directly through technology alone. Control comes through the bureaucratic organization of the corporation, thereby giving a mantle of managerial values to technology. Accordingly, an employee participation program not jointly controlled by rail unions and management is a clear and present danger to labor. Thus, in an industrial democracy, only cooperative programs both bilaterally established and directed should exist (cf. Dilts 1993:128).

In the United States, organized labor has a movement that is weak and declining in membership, power, and influence (Huang 1989). Accordingly, organized labor should consider not just to what extent it agrees to and participates, somewhat passively and sometimes defensively, in cooperative programs initiated by management but also to what degree it demands inclusion in corporate decision making and a voice in formulating the de facto national industrial policy (Sexton 1991:1-2, 274-8). Realization of union goals to achieve the all-important power sharing in the interconnected realms of business and government will not be attained easily, or inexpensively. But without a long-term goal of attaining some codetermination of the control and process of work and some influence over the de facto national industrial policy, American labor unions will decline still further and their membership will become still more downwardly mobile.

Needed is a labor vision for wielding legitimate power in new ways to safeguard a future for workers in our late-industrial age and global economy. Any "new industrial relations" must be novel from the perspectives of both management and labor. Labor must, however, develop broader outlooks than has usually been the case. Samuel Gompers desire for "more" for employees must, in these times of a global labor market, now include more power and control for labor. Otherwise, as has been the experience of recent years, North American employees will continue to receive "less." Power and control are at the bottom of all industrial relations, whether or not labor leaders act upon this truth.

The overall pay scale for unionized employees in American private industry is 35 percent greater and for blue collar workers 70 percent higher than in nonunion firms (Anon. 1993:6). Accordingly, unionization brings a wage advantage to employees in a labor market with firms seeking a competitive advantage by almost any means. Some students of labor feel, however, that this workers' advantage will no longer obtain. One study shows that firms extensively unionized have lower profit rates, market value, and investment in capital and research and development than similar nonunion firms (Hirsch 1991). In other words, with unionization the fruit of labor is redistributed more in favor of workers than would otherwise be the case. Thomas Kochan summarizes a growing problem for North America: "In the international economy of the 1990s and beyond, collective bargaining and industrial unionism can no longer protect worker interests by taking wages out of competition" (1993a:1, 1993b:187-88). During the twenty-first century, in unprotected competition for labor, the higher union wages (and related higher nonunion wages bolstered by unionism) will be detrimental to American and Canadian competitiveness, for example, with the products of Chinese prison labor and other Third World lowly paid labor, sold into the global market. Thus in the dawning world competition to get work, Americans and Canadians are at a great disadvantage. Clearly, if they are to survive in the global labor market of the twenty-first century, unions must develop their own version of a truly new industrial relations. If they do not, it will be developed for them, to their detriment.

THE FUTURE OF WORK IN NORTH AMERICA

The debate in labor circles over participating programs distracts from the enormity of the now-engulfing problem at hand, the devastatingly new nature of work. The new work often means long-term loss of a person's customary kind of employment, life career, and standard of living. The new conditional employment steadily increases, consisting of part-time, temporary, and contract employees—having lesser wages, little or no fringe benefits, and no change of job training—the accursed children of a lesser nation.

The New Nature of Work

In late industrial societies, such as the United States and Canada during the twenty-first century, the future of work may well include not enough of it (or at least not enough work allowing the earning of a customary livelihood) to employ all persons seeking jobs. The two countries have long suffered from a widespread corporate disinvestment in their underlying national productive capacities. Rich corporations milk money from the "cash cows" among their facilities and invest the funds overseas, where labor is cheaper and more controllable by the police. Failure in the two counties of business to compete in the global market has engendered a massive deindustrialization, with attendant loss of the better-paying jobs for ordinary people. In the wake of deindustrialization are closed factories, chronically unemployed workers, dilapidated cities, and decaying infrastructure (Bluestone and Harrison 1982; Harrison and Bluestone 1988; Rodwin and Sazanami 1989; Craypo and Nissen 1993). The globalization of the labor market in the creation of goods and services means that North American assembly-line workers compete with those in southern Asia working for a fraction of their total compensation, and enterers of computer data compete with those in the West Indies and Ireland earning less than half as much.

Jobs for the twenty-first century increasingly will be in the service rather than production industries. Many of the services rendered in the 1990s are shaped by the technological revolutions in electronic communication and in computerization of information handling. The revolutions have allowed great growth in business services. Information for banking; exchange of stocks, bonds, and currencies; and commercial trading of commodities and manufactured goods span the globe electronically in the blink of an eye. Yet these kinds of service jobs are highly susceptible to great automation and rationalization. Thus whether in the traditional, deindustrializing jobs of smokestack production or in the new, automation-probe jobs of electronic service, the outlooks are bleak for both growth in numbers of good jobs and security for employment in such extant jobs.

American and Canadian living standards have eroded since 1980: real wages have fallen, increasing the necessity of working mothers; the number of homeowners continues to decline; higher education becomes ever more unaffordable; and (for America only) the privilege of medical care is denied to growing millions of citizens. In the United States, the needy public picks up the business tab of hundreds of billions of deficit dollars for government's reckless mismanagement of the savings and loans. And, because of over a decade of deindustrialization and decrease in national investments in job skills, capital goods, and infrastructures, workers cannot improve their declining standard of living through increased earnings (Mishel and Frankel 1991; Schor 1991). For further perspectives on these matters, see chapter 7 by Nash, chapter 8 by Blau, and chapter 9 by Weiss.[22]

Today, jobs are permanently eliminated by the scores, often by the thousands, for a single profitable firm. In the job market of the 1990s loyalty has become a one-way street. It does not take much in corporate whim or change in planning to put a long-time employee's job at risk. The employee is supposed to be loyal to the firm, but the employer can, and does, terminate employment at will.[23] In organizations, downsizing of staff is planned in advance. The numbers to be axed are decided well beforehand and divided among the departments. Frequently, a silence rule is enforced on middle managers so that they cannot divulge who will be selected for early retirement or outright firing. Such terminations can be brutal. In some cases, the employee experiences a mass "bug extermination" of firees in a meeting room; sometimes a security guard comes to a firee and orders him to pack his personal effects before he is escorted out the front door. At other times, those not signing a firm's termination document are blackmailed and extorted with threats of no outplacement and related services and of no transitional medical benefits. The employee's family is the hostage of the firm until the extortion demands are met. "Molly Brown," a veteran MBA-level administrator, terminated at a conscienceless Boston teaching hospital for no explained cause, was told to sign a form stating she had resigned voluntarily. At first, she determined to write on the form "I was told to resign." But, then, she said to me, "After sleepless nights, fear took hold"—she had others to support and desperately needed the severance benefits including medical coverage. "It got really nasty toward the end," said this resistance-fighter casualty of the university business conflicts. She now works, from week to week, as a contingent worker.

In democratic North America, stable white- and blue-collar jobs are disappearing structurally (that is, permanently) and workers and their families are compelled to accept a terrifying new labor market. Furthermore, use of contingent employees has become an antisocial corporate addiction. The socioeconomic contract between capital and labor is being torn to shreds. Accordingly, the twenty-first century will be the era of a disposable, rootless worker, giving a graphic new meaning to *proletarian*. Perhaps Marx was wrong about North America. Those with a high school education or less, including many socially disadvantaged citizens, will never participate in the American and Canadian way: work hard, follow the employer's requests, and thereby receive an adequate piece of the economic pie.

Loss of Employment

At one time, North Americans did not talk in public about their sex lives. Similarly, today, as in the past, they find it difficult to tell others that they have been terminated from their job. Shame, embarrassment, humiliation, and anger are typical reactions of a person after being terminated by an employer. In America, a severe anomie is that of the worker who has lost a job. The severest anomie, as in the 1990s, is that of a person who has lost a job with no hope of comparable employment. At a gathering of adults, the unemployed feel ostracized. Their opportunity for conversation is circumscribed because such talk frequently involves the speakers' world of work. People talk about their jobs almost as much as about themselves. But, then, these two entities overlap: "me/my job."

Ordinarily, with no job one has little in the way of public identify or publicly presentable image of the self. ("You mean, you *don't* work [have a job]?") The North American work ethic holds that one should work arduously and diligently and, consequently, one becomes sufficiently rewarded in society.[24]

Being terminated and losing, even temporarily, the attainment of the central societal reward, work, signifies publicly that one might not have labored arduously and diligently. One, therefore, might be a failure in the North American way of life—a loser. Even those in some way forced into retirement develop such a reaction of self-doubt. See chapter 9 by Weiss for depiction of this reaction. Of course, layoffs have a personal and social impact on those not thus fired (O'Toole 1987:110-3, 280-1, 309-13). As Lloyd Warner and others showed in their community studies, downward mobility is the situation dreaded most, not just because of the economic consequences but because of the loss of self-esteem and self-identity.

The traditional American view of working as being sacred and not working as sin persists in the self-chastising and insecurity of the unemployed, the exiles from our society (of workers). "Henry Johnson," one of the casualties of the market, for a time reduced to the ranks of the unemployed in the Boston area, explained to me: "When I was terminated, I became mentally paralyzed; I couldn't think straight. I dreaded facing each new day, and I couldn't sleep at night." The question of his waking nightmare was, "At forty-five, will I ever find work in my field again?" For this electrical engineer, work was more than the comfort of a regular paycheck. He said it was his identity, activities for preventing slipping into a social void. "What am I," he thought. "God! What did *I do* to deserve this," he agonized. He had three children to put through college, a mortgage in jeopardy, and a wife who had to return to the workforce as a minimum-wage sales clerk. I talked to him two years later. He worked outside of his field at little more than half of his former salary, the house was lost, and only one of the children attended college. His familial downward cycle had begun.

To be out of work for a lengthy period is to be out of hope personally and to be out of regard and value socially, that is, without a personally or socially recognizable self. Those without work are the national economy's surplus humans. Moreover, some persons in our society are denied the instructional means and market opportunity to take a job. Rather than unemployed, they are almost never-employed. If work facilitates the integration of a citizen into a country, how united, then, can our increasingly multicultural

American and Canadian societies endure? How realistic can the ideal of participatory democracy remain, if some citizens are condemned to the work on the periphery of society, or sentenced to "hang out" on its street corners?[25] The parallel American and Canadian dreams of workers of all kinds are increasingly becoming part of a global nightmare of work for the twenty-first century.

NOTES

1. In furthering this understanding, in this and related chapter 6 I use considerable literature on work providing information for additional personal reading and instructional use.

2. Reviews with varying emphases on the ethnology of industry, organizations, and work have been done by Tway 1977; Gamst 1977; Holzberg and Giovannini 1981 Gamst 1984a, 1984b; Pennbridge 1985; Baba 1986; Gamst and Helmers 1991; and Götz and Moosmüller 1992. For further considerations of work and related subjects see the journals *Anthropology of Work Review* and *Work and Occupations* and the column of the Society for the Anthropology of Work in the *Anthropology Newsletter* of the American Anthropological Association.

3. Given the diffuseness of the term *work* in English, this chapter could begin by, instead, saying: In this work (writing), now put in the works (in process) is the working out (accomplishing) of a working (on which future work may be based) conception of work (the activity) yielding some kind of a work (the product of this activity). The reason for working (attempting to solve) this issue is to work (influence) people to study our central concept, the working (handling) of which necessitates a time-consuming working (gradual progress requiring great effort).

4. For the Ethiopian Wayto and Qemant, see Gamst's chapter 6.

5. Work occurs with reference to bodies of self-interested and self-serving actors and the individuals within these groupings. (For these actors, see Gamst's chapter 6.) The actor bodies are, minimally, in a dual system, those who conduct work and those who in some way control this work. A web, however, does not encompass "free," all-rational individuals making knowledgeable calculations for their efficient maximization of personal gain and pleasure. Every societal work relations system has a particular *ideology* for each of the bodies of actors. Here, concerning work, ideology is a socially learned and somewhat shared way of thinking about this activity including interactions with fellow individuals inside a body and with other bodies of actors. Such an ideology consists of what could be termed a set of *modalities* guiding behavior, including norms, values, ideals, standards, plans, etiquette, and prescriptive aspects of roles. Because of individual self-interest and other

idiosyncratic variation in behavior, however, the ideas of the modalities are neither static nor absolute requisites for behavior. No person, then, is "natural," that is, free from the behavioral modalities of a culture of subculture. Rational persons behave "rationally" only with reference to an encompassing set of behavioral modalities. Both the emic behavior and the etic conception of a "rational" person are necessarily peculiar products of particular cultures. Accordingly, the precepts of classical and neoclassical economics are culturebound (Gamst 1991).

6. For the timing of industrial work and life see Gamst 1993.

7. Expiation should be included C. Wright Mills feels (1951:215-6).

8. But the arch priest mainly receives as income goods and services through the Qemants' status (nonmarket) exchange of redistribution (Gamst 1988).

9. Because, on railroads, for example, these coordinations and rules are imposed by management upon employees, they are part of the web of rules discussed by Berg and by Gamst in chapters 4 and 6.

10. For work as slavery see P. D. Anthony 1977.

11. For these three kinds of economic exchange, see Dalton 1971; Sahlins 1971.

12. Regarding modern work at least, central to its conception must be recognition of the related concept of skill (cf. Vallas 1990–91). Significant is the ongoing debate about skill requirements of modern work, the controversy over the deskilling of such work, and the place of skill in contests for control of work between employees and employers (Wood 1982, 1989; Attewell 1987, Form 1987; Kern and Schumann 1987; England and Dunn 1988; Haydu 1988; Hyman and Streeck 1988; Zuboff 1988).

13. Regarding auto assemblers, William Form says work "integrates their lives" (1973:1).

14. For reviews of literature on community studies in America see: Galpin 1918; Arensberg 1942, 1954, 1955; Hollingshead 1948; Goldschmidt 1968; Szwed 1979; Gallaher and Padfield 1980; and Spindler and Spindler 1983. Charles Galpin in the 1910s wrote some of the pioneering methodologies on studying the small American community. This information is summarized in chapter 4 of his 1918 *Rural Life*.

15. For a review of ethnological studies focusing on the workplace see Gamst 1990.

16. The Lynds, although labeled as sociologists used then explicitly ethnological methods of field research, centering on participant observation. It was not for nothing that ethnologist Clark Wissler introduced their 1929

study as "a pioneer attempt to deal with a sample American community after the manner of social anthropology" (Wissler 1929:iv).

17. My esteemed colleagues and fellow railroaders the late Nels Anderson (1923:ix–x) and Fred Cottrell (1940:v–vi) told me they worked for and acquired their formative insights into industrial and organizational social science on the same railroad that I did, the Los Angeles & Salt Lake, or "Salt Lake Line" of folk song fame. My views on industrial relations in this chapter are formed in part from over thirty-nine years in railroad labor-management relations as a minor rail union officer, university researcher, and professional consultant in the railroad industry.

18. As an Italian-American, born and raised in such a community, I have always been sensitively interested in depictions of us by writers.

19. Arguments have been made on all sides of the issues raised by the participation programs (Strauss and Rosenstein 1970; Parker 1985; Gold 1986; Parker and Slaughter 1988; Grenier 1988; Banks and Metzgar 1989; Cooke 1990; Grenier and Hogler 1991; Tausky and Chelte 1991).

20. Section 8(a) (2) of the NLRA reads: "It shall be an unfair labor practice for an employer . . . to dominate or interfere with the formation or administration of any labor organization or contribute financial or other support to it. . . . " For further discussion of the consequential issues of this sea change of a case see: Brickley 1992; Reynolds 1992; Schlossberg and Reinhart 1992; and Hogler 1993.

21. For the impairment of family life see Gamst 1980:110–13, and for the devastation of communities, in this instance the railroad community of Caliente, Nevada, see Cottrell 1951.

22. Issues of the elemental restructuring of work have been developed by a number of writers in sundry disciplines including Montgomery 1979; Burawoy 1985; J. Williamson 1985; O. Williamson 1985; Granovetter and Tilly 1988:175–81.

23. For at-will employment, see Gamst's chapter 6.

24. The underlying folk views of work in America have long been fairly well assessed. In his survey research, Daniel Yankelovich finds Americans have four central views of the meaning of work (1974). First, to be a man in America means being a good breadwinner for the family. Second, through work one earns freedom and independence in life. Third, hard work will eventually lead to success in life. And, fourth, one's worth is found in the act of working.

25. For pithy ethnological perspectives on the condemned of the American world of work, see Liebow 1967; Spradley 1970; Keiser 1979; Newman 1988, 1993.

REFERENCES

Anderson, Nels
1961 [1923] *The Hobo: The Sociology of the Homeless Man*. Chicago: University of Chicago Press.

Anderson, Wilbert L.
1906 *The Country Town: A Study of Rural Evolution*. New York: Baker and Taylor.

Andreas, Carol
1994 *Meatpackers and Beef Barons: Company Town in a Global Economy*. Niwot, CO: University Press of Colorado.

Anon.
1993 Wage trends: New data on the union advantage. *LRA's Economic Notes*. September:6.

Anthony, P. D.
1977 *The Ideology of Work*. London: Tavistock.

Applebaum, Herbert
1984a *Work in Non-market and Transitional Societies*. Albany: State University of New York Press.

1984b *Work in Market and Industrial Societies*. Albany: State University of New York Press.

Arensberg, Conrad
1942 Industry and community. *American Journal of Sociology* 48:1–12.

1954 The community study method. *American Journal of Sociology* 60:109–24.

1955 American communities. *American Anthropologist* 57:1143–62.

Attewell, Paul
1987 The deskilling controversy. *Work and Occupations* 14:323–46.

Baba, Marietta L.
1986 Business and industrial anthropology: An overview. *NAPA Bulletin No. 2*.

Banks, Andy, and Jack Metzgar
1989 Participating in management union organizing on a new terrain. *Labor Research Review* 14:1–55.

Bennett, John W.
1969 *Northern Plainsmen: Adaptive Strategy and Agrarian Life*. Chicago: Aldine Atherton.

Bluestone, Barry, and Bennett Harrison
1982   *The Deindustrialization of America: Plant Closings, Community Abandonment, and the Dismantling of Basic Industry.* New York: Basic Books.

Blumenthal, Albert
1932   *Small-town Stuff.* Chicago: University of Chicago Press.

Boal, Ellis
1993   What the law says now. Labor Notes. December:10.

Boggs, Vernon, G. Handel, and S. F. Fava, eds.
1983   *The Apple Sliced: Sociological Studies of New York City.* New York: Praeger.

Bouvier, Pierre
1989   *Le Travail au Quotidien: Une démarche socio-anthropologique.* Paris: Presses Universitaires de France.

Braude, Lee
1983   *Work and Workers.* Malabar, FL: Krieger.

Brickley, Kathleen K.
1992   Labor-management cooperation: Summary of the electromation case. *Labor Law Journal.* June: 395–6.

Bulmer, Martin
1984   *The Chicago School of Sociology: Institutionalization, Diversity, and the Rise of Sociological Research.* Chicago: University of Chicago Press.

Burawoy, Michael
1985   *The Politics of Production.* London: Verso.

Buss, Terry F., and F. Stevens Redburn
1983   *Shutdown at Youngstown: Public Policy for Mass Unemployment.* Albany: State University of New York Press.

Cannon, Walter B.
1942   "Voodoo" death. *American Anthropologist* 44:169-81.

Clegg, Stewart R.
1990   Modern Organizations. Newbury Park, CA: Sage.

Coleman, James S.
1982   *The Asymmetric Society.* Syracuse, NY: Syracuse University Press.

1990   *Foundations of Social Theory.* Cambridge, MA: Harvard University Press.

Cooke, William N.
1990   *Labor-Management Cooperation: New Partnerships or Going in Circles?* Kalamazoo, MI: W. E. Upjohn Institute for Employment Research.

Cottrell, W. Fred
1940   *The Railroader.* Stanford, CA: Stanford University Press.

1951   Death by dieselization: A case study in the reaction to technological change. *American Sociological Review* 16:358-65.

Craypo, Charles, and Bruce Nissen, eds.
1993   *Grand Designs: The Impact of Corporate Strategies on Workers, Unions, and Communities.* Ithaca, NY: ILR Press.

Dalton, George, ed.
1971   *Primitive, Archaic, and Modern Economies: Essays of Karl Polanyi.* Boston: Beacon Press.

Davis, Allison, Burleigh B. Gardner, and Mary R. Gardner
1941   *Deep South: A Social Anthropological Study of Caste and Class.* Chicago: The University of Chicago Press.

Davis, Peter
1982   *Hometown: A Portrait of an American Community.* New York: Simon and Schuster.

de Man, Henri
1929   *Joy in Work.* London: Allen & Unwin.

Dilts, David A.
1993   Labor-management cooperation: Real or nominal changes in collective bargaining? *Labor Law Journal.* February:124-8.

Drake, St. Clair, and Horace P. Clayton
1945   *Black Metropolis.* New York: Harcourt, Brace.

Ellison, Ralph
1964   An American dilemma: A review. In *Shadow and Act.*, pp. 303-17. New York: Random House.

Emerson, Robert M.
1981   Observational field work. *Annual Review of Sociology* 7:351-78.

England, Paula, and D. Dunn
1988   Evaluating work and comparable worth. *Annual Review of Sociology* 14:227-48.

Esman, Marjorie R.
1985   *Henderson, Louisiana: Cultural Adaptation in a Cajun Community.* New York: Holt, Rinehart and Winston.

Firth, Raymond
1955   Function. In *Current Anthropology*, William L. Thomas, ed., pp. 237-58. Chicago: University of Chicago Press.

Fisher, Roger, and William Ury
1983   *Getting to Yes: Negotiating Agreement without Giving In*. Boston: Houghton Mifflin.

Form, William H.
1973   Auto workers and their machines: A study of work, factory, and job satisfaction in four countries. *Social Forces* 52:1–15.

1987   On the degradation of skills. *Annual Review of Sociology* 13:29–47.

Gallaher, Art
1961   *Plainville Fifteen Years Later*. New York: Columbia University Press.

Gallaher, Art, and Harland Padfield
1980   *The Dying Community*. Albuquerque: University of New Mexico Press.

Galpin, Charles J.
1918   *Rural Life*. New York: Century Company.

Gamst, Frederick C., ed.
1977   Golden Anniversary Special Issue on Industrial Ethnology. *Anthropological Quarterly* 50(1).

Gamst, Frederick C.
1969   *The Qemant: A Pagan-Hebraic Peasantry of Ethiopia*. New York: Holt, Rinehart and Winston.

1974   *Peasants in Complex Society*. New York: Holt, Rinehart and Winston.

1980   *The Hoghead: An Industrial Ethnology of the Locomotive Engineer*. New York: Holt, Rinehart and Winston.

1984a   L'ethnologie industrielle Nord-Américaine. *Sociétés: Revue des Sciences Humaines et Sociales* 1(2):11–12.

1984b   Considerations for an anthropology of work. Reprinted in: *Work in Non-Market and Transitional Societies*, pp. 56–61, Herbert Applebaum, ed. Albany: State University of New York Press.

1988   The Qemant theocratic chiefdom in the Abyssinian feudal state. In *Proceedings of the Eighth International Conference on Ethiopian Studies*, Addis Ababa, 1984. Taddese Beyene, ed., vol. 1:793–8. Huntingdon, Cambs.: ELM Publications.

1990   Industrial organizational perspectives on the development and characteristics of the study of organizational cultures. In *Cross-Cultural Management and Organizational Culture*. Tomoko Hamada and Ann Jordan, eds., pp. 13–47. (William and Mary) Studies in Third World Societies No. 42.

1991 Review of James S. Coleman, Foundations of social theory, in *Anthropology of Work Review* 12(3):19–25.

1993 "On time" and the railroader: Temporal dimensions of work. In *Ethnologie der Arbeitswelt.* Sabine Helmers, ed., pp. 105–31. Bonn: Holos.

Gamst, Frederick C., and Sabine Helmers
1991 Die kulturelle Perspektive und die Arbeit: Ein forschungsgeschichtliches Panorama der nordamerikanischen Industrieethnologie. *Zeitschrift für Ethnologie* 116:25–41.

Gans, Herbert J.
1962 *The Urban Villagers: Group and Class in the Life of Italian Americans.* New York: Free Press.

Gold, Charlotte
1986 *Labor-Management Committees: Confrontation, Cooption, or Cooperation?* Ithaca, NY: ILR Press.

Goldschmidt, Walter R.
1946 *Small Business and the Community: A Study in Central Valley of California on Effects of Scale in Farm Operations.* Washington, DC: U.S. Government Printing Office.

1947 *As You Sow.* New York: Harcourt.

1955 Social class and dynamics of status in America. *American Anthropologist* 57:1209–17.

1968 The anthropological study of modern society. *International Encyclopedia of the Social Sciences* 1:330–8.

1978 *As You Sow: Three Studies in the Social Consequences of Agribusiness.* Montclair, NJ: Allenheld Osmund.

Götz, Irene, and Alois Moosmüller
1992 Zur ethnologischen Erforschung von Unternehmenskulturen. Industriebetriebe als Forschungsfeld der Völker-und Volkskunde. *Schweizerischen Archiv für Volkskunde* 88(1–2):1–30.

Granovetter, Mark, and Charles Tilly
Inequality and labor process. In *Handbook of Sociology*, Neil J. Smelser, ed., pp. 175–221. Newbury Park, CA: Sage.

Grenier, Guillermo
1988 *Inhuman Relations: Quality Circles and Anti-Unionism in American Industry.* Philadelphia: Temple University Press.

Grenier, Guillermo, and R. L. Hogler
1991 Labor law and managerial ideology: Employee participation as a social control system. *Work and Occupations* 18:313–33.

Hans, Robert, and Arthur Kleinmann
1983   Belief as a pathogen, belief as medicine. *Medical Anthropology Quarterly* 14(4):3, 16–19.

Harrison, Bennett, and Barry Bluestone
1988   *The Great U-turn: Corporate Restructuring and the Polarizing of America.* New York: Basic Books.

Haydu, Jeffrey
1988   *Between Craft and Class: Skilled Workers and Factory Politics in the United States and Great Britain, 1890–1922.* Berkeley: University of California Press.

Herskovits, Melville J.
1952   *Economic Anthropology: A Study in Comparative Economics.* New York: Knopf.

Hirsch, Barry T.
1991   *Labor Unions and the Economic Performance of Firms.* Kalamazoo, MI: W. E. Upjohn Institute for Employment Research.

Hogler, Raymond L.
1993   Employee involvement and Electromation, Inc.: An analysis and a proposal for statutory change. *Labor Law Journal.* May:261–74.

Hollingshead, August B.
1948   Community research: Development and present condition. *American Sociological Review* 13:136–56.

1949   *Elmtown's Youth: The Impact of Social Class on Adolescents.* New York: Wiley.

Holzberg, Carol S., and M. J. Giovannini
1981   Anthropology and industry: Reappraisal and new directions. *Annual Review of Anthropology* 10:317–60.

Huang, We-Chiao
1989   *Organized Labor at the Crossroads.* Kalamazoo, MI: W. E. Upjohn Institute for Employment Research.

Hughes, Everett C.
1952   The sociological study of work. *American Journal of Sociology* 57:423–6.

Hyman, Richard, and Wolfgang Streeck, eds.
1988   *New Technology and Industrial Relations.* London: Basil Blackwell.

Jacobs, Jerry
1974   *Fun City: An Ethnographic Study of a Retirement Community.* New York: Holt, Rinehart and Winston.

Kalleberg, Arne L., and Ivar Berg
1987   *Work and Industry: Structures, Markets, and Processes.* New York: Plenum.

Keiser, Lincoln R.
1979 *The Vice Lords: Warriors of the Streets.* New York: Holt, Rinehart and Winston.

Kelsen, Hans
1948 *The Political Theory of Bolshevism.* Berkeley: University of California Press.

Kern, Helmut, and M. Schumann
1987 Limits of the division of labour. *Economic and Industrial Democracy* 8:151–70.

Kochan, Thomas
1993a Trade Unionism and Industrial Relations. *IRRA Dialogues.* May:1.

1993b Trade Unionism and Industrial Relations: Notes on Theory and Practice for the 1990s. Industrial Relations Research Association, Proceedings of the 45 Annual Meeting, pp. 187–8.

König, René
1958 *Soziologie.* Frankfurt a/M: Fischer Bücherei.

Landy, David
1990 Toward a biocultural medical anthropology. *Medical Anthropology Quarterly* 4:358–69.

Lantz, Herman R.
1971 [1958] *People of Coal Town.* Carbondale: Southern Illinois University Press.

Leonard, Olen, and Charles P. Loomis
1941 The Culture of a Contemporary Rural Community: El Cerrito, New Mexico. Bureau of Agricultural Economics, U.S. Department of Agriculture, Rural Life Studies No. 1. Washington, DC: U.S. Government Printing Office.

Lewis, Oscar
1946 Bumper crops in the desert. *Harper's Magazine* 193:526–8.

1948a Rural cross section. *Scientific Monthly* 66:327–34.

1948b On the Edge of the Black Waxy: A Cultural Survey of Bell County, Texas. Washington University Studies, n.s., Social and Philosophical Sciences 7 (whole issue).

Lex, Barbara
1974 Voodoo death: New thoughts on an old explanation. *American Anthropologist* 76:818–23.

Liebow, Elliot
1967 *Tally's Corner: A Study of Negro Streetcorner Men.* Boston: Little, Brown.

Lind, Andrew W.
1938   *An Island Community.* Chicago: University of Chicago Press.

Lynd, Robert S., and Helen M. Lynd
1929   *Middletown: A Study in American Culture.* New York: Harcourt, Brace.

1937   *Middletown in Transition: A Study in Cultural Conflicts.* New York: Harcourt, Brace.

Miller, Joanne
1988   Jobs and work. In *Handbook of Sociology*, Neil J. Smelser, ed., pp. 327–59. Newbury Park, CA: Sage.

Mills, C. Wright
1951   *White Collar: The American Middle Class.* New York: Oxford University Press.

Miner, Horace
1939   *St. Denis: A French-Canadian Parish.* Chicago: University of Chicago Press.

1949   *Culture and Agriculture: An Anthropological Study of a Corn Belt County.* Ann Arbor: University of Michigan Press.

Mishel, Lawrence, and David M. Frankel
1991   *The State of Working America.* Armonk, NY: M. E. Sharp.

Montgomery, David
1979   *Workers' Control in America: Studies in the History of Work, Technology and Labor Struggles.* New York: Cambridge University Press.

Myrdal, Gunnar
1944   *An American Dilemma: The Negro Problem and Modern Democracy.* New York: Harper.

Nash, June
1989   *From Tank Town to High Tech: The Clash of Community and Industrial Cycles.* Albany: State University of New York Press.

Nelson, Lowry
1930   *The Mormon Village: A Study in Social Origins.* Provo, UT: Brigham Young University Studies No. 3:(whole issue).

Newman, Katherine S.
1988   *Falling from Grace: The Experience of Downward Mobility in the American Middle Class.* New York: Free Press.

1993   *Declining Fortunes: The Withering of the American Dream.* New York: Basic Books.

Noble, David F.
1986   *Forces of Production: A Social History of Industrial Automation.* New York: Oxford University Press.

Norbeck, Edward
1959   *Pineapple Town—Hawaii.* Berkeley: University of California Press.

OED (Oxford English Dictionary)
1971   [1884-1928] *The Compact Edition of the Oxford English Dictionary,* vol. 2, P-Z. New York: Oxford University Press.

O'Toole, James
1972   *Watts and Woodstock: Identity and Culture in the United States and South Africa.* New York: Holt, Rinehart and Winston.

1987   *Vanguard Management: Redesigning the Corporate Future.* New York: Berkley Books.

Pahl, R. E., ed.
1988   *On Work: Historical, Comparative and Theoretical Approaches.* Oxford: Basil Blackwell.

Parker, Mike
1985   *Inside the Circle: A Union Guide to QWL.* Boston: South End Press.

Parker, Mike, and Jane Slaughter
1988   *Choosing Sides: Unions and the Team Concept.* Boston: South End Press.

1993a   What is the Reich Commission? *Labor Notes.* December:9.

1993b   AFL-CIO may trade away law against company unions. *Labor Notes.* December:7, 11.

Pennbridge, Julia N.
1985   *Industrial Anthropology: A Selected Annotated Bibliography.* Society for Applied Anthropology, Monograph No. 14.

Powdermaker, Hortense
1939   *After Freedom: A Cultural Study in the Deep South.* New York: Viking.

1941   *Probing Our Prejudices.* New York: Harper.

1950   *Hollywood the Dream Factory: An Anthropologist Looks at the Movie Makers.* Boston: Little, Brown.

1966   *Stranger and Friend: The Way of an Anthropologist.* New York: Norton.

Reynolds, Joy K.
1992   A perspective on the Electromation case from the U.S. Department of Labor. *Labor Law Journal.* June:397-402.

Richardson, Frederick L. W., Jr.
1941   1942, 1948 Community resettlement in a depressed coal region. *Applied Anthropology* 1(1):24–53, 1(3):32–61, 7(4):1–27.

Richter, Curt P.
1957   On the phenomenon of sudden death in animals and man. *Psychosomatic Medicine* 19:191–8.

Rivers, Andrew
1993   How one company is using a modern 'company union' to keep out the CWA. *Labor Notes*. December:11–12, 14.

Rodwin, Lloyd, and H. Sazanami, eds.
1989   *Deindustrialization and Regional Economic Transformation: The Experience of the U.S.* Boston: Unwin Hyman.

Sahlins, Marshall
1971   *Stone Age Economics*. Chicago: Aldine.

Schor, Juliet
1991   *The Overworked American: The Unexpected Decline of Leisure*. New York: Basic Books.

Schlossberg, Stephen I., and Miriam B. Reinhart
1992   Electromation and the future of labor-management cooperation in the U.S. *Labor Law Journal*. September:608–20.

Schuster, Michael H.
1984   *Union-Management Cooperation: Structure-Process-Impact*. Kalamazoo, MI: W. E. Upjohn Institute for Employment Research.

Sexton, Patricia C.
1991   *The War on Labor and the Left: Understanding America's Unique Conservativism*. Boulder, CO: Westview.

Sleigh, Stephen R., ed.
1993   *Economic Restructuring and Emerging Patterns of Industrial Relations*. Kalamazoo, MI: W. E. Upjohn Institute for Employment Research.

Spindler, George D., and Louise Spindler
1983   Anthropologists view American culture. *Annual Review of Anthropology* 12:49–78.

Spittler, Gerd
1991   Die Arbeitswelt in Agrargesellschaften. *Kölner Zeitschrift für Soziologie und Sozialpsychologie* 43(1):1–17.

Spradley, James P.
1970   *You Owe Yourself a Drunk: An Ethnography of Urban Nomads*. Boston: Little, Brown.

Strauss, George, and E. Rosenstein
1970   Workers' participation: A critical review. *Industrial Relations* 9:197–214.

Szwed, John F.
1979   The ethnography of ethnic groups in the United States, 1920–1950. In *The Uses of Anthropology.* Walter Goldschmidt, ed., pp. 100–9. Washington, DC: American Anthropological Association.

Tausky, Curt, and Anthony F. Chelte
1991   Employee involvement: A comment on Grenier and Hogler. *Work and Occupations* 18:334–42.

Tilgher, Adriano
1958   [1929] *Work: What It has Meant to Men through the Ages.* Chicago: Henry Regnary.

Tway, Patricia, ed.
1977   Special issue: Anthropology and the public sector. *Anthropological Quarterly* 50(4).

Vallas, Steven P., ed.
1990   -1991 Special issues: The meaning and measurement of skill. *Work and Occupations* 17(4):379–483, 18(1):4–45.

Vidich, Arthur J., and Joseph Bensman
1958   *Small Town in Mass Society: Class, Power and Religion in a Rural Community.* Garden City, NY: Doubleday.

Vidich, Arthur J., Joseph Bensman, and Maurice Stein
1964   *Reflections on Community Studies.* New York: Wiley.

Wadel, Cato
1979   The hidden work of everyday life. In *Social Anthropology of Work,* Sandra Wallman, ed., pp. 365–84. New York: Academic Press.

Wallace, Anthony F. C.
1988   *St. Clair: A Nineteenth-century Coal Town's Experience with a Disaster-prone Industry.* Ithaca, NY: Cornell University Press.

Warner, W. Lloyd
1949   *Democracy in Jonesville.* New York: Harper.

Warner, W. Lloyd, and J. O. Low
1943   *The Strike: A Social Analysis.* New Haven: Yale University Press.

1946   The factory in the community. In *Industry and Society,* W. F. Whyte, ed., pp. 21–45. New York: McGraw-Hill.

1947   *The Social System of the Modern Factory.* New Haven: Yale University Press.

Warner, W. Lloyd, and Paul S. Lunt
1941   *The Social Life of a Modern Community*. New Haven, CT: Yale University Press.

Westrum, Ron
1991   *Technologies and Society: The Shaping of Peoples and Things*. Belmont, CA: Wadsworth.

Whyte, William Foote
1955   [1943] *Street Corner Society: The Social Structure of an Italian Slum*, 2nd ed. Chicago: University of Chicago Press.

Williams, James M.
1906   *An American Town: A Sociological Study*. New York: no publisher.

Williams, Melvin D.
1992   *The Human Dilemma: A Decade Later in Belmar*. Fort Worth: Harcourt Brace Jovanovich.

Williamson, Jeffrey
1985   *Did British Capitalism Breed Inequality?* London: Allen and Unwin.

Williamson, Oliver
1985   *The Economic Institutions of Capitalism*. New York: Free Press.

Wirth, Louis
1928   *The Ghetto*. Chicago: University of Chicago Press.

Wissler, Clark
1929   Foreword. *Middletown: A Study in American Culture*. In Robert S. Lynd and Helen M. Lynd., pp. v–vii. New York: Harcourt, Brace.

Withers, Carl
1945   *Plainville, U. S. A.* New York: Columbia University Press.

Wood, Stephen, ed.
1982   *The Degradation of Work? Skill, Deskilling, and the Labour Process*. London: Hutchinson.

1989   *The Transformation of Work? Skill, Flexibility, and the Labour Process*. London: Unwin and Hyman.

Yankelovich, Daniel
1974   The meaning of work. In *The Worker and the Job*. Jerome S. Rosow, ed., pp. 19–47. Englewood Cliffs, NJ: Prentice-Hall.

Zorbaugh, Harvey W.
1929   *The Gold Coast and the Slum: A Sociological Study of Chicago's Near North Side*. Chicago: University of Chicago Press.

Zuboff, Shoshana
1988   *In the Age of the Smart Machine: The Future of Work and Power*. New York: Basic Books.

2

The Concept of Work in Western Thought

INTRODUCTION

As background to the necessarily Western concepts in social science found in this book, the present chapter reviews salient aspects of the Western tradition of culture and work. I present a general perspective on work across three historical periods—ancient, medieval, and modern. Next, I discuss work and technology and, finally, I consider work, leisure, and the future of work.

What is work? The human condition compels the existence of work as a condition of life. Work creates our human-made environment. Human beings are both in nature as biological beings subject to the laws of nature and outside of nature through the material and social environment they create as extensions of their culture. Since work relates to all human activity, no definition of work is satisfactory short of explaining all human culture. Humans at work use materials, forces, and living organisms of nature to fashion tools with which to make, grow, and build things to satisfy human needs. Making things is not the only kind of work. Teachers, clerks, engineers, scientists, nurses, doctors, accountants, secretaries, guards, and so on do not make anything. These people satisfy needs through service to others. Both making things and performing services are useful work.

The role of technology is crucial to human work. The human mind must have some idea of the thing to be made before it is created. In the modern world ideas about what and how things are made are part of technological information controlled by specialists. But there is an ongoing struggle to prevent technology from getting beyond human control, from leading to deskilling of work and to giving employers and management inordinate control over the workplace (Trice 1993:17–9). Regardless of the power of technology, it is always a human decision as to how, when, and where to use that technology.

There is a big difference between a tool, controlled by human hands, and a machine to which human hands must adapt. Once the machine appears, humans cease to be the subjects of their own work. Only in their own workshops and in their homes can people have control over their own work, not in the factory. We no longer design products to fulfill needs as our primary goal. Products are designed that are adaptable to present technology, and then the "need" is created for these products through advertising and marketing. When markets and profits dominate the work process, the quality, beauty, usefulness of product, and satisfaction from work, are all secondary to the sale and the profit. Technology then spawns products like a biological process run wild. Whether mankind wants or needs these products becomes irrelevant relative to economic success. Marketing, as well as technology, leads to the flood of goods that pours over and coats our perspectives on quality of life.

A commercialized, market-type of society fits well with cultures dominated by materialism, scientific rationalism, and technological primacy. However, if we think it important to establish human control over work and over technology, structural changes will be required in the organization of work and in the nature of social and political organization in industrial cultures. Whether the work ethic is strong or not, accepted or not, needs to be revised or not, our survival as a species depends on the need to work. Work is the cooperative effort of humankind, the sharing knowledge and skill to create our human-made world. Work is still associated with self-esteem, social progress, and quality of life. Work is still the precondition for releasing people to enjoy self-fulfilling leisure. Work is still associated with maturity, self-discipline, and moral values. For all these reasons, work is the precondition for the human condition.

THE CONCEPT OF WORK IN ANCIENT GREECE AND ROME

Homeric Society

Homeric society is that complex of institutions, relationships, and social values depicted in the Homeric epics. The key institution was the aristocratic "oikos," a family group residing on a landed estate, which included father, mother, unmarried children, sons with wives, grandparents, slaves, retainers, itinerant craftsmen, visiting relatives, and wandering strangers, including minstrels. Gift-exchange and reciprocity was the single most important social merchanism for establishing alliances between different household groupings (Finley 1979:65). This mechanism is common among small-scale, preindustrial cultures. Reciprocity preserves orderly relations between persons and groups through the flow and exchange of gifts and hospitality (Mauss 1967).

Work in Homeric society, similar to work in other nonmarket, small scale cultures, was embedded in all the activities of the society (Applebaum, 1984:3–4). In these cultures, just as in Homeric society, there is no separate word for work, as it is part of the life-course. Thus, we find work is acceptable to all ranks and groups in Homeric culture, to nobles as well as commoners. Noble men and women did not disdain to participate in work. Odysseus built his own bed-chamber. Paris helped with the construction of his home. Penelope spins and weaves and makes garments. Nausicaa washes clothes. Odysseus challenges the suitors to a ploughing contest, boasting that he could cut grass with a scythe, drive a pair of oxen, and plow a clean furrow (Iliad 61.23–24; 22.440–41; *Odyssey*, 2.97; 6.30). In Homer's time, the specialist was the *demiourgoi* (the artisan who worked for the people) and the term, *techne*, referred to their know-how, demanding experience and dexterity such as that of metalworkers and carpenters, and among women to the art of weaving. There was no clear distinction between technological achievement and feats of magic, and the social category of the *demiourgoi* included healers and diviners as well as workers in wood and metal (Vernant 1983:279).

Classical Greece

During the classical period, the attitude toward work contrasted with that of the Homeric period. Farming work was esteemed, but any form of wage work was considered a form of slavery. Service to others was considered unworthy of a truly free man. The free man was the active man of leisure, free to engage in politics and contemplation. The free man was a user of products, never a maker of products. The literature from classical Greece is filled with observations about the inferior nature of those who must perform manual work (Plutarch 1934:171-2; Xenophon *Oeconomicus*, 1970:IV.2; Aristotle, *Politics*, 1946:VII, 1328b.37-1329.2). Plato stated that those who needed to work must be willing to accept an inferior status, nor was Plato interested in training people who must work to make them fit for governing.

Like Plato and Socrates, Aristotle believed that the mechanical arts had a degrading effect on the body and mind. To perfect a skill, in Aristotle's view, was to be stricken with a bent of mind that made one unfit for contemplation and philosophy. Aristotle believed that the bodies of artisans became cramped and warped by the monotonous movements of their trades. Like Plato, Aristotle believed that working people, even farmers, could not be trained to rule the state. It is ironic that Plato and Aristotle, who both believed that democracy was the best form of government, should have devised models that resembled the oligarchy of Sparta. Both tried and failed to reconcile the nature of work with the nature of the democratic city-state.

While philosophers of classical Greece reflected a disdain for work, craftsmen themselves were not necessarily ashamed of their craft. Epitaphs survive that show manual workers proudly proclaiming what work they performed and how well they did it. Crowns given for craftsmen competitions is further evidence of respect accorded tradesmen. The signing by workers, particularly pottery, is a mark of self-esteem. Pottery, plaques, stelai, sculptures, and bas refliefs survive from ancient classical Greece portraying men and women at work (Burford 1972:177-8). The craftspersons who created these scenes were making proud statements about themselves, perhaps with the approval of their patrons who permitted such portrayals.

Hellenistic Greece

Stoicism was one of two main philosophical trends during the Hellenistic period, Epicureanism being the other. Stoics postulated a universe of rational structures subject to rational explanation. According to Stoic philosophy, cosmic events and human actions were part of the same order (logos). Wisdom was a step beyond rationality, being harmony between actions and events. Work, like all other aspects of the universe, was part of the order of things.

"Through Stoic teaching, work is moralized . . . an ethos of work and workmanship arises" (Edelstein 1966:76). Unlike the Aristotlean view, which saw the user as the one to evaluate work, Stoicism stressed the workman's relation to product, along with the worker's moral life. Stoicism reshaped attitudes toward manual work, postulating the notion of "calling," a concept later developed by Christian thinkers into the idea that everyone, even the lowliest person, had a mission in life to fulfill (Edelstein 1966:77–8).

Roman Republic and Roman Empire

Cicero, a leading statesman and thinker during the late Roman Republic, representative of the ruling elite, considered as "vulgar and undesirable" all hired workmen and manual laborers, whose very wage was a mark of their slavery (Cicero, *De Officiis*, L.XLII.150–1). The important distinction in the ancient world was between the man who worked for himself and the man who worked for others, with only the former considered to have social prestige (Heitland 1970:458).

Rome put its slave system in place during the late Roman Republic. Writers on agriculture like Cato, Varro, and Columella assumed an agricultural system based on large estates, run for profit and manned by slave men and women. The small proprietor was still in the majority but losing out to absentee landlords with large estates. In the cities, small workshops increasingly used slave labor. The Roman bureaucracy increasingly used slaves, as in the case of the water system, which was maintained by a work force of 700 slaves (Frontinus, *Aqueducts of Rome*, II.116). Work in the mines was mostly done by slaves and condemned criminals. Both small and large households employed slaves, with the large aristocratic households having slave specialists ministering to the needs and wants of the wealthy (Petronius, *Satyricon*, 1987).

One significant aspect of Roman society was the existence of *collegia*, clubs made up of people sharing the same craft. They were mutual aid societies, providing benefits for members. Collegia provided an outlet where working people could mingle with peers. Collegia gave commoners a sense of importance. They could run for and elect collegia officers, worship collegia patron gods, and attend collegia dinners and festivals. They were not unions or guilds since they did not try to control wages or prices. The collegia were active in city ceremonials. They were important politically, as Roman statesmen sought to mobilize their vote during elections. More than 150 of them have been traced and accurately defined (Carcopino

1968:178). At one juncture in Rome's history they appeared so powerful, and dangerous, that Augustus outlawed them.

Agricultural work was always extolled in Rome, particularly the small, working farmer, as exemplified by Virgil's great tribute to farming, *The Georgics* (1987). In the ideal, farm work was linked to citizenship and citizenship linked to military service. It was modeled on the story of Cincinnatus, a legendary hero who left his plough to save the State and then returned to his farm (Bowder 1980:58).

Handicraft and artisan work, considered manual work, was never held in high esteem by the elite of Rome. During the Empire, however, artisans began to have higher status as their importance grew in proportion to the decline of slave labor. Free men found it profitable to undertake craft work. Masses of free men were employed in public works projects (Brunt, 1980:81–100). Still the prejudice against manual labor did not disappear. Roman opinion was articulated by Seneca who said that "wisdom does not teach our fingers but our minds." (Guinagh and Dorjahn, 1942:498).

During the Roman period, women shared in their husband's work, particularly in the finer crafts, luxury trades, perfumery, and tailored clothing. The mother of Emperor Marcus Aurelius was prominent in the brick manufacturing business. Women worked in service occupations like nursing and midwifery, where there were opportunities to achieve some distinction. The social role of women was predominant in the home and in the upbringing of children. Roman attitudes toward mothers was generally positive, intense, and emotional.

THE EARLY JEWISH AND CHRISTIAN ATTITUDES TOWARD WORK

Arthur Geoghegan (1945:60) characterizes the ancient Hebrew attitude toward work: "Surely, if the Most High is described as the Divine Laborer, it cannot be dishonorable for a man to work." Mosaic law showed solicitude for the man who worked for wages, something neither the Greeks nor the Romans ever did (Deuteronomy, 24.14). The Old Testament depicts many of the Hebrew leaders performing work—Gideon in the wine press, Saul working in the fields, David keeping sheep, Elisha plowing (Judges, 6.11; I Samuel 11.5; I Samuel 16.11; I Kings 19.19). Most of the Rabbinical teachers were workingmen—masons, woodcutters, charcoal makers, sandal makers, scribes, bakers, grave diggers (Geoghegan 1945:75–6).

The New Testament is the source for Christ's attitude toward work. He was born into the home of an artisan and was one himself, a carpenter. His companions were workers. And in his preaching he drew material from the world of work. Early Christian thinkers had a positive attitude toward work, particularly St. Paul and St. Augustine. Paul was a tentmaker, practiced his trade and used the expression, "my fellow workers." One of his most often quoted sayings was, "If anyone will not work, let him not eat." Saint Augustine wrote an important treatise on the subject of work, *De Opere Monachorum*, in which he extolled work as a means of moral perfection. In his *City of God*, Augustine presents one of the great tributes to human work, referring to the genius of man and his astonishing arts. Augustine saw work partly as a necessity for sustenance, and partly as the result of exuberant invention and the remarkable vigor of the human mind. Ernst Benz calls Saint Augustine "the first Christian theologian of technology" (1966:128).

The teachings of St. Paul and St. Augustine reinforced the respect for work. They saw work as providing independence for the individual, as offering a pathway to humility, and as a means of offering charity to others. Many wealthy Christians followed their preachings, gave up their wealth, and distributed their goods to the needy. Christian communities of the third century were social welfare communities, providing work for the unemployed and supporting the unemployable. Work and charity were the two important messages of the early Christian Church, along with the word of God and the teachings of Christ.

Monasticism and the Concept of Work

A number of writers and thinkers have pointed to the connection between positive attitudes toward work in Western civilization and the monastic movement (Ovitt 1987; Weber 1950; Benz 1966; Mumford 1967; Le Goff 1980). The Benedictine rule for monastic life made work an integral part of daily life, which was divided into three parts—one for prayer; one for sleep, meals, and recreation; and one for work. The Benedictine monastery provided the basis for the later development of the positive attitude toward work by placing in the social fabric an institution that accepted work as part of a person's moral commitment.

The Concept of Work During the Middle Ages

The ninth and tenth centuries in northern Europe saw the introduction of a number of new inventions and techniques. These included the three-field system in place of the two-field system, the use of the horse in agriculture facilitated by a new horse collar, and the use of the heavy plow to work the heavy soils of northern Europe. With the advent of the Carolingians and the reign of Charlemagne, great attention was paid to the nature of work. In his capitulary, *de Villis*, Charlemagne addresses improvements in the organization of work on the royal estates, along with recognition of the crafts and training and education for artisan work.

The church's position was that spiritual life was enhanced by work on three counts: first, work helped to protect against the dangers of idleness; second, work created opportunities for both charity and communal self-sufficiency; and third, work was the means through which humans exercised their stewardship over nature (Ovitt 1987:164). On a more profound level, man's work was viewed as being in the image of God's work, which was the work of creation. Any profession or trade that did not create was inferior. A peasant's work during the harvest, or the artisan who transformed materials into objects, performed creative work. But the merchant who created nothing was condemned. This attitude changed when cities grew in importance and merchants through their power and wealth were able to get the recognition they sought.

When we think of the Middle Ages, we think of guilds and the apprenticeship system for the learning of craft. Indeed, our romanticized concept of work stems from this period and this system (Lucie-Smith 1984:113-4). It is a concept based on the idea of the craftsperson working with her/his own tools and materials, controlling the work process, possessing technical knowledge and skill, and selling the product. Craft work was also associated with the great period of cathedral building during the Middle Ages, 1100 to 1400. With inexact technology, master craftsmen and journeymen, with their apprentices and laborers, created lasting monuments to their work skills, their organizing and administrative abilities, and their religious zeal (Delort 1983:73-74; Gimpel 1980:1). It was during this period that towns and cities arose after the disruptions of invaders from the east and north ceased. It was in the cities where guilds were created to form an integral part of the economy and administration of these centers. In the cities and towns people were free of feudal restrictions. A German expression, "the city makes you free," reflected the fact that in the cities people were free to learn a craft and become independent.

There is a thesis, not without controversy, that during the three centuries that closed the Middle Ages, men were in short supply and that women were impelled into the work world (Howell 1988:1–6; 193–7). The unlucky ones became prostitutes and street people. Luckier ones found work in textiles, domestic service, peddling, or in entering convents. The luckiest worked in their own craft, training as apprentices and becoming master craftspersons in their own right.

Masonry was held in high esteem during the Middle Ages, largely due to its association with the building of churches and cathedrals. Stone was the symbol of the church building. There were two types of masons, the hardstone masons and the freestone masons. The term, "freestone" referred to the soft stone used for sculpture. Those who worked the soft stone were called freemasons, a term later associated with the freemasonry and the freemason's lodge. Lodges were places set up near building sites where masons could sleep, keep their tools, and hold discourses among themselves. It was from this social system at the work site that the masonic lodge and the freemason movement came into being (Knoop and Jones 1967).

The Middle Ages was based upon the interdependence between the three orders—priests (oratores), warriors/nobles (bellatores), and workers (laboratores) (Duby 1980). Even though workers were at the bottom of the social ladder, they did have a recognized place in society. They had duties, but they also had rights, just as the other orders. Ovitt believes that medieval society aimed at, but never achieved, a social order based upon a morally centered culture, cooperative labor, and an honored place for the concept of work. This was reflected in the monastic movement, but it never spread to the rest of medieval society and culture (1987:204).

THE MODERN PERIOD: THE SIXTEENTH THROUGH THE EIGHTEENTH CENTURIES

Luther and Calvin

Protestantism and the ideas of Luther and Calvin on work is the beginning of the modern concept of work. For Luther, work was a basis for charity and a defense against idleness. However, Luther broke with monastic thinking, which he considered selfishness and an abdication of responsibility to the world at large. Luther saw work as the base of society and the basis for differing social classes. He believed everyone should work within the confines and according to the traditions of one's trade or profession into which one was born. Luther's doctrine of "calling" was his most important idea about the work ethic. It was a message of action and a message of individualism. Luther rejected the Roman Catholic double standard of higher and lower callings, shifting the idea of work from its punishment quality to its positive and creative aspects.

Unlike Luther, Calvin considered it unworthy for one to remain satisfied with one's station in life. Calvin freed work from the hampering ideas of caste. In his hands, work became mobile, fluid, and man-made rather than God-given. Work was rationalized by Calvin, who viewed life from the standpoint of the peasant. Unlike Luther, Calvin praised trade, profits, and finance, considering them as on the same level as the earnings of workmen when based on diligence, industry, and hard work. Calvin believed that profit was a sign of God's blessing.

There is a continuing debate over Max Weber's thesis regarding the connection between Protestantism and the rise of capitalism (Telos, Issues 75 and 81). However, the connection between Protestantism and the work ethic is quite clear and indisputable, particularly as regards Calvinism. Protestantism emphasized order in one's life. This goal was also emphasized by Catholic monasticism, with the difference being that the monks sought to achieve their goals within their self-contained communities, while Calvinists and Lutherans participated in the affairs of the world-at-large. Both the Calvinists and the monasticists sought an ordered existence based on a strong work ethic and rationally formulated rules of behavior (Weber 1950:119).

The English Enlightenment

The English Enlightenment of the seventeenth century marks a further advance in the development of a modern view of work. It wedded the mechanical arts and the knowledge of skilled craftsmen to the theories of science. Francis Bacon, son of Sir Nicholas Bacon, Lord Keeper of the Great Seal, who lived from 1561 to 1626, was one of the first to advocate the importance of the mechanical arts in the development of scientific knowledge (Bacon 1967:85-6). Thomas Hobbes (1588-1679), author of the great work in political philosophy, *Leviathan*, shared Bacon's rejection of the status quo of medieval scholasticism and advocated experimental science as the path for human progress. Hobbes believed that all people in a commonwealth should be required to work as an obligation to society, which, in turn, gave them rights as citizens. In order to eliminate the reason for people not being able to find employment, Hobbes urged the government to develop the mechanical trades so that everyone would be able to find some form of work (The *Leviathan* 1939:334). Hobbes believed that labor was the principal element in the value of goods and saw mankind's development as based on the mechanical arts and inventions. He believed human beings created governments just as they created any other object through their work. Hobbes described government as an artificial person created by man, the *artificer*, significantly choosing a term of work rather than one of mind. Hobbes stated that knowledge of the world can only be gained through knowledge of craft and science rather than magic, which was part of his materialist approach to the natural world.

John Locke (1632–1704), son of a country lawyer, grew up amid the disorders of the English Civil War and was later involved in the struggle against James II. In his concept on the origins of property Locke relied on his concept of work. Locke's view was that the labor of one's body was the foundation of property. Locke sought an explanation of how private property could be taken out of the public domain and be appropriated to one's self. His solution was that since work or labor added something to nature's products, one was entitled to that which one added his labor to, and that no one could take the right of one's labor from him. A hundred years before Adam Smith, Locke propounded a labor theory of value, stating that "'tis Labour indeed that puts the difference of value on every thing" (*Two Treatises of Government*, Laslett translation, 1967:314). The labor theory of value, as further developed by Marx and Adam Smith, assets that all goods, regardless of price, receive their value from the labor-time expended upon them. Wood comments that Locke was the first classic political theorist to place such great emphasis on labor, making it the cornerstone of his edifice of political ideas (Wood 1984:53). Locke had a concept of God as maker, stating that humans have property through their own work by working in a "God-like fashion" (Tully 1980:36). Work now becomes a moral activity. Locke said, "God, when he gave the world in common to all mankind, commanded man also to labour" (*Two Treatises*, p. 35). To work now becomes a direct command of God. Work becomes the logical extension of human beings, part of the natural law of human existence.

The French Enlightenment

The eighteenth-century French Enlightenment was reflected largely in the work of Diderot, Voltaire, and Rousseau, while the Scottish Enlightenment was represented by Adam Smith, David Hume, and Adam Ferguson.

Denis Diderot sought to weld the mechanical arts to the physical and social sciences. His underlying philosophy was rationalism and faith in human progress. Diderot insisted that all arts, the mechanical as well as the liberal, must have both a theoretical as well as a practical side (Diderot, *On Art*, 1953:292). Diderot wanted to give artisans their due and admonished the liberal arts for having contempt for the mechanical arts. He observed that artisans believed themselves contemptible because people looked down upon them. Diderot felt his mission was to teach workers to have a better opinion of themselves (1953:301).

Voltaire propagated the idea of progress through human effort rather than reliance on the deity. In *Candide*, Voltaire concludes with the concept that life become bearable through work, embodied in the memorable words, "we must cultivate our garden" (*Candide* 1959:119–20). At Ferney, Switzerland, Voltaire established a watchmaking industry. He built homes for workers and attracted craftsmen to his model town. Maurois states that the Voltaire of Ferney was no longer the "fashionable man" but was a Benedictine of rationalism (Andre Maurois, Introduction to *Candide*, pp. 4–5). Voltaire believed he had done more in his own time than Luther or Calvin to promote the good life based on craft and control over one's calling (Tilgher 1930:84).

Jean-Jacques Rousseau, born in 1712, had an early taste of the atmosphere of the workshop, being the son of a watchmaker. Born in Geneva, Rousseau was influenced by the Calvinist work ethic. He also had a first-hand experience of work, being apprenticed to an engraver at the age of twelve (Jean-Jacques Rousseau, *Confessions*, 1923:36). Rousseau's respect for the artisan way of life was especially clear in his tract on education, *Emile*, in which he said "Man in society is bound to work. . . . Emile shall learn a trade. I would rather have him a shoemaker than a poet, I would rather he paved streets than painted flowers on china. . . . We have made him a worker and a thinker" (*Emile*, 1953, p. 66).

The Scottish Enlightenment

With Adam Smith we have a developed formulation of a theory of work. Not only did he postulate a labor theory of value, but he foreshadowed the modern malaise of work, with its severe division of labor and its monotonization of work. Smith pioneered in his theory of the free market and the place of work within the factory system. He was a true Enlightenment figure, as a professor of ethics and political economy and as one of the founders of the *Encyclopedia*

Britannica. Smith believed that the understandings of men are formed by their ordinary employments (*Wealth of Nations*, 1937:302). His associate in the Scottish Enlightenment, Adam Ferguson, also believed that a man's character was formed by his "work function" (Reisman, 1976:153). Smith and Ferguson saw that the division of labor increased worker productivity through specialization, but they also observed that extreme subdivision of labor led to human deprivation by contracting the mind through the repetitive nature of overly subdivided work. Adam Smith thought the ill effects of the subdivision of labor in industry could be overcome by education. He was sympathetic to the working man and advocated high wages to provide incentives to work. In essence he viewed work, or labor, as the basis of a nation's wealth and also as the measure of value of all goods in a society.

Benjamin Franklin

Benjamin Franklin certainly deserves to be ranked as an Enlightenment man. His life, his writings, his public career, his mastery of the craft of printing, all combined to make him a model of the blending of hand and mind, of intellectual and manual laborer, of the public and private man of action, i.e., the model of Enlightenment man. He was also a man of science with his experiments in electricity, which earned him membership in both the British and French Academies of Science. Franklin espoused the Puritan work ethic of Calvinism. His publication, *Poor Richard's Almanac*, was filled with the thoughts of Enlightenment thinkers. In this publication Franklin exhibits his principles as a philosopher of the work ethic, a fact recognized by both Karl Marx and Max Weber. Marx credited Franklin with coining the concept of man as a "tool-making animal" (*Capital*, 1906:358). Given his views on work and his attitude toward the importance of labor, it is not surprising to find that Franklin developed a labor theory of the value of goods (*Writings*, 1987:119–35). Throughout his long career Franklin maintained his belief in the importance of work as the foundation of society (*Writings*, 1987:977).

Utopian Socialists

During the early decades of the nineteenth century, a group known as Utopian Socialists sought to reform existing European society, which was in the throes of developing industrialism and suffering the consequent birth pangs of broken lives, pollution, demeaning work, and unsanitary conditions. Three of the most prominent of these early reformers were Robert Owen, an Englishman, and two Frenchmen, Charles Fourier and Claude Henri de Rouvroy de Saint-Simon.

The Utopians believed that work and its improvement was a key to a better world. They rejected the capitalist view of work, which was based mainly on rationalism and cost efficiency. Instead, they saw work as a liberating, creative force that could transform workers as well as the world for the better. What was needed, in the view of the Utopian Socialists, was a transformation of societal institutions, which would help to make work more meaningful. Taking their cue from the Enlightenment, these utopians believed that by reason and through the education of society's leaders, as well as through the example of model communities, that social conditions could be reformed. A number of utopian communities were established in the United States during the first half of the nineteenth century. However, the ideas of the utopians failed to reform society at large, since it was based on convincing those in power in European and American society to give up their power by means of reason alone, an unrealistic hope at best. Nevertheless, these Utopian Socialists left a legacy of good works, creative ideas, and a strong belief in the creative and transforming power of work as part of the condition of mankind.

THE MODERN PERIOD: THE NINETEENTH CENTURY

The nineteenth century is the century of industrialism, and work as we know it is based on industrial cultures. Work in industrial society holds a central place in the life of the individual and belongs to the public sphere where it is wage work. Work in the home, unpaid work, voluntary work is not recognized in economic terms. Work in the public sphere enables one to acquire a social existence and a social identity. Work becomes part of a network of exchanges, in which persons are measured against each other. Work requires obligations and duties, but it also confers rights upon those who engage in work in the marketplace. Andre Gorz identifies industrial society as a "society of workers," which distinguishes it on these grounds from all earlier forms of society (Gorz, *Critique of Economic Reason*, 1989:13-14).

Karl Marx

During the nineteenth century, it was Karl Marx, above all, who advanced the modern theory of work, giving it a profound and distinctive dimension within his overall social theory and his philosophical viewpoint. Marx's view of the importance of work stemmed from his notion that productive relationships were the most important ties in modern society. He stated that by acting upon nature through work mankind creates its own nature (*Capital*, 1906:198).

Like Adam Smith, Marx saw that cooperation in work and the division of labor led to great productivity and efficiency. But Marx went beyond Smith in viewing the effects upon human beings of the extreme subdivision of labor. Where Smith saw monotonization, Marx saw alienation, man separated from the products of his own hands. Hegel's ideas influenced Marx on a number of questions, including that of alienation. Alienation according to Hegel, was not a marginal aspect of work, but fundamental and imminent. Hegel believed the nature of work made man alien to his own objective world, which, once it comes into being, stands outside of man, and in some sense over and against him (Avineri 1973:196–215). Marx wished to create a society where mankind would do away with the alienation of work by eliminating its coercion and by turning it into an end-in-itself as part of the self-fulfillment of human beings. Marx pictured a society that would "make it possible for me to do one thing today and another tomorrow, to hunt in the morning, fish in the afternoon, rear cattle in the evening, criticize after dinner, just as I have a mind, without ever becoming hunter, fisherman, shepherd, or critic" (*Basic Writings*, edited by S. Feuer, 1959:254).

Marx saw the possibility that work could become a positive, creative activity, and not necessarily a curse, only if work was associated with choice and pleasure (*Grundrisse*, 1971:435). Marx saw the future as one of increasing productive power of the forces of production that would release all persons for the enjoyment of free time. He sought to close the gap between work and leisure, not by turning work into play, but by transforming leisure into something close to creative work (*Grundrisse*, 1971:290). Marx saw the joy to be derived from work as not mere pleasure but as an earnest kind of joy linked with the fulfillment of purpose. "Not Playboy but Prometheus was Marx's model; a heroic individual engaged in a variety of challenging, self-directed activities of social value" (Campbell 1989:22).

Other Thinkers

Marx, Hegel, and the Utopian Socialists were not alone in considering the problem of work in the nineteenth century. Thomas Carlyle (1843) and William Morris (1946) in England extolled the virtues of work and workmen. In the United States, the Puritan New England and Quaker Pennsylvania, in the mouth of preacher Henry Ward Beecher and in the writings of Thoreau, Melville, and Hawthorne, work was the gospel. It was, above all, the gospel of the Protestant bourgeosie, the middle classes, and among the independent craftsmen, farmers, merchants, ministers, professionals, and nascent industrialists. At the same time, it was not without challenges from the working classes who had not yet been disciplined to the rigors of the factory system, which required a long period of socialization both in England and the United States (Rodgers 1978:Chapters 1, 3, and 4; Thompson 1967:56–97).

THE MODERN PERIOD: THE TWENTIETH CENTURY

The twentieth century has witnessed the most successful application of the work ethic and, ironically, it has witnessed a weakening of the work ethic in the wake of its success. The twentieth century is a century of frenzied activity and striving. Modern men and women do not passively reflect upon a God-given world, but rather organize, administer, plan, and regulate their social order. Economics is at the center of the modern world as humans work to attain continuity. In precapitalist society work performed was determined by demand, known beforehand. Today, supply, frantic to dispose of itself, rushes out to engender demand, to command it, insinuate it, and create it. And the means for doing this is marketing, advertising, and huckstering.

While the modern factory makes a cog out of the working man, life is easier today through a shortening of the work day, paid holidays, paid vacations, health and insurance benefits, mortgages for homes, installment buying, and greater access to education and culture. However, there seems to be little optimism that satisfying work is attainable for the majority of people in industrial cultures. Only those who have acquired education and skills of the mind have the hope for satisfying work. For most people work is considered time spent for the benefit of others. People seek satisfaction outside of the workplace. And there is fear, as the example of the Soviet Union exhibits, that a society resting on a weak work ethic is in danger of collapse.

I will now examine the subject of work as it has been dealt with by various social theorists in the twentieth century. This is being done not with the purpose of developing a new theory of work. The thinkers who have been singled out are those who used their ideas about work to tell us something about the social structure and organization of modern industrial society.

Thorstein Veblen

Thorstein Veblen was born in Wisconsin in 1857 and died in 1929. He received a Ph.D. from Yale and taught economics at the University of Chicago, the University of Wisconsin, and the New School for Social Research. In the *Theory of the Leisure Class*, he presents the idea that the industrial system required men who are technically competent, efficient, and rational, whereas those who ran American business were incompetent, wasteful, and irrational (1934). Veblen saw a conflict between producing goods to satisfy human needs and producing goods to make a profit.

Veblen's most developed analysis of work is contained in his book, *The Instinct of Workmanship* (1914). Veblen viewed the handicraft tradition of work as a constellation of beliefs, customs, habits, and values, shared by members of a given craft or trade. Veblen believed that nothing like this paradigm existed for modern workers, except for the professions. Veblen saw modern technological exigencies enforcing attitudes that affected the principles of workmanship. He believed that habituation to the principles of business and pecuniary goals undermined and invaded the sense of workmanship. Work, workmen, equipment, and products were all rated by businessmen on the scale of money values. Veblen thought this was a pernicious practice that had a negative effect on workmanship. As Veblen saw it, workmanship was confused with salesmanship. He said that selling rather than science and technology had become the focus of American industry. Veblen saw modern industrial society headed for ruin as pecuniary goals replaced the goals of workmanship (1914:348-9). Veblen predicted the great depression of the 1930s, and when it arrived, sociologists and economists took notice of his ideas and posthumously gave him his deserved respect.

Henri Bergson

Adriano Tilgher said of Henri Bergson "No philosopher has placed higher, has more worthily celebrated, the productive labor of man. No one before him stated clearly that it is as an artisan that man celebrates his divinity. It is thanks to Bergson that homo faber becomes synonymous with homo sapiens" (1930:100). For Bergson, man is essentially an inventor who knows how to make tools and in intelligent being insofar as he is an artisan. Bergson saw man as a maker, a fabricating being with an intelligence that treats all things mechanically. Bergson believed that work bestowed upon man feelings that elevate him and make him rise in every direction. In essence, Bergson was identifying work with its *expressive* aspects, a value in work that was later associated with the human relations movement in industry. It is being stressed today as a hoped-for value in future postindustrial society (Daniel Yankelovich, et al., 1983:52).

Hendrik de Man

The Belgian sociologist, Hendrik de Man (1885-1953) lived and studied work in many countries, participated in working-class movements, and was also an academic. His most important book, *Joy in Work*, was based on his experiences and first-hand studies in Belgium, France, Germany, Russia, England, and the United States. De Man believed that most workers generally aim at joy in work and do not simply view work as only a means to gain a livelihood. He thought it a mistake to look for variables to measure joy in work. Particular occupations, levels of income, age, sex, country, and family may all combine in various complex syndromes to either permit or frustrate satisfaction in work. These variables also shift over time. Thus, de Man sought impressionistic insights dealing with meanings with which workers invested their actions. He also sought to relate the study of work to the totality of social institutions—political, economic, ideological forces, including the family.

Like Marx, de Man was convinced that with the advance of machine technology, workers were increasingly controlled by their own creation (*Joy in Work*, 1929:130-4). Thus, they are destined to be passive, not active subjects in the work process, with work increasingly losing its intrinsic meaning for workers. What they could hope for was a reduction in the work day, an increase in their standard of living, and a seeking for satisfaction outside of the workplace. There are many theorists today, as well as entire movements to humanize the workplace, who disagree with de Man and still believe that it is possible to revitalize industrial work and permit more creativity, autonomy, and satisfaction from many modern occupations (Blauner 1964; O'Toole, 1975).

Hannah Arendt

Hannah Arendt (1906–75) was born in Germany and became a United States citizen in 1951, the same year that her book, *Origins of Totalitarianism*, established her as a major social theorist. Her views on work are contained in her book, *The Human Condition* (1958). Other than activities of the mind, Arendt sees work, labor, and action as the three fundamental human activities. She considers labor as the undifferentiated use of the body to perform work, while work is the use of the hands and head to create man-made things that are durable and that can be used to create other things. Laboring disappears in consumption. Work creates the man-made world of things.

Arendt uses the distinction between work and labor to analyze the human condition in the modern world, relating work to larger social issues. She sees use-values associated with work giving way to exchange-values associated with labor. She sees quality giving way to quantity. She sees the emphasis on machines, technology, and profit sacrificing purpose and beauty in man-made things. The decrease in skill, the thrusting aside of the craftsman by the machine and the message of industrial society to consume and waste, are all signs for Hannah Arendt of the sacrifice of human values in industrial cultures.

While acknowledging that the distinction is not absolute, Arendt sees labor and work as comparable to Marx's distinction between abstract and concrete labor. Labor assimilates man to nature, work distinguishes man from nature. Labor is mechanical and cyclical, adjusting man to nature, while work distances man from nature. With labor man accepts external nature, with work man puts his own stamp on nature. Labor is judged by subjective criteria of human desires, while work is judged by objective criteria that give man a measure of independence. Above all, through work, man creates his own world that endures and outlasts generations (Arendt 1958:173). Hannah Arendt sees work as the defining characteristic of homo faber. Like Bergson, she believes it is the crafting nature of mankind that is necessary for the survival of all the works of mankind, from the works of artists to that of monument builders.

John Paul II

It is no exaggeration to state that Pope John Paul II is one of the most important Catholic theoreticians in the modern world. This gives added weight to his views on work, which are contained in his encyclical *Laborem exercens (On Human Work)*. In the introduction to the encyclical, the Pope presents the thesis that work is the distinguishing characteristic of man: "Only man is capable of work, and only man works, at the same time by work occupying his existence on earth" (1982:3). Pope John Paul II believes that work and its problems are at the heart of the social problems of the modern age. If the work ethic is in danger, the Pope believes so are certain important values of mankind, since work engenders fidelity, responsibility, and self-realization.

The Pope is critical of both capitalist and socialist nations for making human beings the objects of work rather than the subjects of their own work (1982:121–5). In *Laborem exercens*, the Pope asserts the principle of the "priority of labor over capital." He believes that the ultimate aim of work is to give one a sense of working for oneself, and that in a system of excessive bureaucratization, whether under a system of private property or socialist property, workers are made to feel they are just cogs in a huge machine moved from above. In this situation, the worker is a mere instrument rather than a true subject of his own work, with initiative and autonomy.

The encyclical, *Laborem exercens*, contains the concept that man makes himself through his work, an idea espoused by Hegel, Marx, and Arendt. The Pope states that "Everyone becomes a human being through, among other things, work" (1982:113). The Pope states that because man combines his deepest human identity with membership in a nation or a community, through his work he comes to understand his obligation and service to his own people, and, in addition, his service to all people on earth. Like Saint Paul, Pope John Paul II views work as an obligation to society and community. Thus, as each person has the moral obligation to work, each person has fundamental rights both as a person and as a worker. For Pope John Paul II, work is the foundation for individual respect and freedom, as well as the support of the community, if it is organized in such a way that humans become the subjects of their own work, and if labor takes priority over capital.

WORK AND TECHNOLOGY

Modern technology comes upon the historical scene by destroying the traditions of handicraft. The steam engine was a crucial accelerator of this development. As a prime mover it was free of the constraint of time and place. It also led to the building of large, complex machines (Borgmann 1987:116). These machines were not only more productive than humans, but they were more reliable since they liberated work from the risks of human judgments and the varying moods of workers. The goal of modern management in industry is to develop machines so that their users are largely replaceable or dispensable. Research and development of modern industry is directed toward a division of work based on machines, not operators (Braverman 1974:185-7).

The central element in modern technology is the use of scientific knowledge and engineering expertise. Common sense and experience gives way to rationalization and professional education. Modern technology is hailed as liberating mankind from hard, physical work. Robots can relieve people from hazardous, dirty, and monotonous work. Furthermore, robots do not get sick, take vacations, organize unions, or ask for higher wages. Technology has decreased the circle of expertise in the organization of work. But industrial cultures have paid the price for the abundance of goods that technology made possible. That price is the ongoing deskilling of work and the erosion of the work ethic (O'Toole 1975:29-75). Jacques Ellul believes that technology is the new social milieu of modern society, supplanting the old milieu of nature. Like nature, Ellul believes that technology is a closed circle, self-determinative and independent of human intervention (1983:86). Technology has become so powerful that it determines ends and enslaves people to means. Thus, ends such as safety, health, comfort, nutrition, shelter, mobility, and even happiness become instrument-specific. The desire to move becomes the desire to possess an automobile; the need for communication becomes the need to have a telephone; the necessity to eat becomes the need for a refrigerator, a stove, and a supermarket close by. Whether we like it or not, whether we can do something about it or not, the technological paradigm often gives meaning and affects our goals and values in modern society (Winner 1977:234).

The technological paradigm confronts mankind with the problem of how to control it. Machinery, science, engineering, and technological invention are an integral part of the present and future social order. Mumford calls for a change in our view of technology (1983:85). Instead of seeing it as a liberation *from work* he would reorient technology toward a liberation *for work*. Mumford advocates a more educating, mind-forming, self-rewarding work, on a voluntary basis within a culture where technology is "life-centered." Marcuse considers the control of technology as a crisis of the essence of human values (1964:231-2). Few philosophers argue for the elimination of technology. Most agree on the need for its control and reform, so that work, which is dependent upon it, can be humanized. Then, hopefully, the promise of technology as offering greater freedom and prosperity can be realized.

WORK, LEISURE, AND THE FUTURE OF WORK

Throughout history, starting with Aristotle, and continuing through Fourier, Saint-Simon, Marx, Mumford, Marcuse, Arendt, Tilgher, deGracia, and Gorz, leisure time, or free time, has been viewed as an alternative value for seeking self-fulfillment, which was once thought to exist only through work. An increase in leisure depends upon a decrease in work and, thus, the old duality of work and leisure is no longer adequate for an understanding of these two social forces. In the late twentieth century, we find in all industrial societies, and even in developing ones, that there has been an increase in free time as a result of improved technology and the consequent reduction in the amount of labor time required to produce our goods and services.

Time has become an important dimension of social life—how much time do we owe to society, to family, to ourselves? How will free time be utilized? Will free time be used passively, abdicating our right to criticize or ratify decisions of political leaders, or will citizens organize "publics" to make our democracy truly participatory? (Habermas 1985:167–90). Will free time be used strictly for play and pleasure, or can more individuals be trained and educated to use free time for services to others or for their own creative self-fulfillment?

In the modern world we tend to understand leisure as a set of contrasting values differing from work (Andrew 1981:19). Work involves strain, effort, exertion, and pain, while leisure is easy, effortless, and pleasurable. Work is done through compulsion and necessity, while leisure is unforced. Work is a means to an end, while leisure is considered an end-in-itself. Work is time spent for others, while leisure is "one's own time." Work is seen as socially useful and an obligation to society, while leisure is individually enjoyed and has no other purpose than one's own self-satisfaction. Work is monetarily rewarded, while leisure is its own reward. Work is often routine, whereas leisure is a liberation from routine. Work is organized by others and strictly scheduled, while leisure is free from employers and time clocks. However, there is "leisure" that is not volitional, which is the result of unemployment or unpaid "furloughs," which in these cases can hardly be called leisure or pleasurable.

As we approach the end of the twentieth century we see high technology moving so rapidly that while 25 percent of our work force currently produce all of our material goods, by the year 2010, it is possible only 10 percent will be required to produce our necessities of life (Jones 1982:202–3). If this proves to be true then it may be possible to choose more leisure in place of more goods. There is no consensus for this at present, but this can change as industrial societies become more affluent and reach a stage that might be called "postmaterialist." Part of the current increase in consumption is the increase of leisure, which now accounts for 30 percent of consumer spending in the United States and England. The connection between work and leisure varies with occupation, age, gender, country, history, and culture and most studies on leisure are too specific for one to draw generalizations. It is still not clear whether moving toward a leisure-oriented society is possible, and if it is so, whether it would come from evolutionary change based on present institutions or whether it would require a basic restructuring of society.

In the 1980s, a number of studies appeared suggesting that high-tech society had changed so drastically that work, along with other social spheres, would also have to change drastically. One of the prominent and influential thinkers about work in the future is Andre Gorz. In three separate books and a number of articles, he provides a systematic theory that analyzes work in a changing technological and social context (1982, 1985, 1989, *Telos*, No. 55, 1983, *Telos*, No. 67, 1986). In *Paths to Paradise* (1985), Gorz contrasts the megatechnologies of the industrial age with the microelectronics technology of the last fifty years. The older technologies lead to centralization and hierarchies of power, whereas the new technology had the potential for organizing work in autonomous, decentralized settings. Gorz believes that the new technology can do away with exchange value as the measure of economic values and overturn traditional economics (1989). He predicts that the living labor portion of value in the fully automated factory will fall close to zero. As a consequence, the work force of the future will have a smaller percentage of permanently employed workers. In Gorz's view, automation will take industrial society beyond both capitalism and socialism.

Given the productivity of modern industry, Gorz sees the possibility that each person could receive the necessities of life in exchange for a lifetime of work that would not exceed 20,000 hours. This represents ten years of full-time work or twenty years of part-time work. Under these conditions, work would no longer be anyone's full-time occupation, nor the center of one's life. Free time, or leisure hours, could be devoted to a wide range of lifestyles, with a person having the possibility of moving into several spheres of life, passing from one to another. The standardization of skills that Braverman and others decried as representing a degradation of work, is considered a plus by Gorz. He looks upon deskilling as a precondition for the distribution of socially necessary work among the greatest number of people. With skills reduced to some minimum standard, everyone can work and everyone can work less and less as technology becomes more efficient. High technology reduces both the need for specialized labor and reduces the time necessary for production. Unlike others, like Blauner (1964), who thought that automation could and should increase skills, Gorz sees automation as emancipatory only if skills are simplified, so that everyone, after a universal, basic training, could be able to apply for any job (Gorz 1985:47).

Gorz's concept of work leads to the idea that free time for everyone can result in changed social relations. If work and other social relations are no longer dominated by money and the market, then human existence is enriched by being based on affection, friendship, and solidarity. Gorz shares with Aristotle and other philosophers, the belief that noneconomic activities are the very fabric of life. The only work that will be performed for the sake of money will be time spent in producing the necessities of life. The rest of one's time can be spent in some form of voluntary work or activity that will be free and autonomous and taken up for pleasure (Gorz 1985:53). For the most highly qualified work, such as that of surgeons, engineers, researchers, scientists, therapists, journalists, lawyers, there have always been more candidates than jobs available. By reducing work time among professionals, there can be a spreading of the work to allow more people with talent and expertise to practice their profession and maintain their skills. If professional people work less they can work with more intensity and greater proficiency. Talent often requires periods of rest and sabbaticals for renewal.

Time is one of the precious human resources. Minimizing time devoted to necessities and maximizing free time can give people opportunities for creative and autonomous activities of all kinds. Gorz identifies some of these activities (1989:233): caring and mutual-aid in neighborhoods and localities; development of friendships; educational and artistic activities; mutual help in household and repair work; growing food and producing objects for one's own use; service-exchange cooperatives; small enterprises based on neighborhoods and localities.

Gorz sees the possibility of organizing work in the future on three levels (1985:63): (1) *Macro-social work*, organized across society as a whole, which is devoted to producing necessities for the basic needs of all citizens. (2) *Micro-social activity*, which is self-organized on a local level and which is voluntary work. It can include work for basic needs as well as work for individual self-fulfillment. (3) *Autonomous activity*, which is based on the particular desires of individuals, families, and groups. This kind of organization of work will shift responsibility to the local community, which can decide for itself how to participate in macro and micro work. It would permit both communal and individual choices over work and give work more meaning.

Whether one agrees with Gorz or not, the significance of his ideas is his concept that the future of work and the future of society are inextricably intertwined. Like Aristotle, Gorz sees the good life as that which eliminates the constraint of necessity. Lifting the constraints of necessity can create the conditions for a free and just society. This utopian vision has been in the minds of thinkers from the early Christians through the philosophers of the Enlightenment to modern and futurist thinkers at present. Restructuring work will require difficult political decisions and the course of development, if it takes place, will not occur in a straight line. The difference from the past, however, is that possibilities for self-fulfillment are now open to the majority of the population and not just for a small elite, as was the case in Aristotle's time.

Gorz's scenario about the future of work is similar to the projections of Herman Kahn and his associates at the Hudson Institute (Kahn et al. 1977). They see a future in which wealth and affluence will increase to the point where people will opt for more free time rather than more goods. The marginal utility of more material wealth will fall and people will desire more leisure. If the demand side for material goods is lowered, it will lower the supply side and put less strain on the world's resources. The world that Kahn and his associates visualize for the future is reflected in their list of the characteristics of a postindustrial society (Kahn et al. 1977:23), as follows: ritualistic and aesthetic activities; reading, writing, painting, acting, composing, performing, gourmet cooking and eating; hunting and fishing, hiking, camping, boating; exercise of nonvocational skills; gardening and decorating; conversation, discussion, debating and politicking, cultural and social activities;

welfare and social security functions; search for adventure, excitement, and amusement; public works projects; creation of taboos, totems, and demanding religions. Veal calls this list the traits of a "leisure society" (1989:61).

Some surveys are beginning to reveal that people in industrial society may be interested in other values than the accumulation of material goods. A Harris poll in the United States in 1977 revealed that 64 percent of respondents thought that finding more inner and personal rewards from work was more important than increasing the productivity of the work force. Seventy-five percent thought that learning to get pleasure out of nonmaterial experience was preferable to satisfying our needs for more goods and services (Jones 1982:230–1).

Some theorists on work have suggested alternatives to the work ethic. Jenkins and Sherman postulate a usefulness ethic, based on the idea that the need to be wanted is more in tune with the human conditions than the need for formal work (Jenkins and Sherman 1981:15, 185). Clemiston and Rodgers would like to see a life ethic replace the work ethic, a life ethic concerned with the full development of human beings to replace the notion that occupation is the major contribution to society (1981:13, 196). R. Clarke talks about a contribution ethic based on the belief that we can find fulfillment doing things for others (1982:196). James F. Murphy advocates a leisure ethic based on free time liberated by technology, which leads to personal options, diversified lifestyles and a merging of work/leisure relationships (1974:22). While there is the possibility of replacing the work ethic with another, it would be naive to believe that it can be done through some kind of educational or missionary program to convert people to a new ethic (Veal 1989:61, 267). Veal contends that it is more likely that a new ethic will emerge as a result of structural and economic changes within the fabric of society. Gorz, on the other hand, believes that changing the work ethic itself can be the agent of social change.

Tom Stonier sees knowledge and information as the key ingredient of future society. Stonier postulates a future with education as the number one employer (1989:28–9). The utility of the education sector is that it is labor intensive and able to absorb jobs replaced by technology in the manufacturing and service sectors.

One of the important issues that affect the modern workplace is the question of power. While the individual is given a set of rights and responsibilities by the state, rights, responsibilities, and power in modern society extend to organization. These rights, coupled with size, give organizations an enormous amount of power within the state. The state or government is more comfortable dealing with other organizations that with individual persons. Thus, corporations, the government, labor unions, professional associations, and social-reform organizations are the centers of power in the modern, industrial state. (Hall 1994:319–20).

Existing power relationships based on institutional structures make the prospect of replacing a work-oriented society with a leisure-oriented society far from certain or even probable. Still, such a restructuring with regard to society's values seems to be on the agenda in looking at the future of industrial society in the twenty-first century. Human history and social development are too complex for either blueprints or predictions. However, it is reasonable to expect that individual and collective choices can be promoted to decide how we will work and live in the future. The political rhetoric at least offers the possibility that each person should have access to work, education, and culture for individual self-fulfillment. Whatever the future, work will continue to be the spine into which and out of which social relations radiate and are given meaning.

REFERENCES

Andrew, Ed
1981   *Closing the Iron Cage.* Montreal: Black Rose Books.

Applebaum, Herbert A.
1984   *Work in Non-Market and Transitional Societies.* Albany: State University of New York Press.

Arendt, Hannah
1958   *The Human Condition.* Chicago: University of Chicago Press.

1958   *The Origins of Totalitarianism.* New York: Viking.

Aristotle
1946   *The Politics.* Translated by Ernest Barker. New York: Oxford University Press.

Avineri, Shlomo
1973   Labor, Alienation and Social Classes. In *The Legacy of Hegel,* edited by J. J. O'Malley, et al. The Hague: Martinus Nijhoff, pp. 196–215.

Bacon, Francis
1967   Modern Library Edition. *The Great Instauration.* New York: Random House.

Benz, Ernst
1966   The Christian expectation of the end of time and the idea of technical progress. In *Evolution and Christian Hope*. Garden City, NY: pp. 121–42.

Bible, Old and New Testaments
1962   Cleveland: World Publishing Company.

Borgmann, Albert
1987   *Technology and the Character of Contemporary Life*. Chicago: University of Chicago Press.

Bowder, Diana, ed.
1980   *Who Was Who in the Roman World, 753 B.C.–A.D. 476*. Oxford: Phaidon.

Blauner, Robert
1964   *Alienation and Freedom in American Industry*. Chicago: University of Chicago Press.

Braverman, Harry
1974   *Labor and Monopoly Capital*. New York: Monthly Review Press.

Brunt, P. A.
1980   Free labor and public works at Rome. *Journal of Roman Studies*, vol. 70, pp. 81–100.

Burford, Allison
1972   *Craftsmen in Greek and Roman Society*. Ithaca, NY: Cornell University Press.

Campbell, Joan
1989   *Joy in Work*. Princeton, NJ: Princeton University Press.

Carcopino, Jerome
1968   *Daily Life in Ancient Rome*. New Haven, CT: Yale University Press.

Carlyle, Thomas
1843   *Past and Present*. Everyman's Library. New York: E.P. Dutton.

Cicero
1938   *De Officiis*. Loeb Library. London: William Heinemann, Ltd.

Clarke, R.
1982   *Work in Crisis*. Edinburgh: St. Andrew's Press.

Clemitson, I. and G. Rogers
1981   *A Life to Live: Beyond Full Employment*. London: Junction Books.

Delort, Robert
1983   *Life in the Middle Ages*. New York: Crown Publishers, Inc.

de Man, Henri
1929   *Joy in Work*. London: George Allen & Unwin, Ltd.

Diderot, Denis
1953   The Encyclopedia, "Art." In *French Thought in the Eighteenth Century*, edited by Rolland Maurois and Herriot. London: Cassell & Co.

Duby, Georges
1980   *The Three Orders, Feudal Society Imagined*. Chicago: University of Chicago Press.

Edelstein, Ludwig
1966   *The Meaning of Stoicism*. Cambridge, MA: Harvard University Press.

Ellul, Jacques
1983   The Technological Order. In *Philosophy and Technology*, edited by Carl Mitcham and Robert Mackey. New York: The Free Press, pp. 86–108.

Finley, Moses I.
1979   *The World of Odysseus*. New York: Pelican Books.

Franklin, Benjamin
1987   *Writings*. New York: The Library of America.

Frontinus
1925   *Strategems and Aqueducts*. Loeb Library. London: William Heinemann, Ltd.

Geoghegan, Arthur T.
1945   *The Attitude Towards Labor in Early Christianity and Ancient Culture*. Washington, D.C.: Catholic University of America Press.

Gimpel, Jean
1980   *The Cathedral Builders*. New York: Harper & Row.

Gorz, Andre
1982   *Farewell to the Working Class*. London: Pluto Press.

1985   *Paths to Paradise: On the Liberation from Work*. Boston: South End Press.

1986   The socialism of tomorrow. *Telos*, No. 67, Spring, pp. 199–205.

1989   *Critique of Economic Reason*. New York: Verso.

Guinagh, Kevin, and Alfred P. Dorjahn
1942   *Latin Literature in Translation*. New York: Longmans, Green.

Habermas, Jurgen
1985   *Philosophical-Political Profiles*. Cambridge, MA: M.I.T. Press.

Hall, Richard H.
1994   *Sociology of Work*. Thousand Oaks, CA: Pine Forge Press.

Heitland, W. E.
1970   *Agricola*. Westport, CT: Greenwood Press.

Hobbes, Thomas
1939   *Leviathan*. Modern Library Edition. New York: Random House.

Howell, Martha C.
1988   *Women, Production, and Patriarchy in Late Medieval Cities*. Chicago: University of Chicago Press.

Iliad
1939   Loeb Library, 2 vols. London: William Heinemann, Ltd.

Jenkins, C. and B. Sherman
1981   *The Leisure Shock*. London: Eyre Methuen.
       Jones, Barry

1982   *Sleepers, Wake. Technology and the Future of Work*. Brighton, England: Wheatsheaf Books.

Kahn, H., W. Brown, and L. Martel
1977   *The Next 200 Years*. London: Abacus.

Knoop, Douglas, and G. P. Jones
1967   *The Medieval Mason*. New York: Barnes and Noble, Inc.

Le Goff, Jacques
1980   *Time, Work, and Culture in the Middle Ages*. Chicago: University of Chicago Press.

Locke, John
1967   *Two Treatises of Government*. Cambridge: Cambridge University Press.

Lucie-Smith, Edward
1984   *The Story of Craft, The Craftsman's Role in Society*. New York: Van Nostrand.

Marcuse, Herbert
1964   *One-Dimensional Man*. Boston: Beacon Press.

Marx, Karl
1906   *Capital*. Modern Library Edition. New York: Random House.

1959   *Basic Writings*, edited by Lewis S. Feuer, Garden City, NY: Doubleday & Co.

1971   *The Grundrisse*, translated by David McLellan. New York: Harper & Row.

Mauss, Marcel
1967   *The Gift*. New York: W. W. Norton.

Morris, William
1946   *Writings*, edited by G. D. H. Cole. London: Nonesuch Press.

Mumford, Lewis
1967–   *The Myth of the Machine.* 2 vols. New York: Harcourt, Brace and World.
1970

1983   Technics and the nature of man. In *Philosophy and Technology*, edited by Carl Mitcham and Robert Mackey. New York: The Free Press, pp. 77–85.

Murphy, James F.
1974   *Concepts of Leisure: Philosophical Implications.* Englewood Cliffs, NJ: Prentice-Hall.

Oakes, Guy
1989   Four questions concerning the protestant ethic. *Telos*, No. 81, pp. 77–85.

Odyssey
1945   Loeb Library. 2 vols. London: William Heinemann, Ltd.

O'Toole, James
1975   *Work in America.* Cambridge, MA: The MIT Press.

Ovitt, George, Jr.
1987   *The Restoration of Perfection*: *Labor and Technology in Medieval Culture.* New Brunswick, NJ: Rutgers University Press.

Pellicani, Luciano
1988   Weber and the myth of Calvinism. *Telos*, No. 75, pp. 57–86.

Petronius
1959   *The Satyricon.* Ann Arbor: University of Michigan Press.

Plutarch
1934   *Lives.* Modern Library. New York: Random House.

Pope John Paul II
1982   Laborem Exercens, Encyclical Letter. In Gregory Baum, ed., *The Priority of Labor.* New York: Paulist Press.

Reisman, David A.
1976   *Adam Smith's Sociological Economics.* New York: Barnes and Noble.

Rodgers, Daniel T.
1978   *The Work Ethic in Industrial America, 1850–1920.* Chicago: University of Chicago Press.

Rousseau, Jean-Jacques
1923   *The Confessions.* New York: Alfred A. Knopf.

1953   The Education of Emile. In *French Thought in the Eighteenth Century*, edited by Rolland, Maurois, and Herriot. London: Cassell.

Smith, Adam
1937   *Wealth of Nation*. Modern Library. New York: Random House.

St. Augustine
1950   *City of God*. Modern Library. New York: Random House.

Stonier, Tom
1989   Technological Change and the Future. In *Freedom and Constraint: The Paradoxes of Leisure*, edited by Fred Coalter. New York: Routledge.

Telos
1983   and 1989, Numbers 75 and 81. New York: Telos Press.

Thompson, E. P.
1967   Time, work-discipline and industrial capitalism. *Past and Present*, no. 38, pp. 56–97.

Tilgher, Adriano
1930   *Work, What It Has Meant To Men Through the Ages*. New York: Harcourt, Brace & Co.

Trice, Harrison
1993   *Occupational Subcultures in the Workplace*. Ithaca, NY: ILR Press.

Tully, James
1980   *A Discourse on Property: John Locke and his Adversaries*. Cambridge: Cambridge University Press.

Veal, A. J.
1989   Leisure and the Future: Considering the Options. In *Freedom and Constraint*, edited by Fred Coalter. New York: Routledge.

Veblen, Thorstein
1899   *The Theory of the Leisure Class*. New York: Macmillan Co.

1914   *The Instinct of Workmanship*. New York: Macmillan Co.

Vernant, Jean Pierre
1983   *Myth and Thought Among the Greeks*. London: Routledge and Kegan Paul.

Virgil
1987   *The Georgics*. Penguin Classics. New York: Viking/Penguin.

Voltaire
1959   *Candide*. New York: Bantam Books.

Weber, Max
1950   *The Protestant Ethic and the Spirit of Capitalism.* New York: Charles Scribner's Sons.

Winner, Langdon
1977   *Autonomous Technology.* Cambridge, MA: MIT Press.

Wood, Neal
1984   *John Locke and Agrarian Capitalism.* Berkeley: University of California Press.

Xenophon
1970   *Oeconomicus.* Ithaca, NY: Cornell University Press.

Yankelovich, Daniel, et al.
1983   *Work and Human Values.* New York: Aspen Institute for Humanistic Studies.

WALTER GOLDSCHMIDT

3

Task Performance and Fulfillment: Work and Career in Tribal and Peasant Societies

Everyman's work . . . is a portrait of himself.
—Samuel Butler

THREE EXAMPLES OF TASK PERFORMANCE

Haejoang Cho (1979) describes the activities of the diving women of Cheju Island in South Korea. As girls, these women had long training for this demanding activity; they spend many hours in the arduous task of diving for abalone, seaweed, and other products of the ice-cold sea. They also do most of the farm work, keep house, and care for their husbands and raise their children. They take great satisfaction in their efforts, endeavor to be the best diver and enjoy the camaraderie of their sister divers. They are proud of their ability to care for their husbands, finding them more handsome than the men of the mainland. Life is both arduous and rewarding. Their men are largely idle; they are fops, spending a great deal of time performing tea ceremonies or in idleness; they often are depressed and alcoholic.

Heizo Harako (1976) has given us a careful analysis of Mbuti net-hunting practices. Every second day or so, most of the people of the band go out into the forest, the men carrying nets weighing at least a fourth of their own weight, set the nets side by side in a long arc and, while the women and children act as beaters, wait to club the duikers or francolin that are caught in their net. They then move their nets, perhaps as much as eight or ten times, and repeat the process. Each man has his turn at the center of the arc, where it is more likely that they will make a kill, for which they want the credit—though in the end the meat is divided equitably among the people of the band. Sometimes men shirk this arduous labor, though Colin Turnbull (1961, 1965a, 1965b) tells us that the old men do not enjoy the leisure that is forced upon them when they are "retired" and are expected to stay in camp and care for the small children. Among the Mbuti, a man gains standing for his display of energy and prowess as a hunter. A half century earlier, Radcliffe-Brown (1933) described a quite similar pattern of behavior among the Andamanese pygmies, including differences in industry and ability among the men. Neither Mbuti nor Andamanese men get any special rewards or privileges from such industriousness or talent other than prestige, though their greater respect may give them some increased public influence.

When a woman of Sebei in Uganda has a field to cultivate she brews beer (Goldschmidt 1976). Her neighbors and friends come with their heavy hoes to loosen the hard soil over a carefully measured area for which in return they enjoy an afternoon around the beer pot. Women are known for their generosity or stinginess and for the quality of beer they brew—though there never seems to be a dearth of workers. Thus the work women do is a social occasion, and the guest on one day will be the host on another. The cost of the beer, I discovered by examining a sample of such work-parties, averages precisely what common labor received at the time—two shillings a work-day. And that, in turn, is also the cost of an afternoon of drinking at a native beer bar. Obviously there is some quiet calculation going on behind this reciprocity.

All of these Korean, Mbuti, and Sebei men and women would recognize these activities as work in the sense that they are tasks that need doing, in the sense that they constitute tiring and sometimes onerous activity. But I am not sure that they have a concept of work that stands in contrast to leisure or to play. I think it is more appropriate to use words like task and task performance for such activities.

CAREERS

Some important generalizations arise from these examples of task performance. First, they produce the necessities of life for these peoples; they are therefore essential to the livelihood and welfare of the individuals and the community. Second, the rewards for performance are not measured merely in the output of product but in social gratification. Third, individuals vary both in their attitudes toward such task performance and in their abilities to perform them. Fourth, though such work is done by individuals, it often involves collaboration and group effort, which makes them social events. These elements are central to what I have come to call the *human career*, a thesis I have recently set forth at length in a book using this phrase as its title (Goldschmidt 1990).

We are all well aware of careers in our own society; as you read this you are busy working on yours. But we have not thought that tribal peoples also have careers nor what such careers mean to the very character of such societies. Indeed, we have lost sight of the individual as an actor, burying him in the notion of social role and wiping him out for a *tabula rasa* on which his culture is to be imprinted, or living out a life cycle as a culturally programmed automaton. These perceptions derive from the fallacious effort to treat social and cultural matters as if they constituted a separate level of reality with its own "laws," independent of the needs and the wills of individuals.

I have turned these notions around, seeing social institutions and cultural forms as products of the cumulated social actions of the members of a community. In this view, each individual has a personal agenda, the central element of which is to achieve standing in his community; this he or she must do through performance of the essential tasks required for the welfare of that community, as these are set by custom and are appropriate to gender and age. Such task performance requires collaboration, so institutional frameworks are provided for such cooperative endeavor. Social systems are dynamic, and the force behind this dynamism is the motivation of the individual actor.

I cannot here develop this theory of careers in any detail. Let me just say that I see the human individual as being primarily motivated by something I call *affect hunger*; that this is a part of his biological make-up and is the basis for the infant's dynamic interaction with his mother. In the process of the infant-mother dialogue the child acquires the cultural definitions of behavior appropriate to the fulfillment of these affective desires; that is, the biological demand for affect is translated into the cultural need for acceptance and prestige.

This means that every human being enters into the social order with a personal agenda. Of course, this agenda is contextualized; its shape is set by the culture and the society in which he is to grow. But such contextualization must be seen as just that; it is not a die that stamps him into a clone of his cultural compatriots, however much his parents might wish this to be the case. This motivated individual is seeking his (or her, of course) own ego gratification, own sense of self; that is the central dynamic force in social life. While the infant accepts the cultural definitions of the appropriate and fits himself into the existing social order, he does so with a strong sense of his own individuality and is ready to move out in novel directions when circumstances make such actions seem appropriate. Thus social forms are subject to constant redefinition; the individual and his community are in a kind of dialectic relationship, a circularity that not only enables change to take place, but actually fosters it.

TASK DEMANDS AND SOCIAL STRUCTURE

One of the things—perhaps the most important thing—that each man and woman must do is to "earn a living," as we would put it. Other activities contribute to the satisfactory sense of self, notably sexuality, reproduction, the nurturance of children, and even such more removed matters as aesthetic performance and play. But inasmuch as this volume deals with work, I will focus on those tasks that fit our more usual idea of what constitutes work. As a matter of fact, I find task performance to be the most important element in this dynamic because it is closely related to the ecological conditions of the society; it is most sensitive to the technological competencies of the community and the means of gaining sustenance from the land.

In the homogeneous tribal and peasant communities to which anthropologists traditionally give attention, the manner of earning a living tends to be very nearly uniform and the activities therefore very nearly standardized for persons of the same sex and similar age. There may be some regional variation or specialization involving particular skills, but for the most part the expectations in task performance are consistent and the career trajectory has a uniform contour.

The contour of such careers varies from one culture to another precisely because it is shaped by the nature of the major economic enterprises. If we ponder for a moment the kind of action expected from men in pastoral societies, who must protect their herds from animal and human predators and move them about over great distances in search of graze and water, and then compare these with what is expected of horticulturalists living in permanent close-knit villages, we can see that the nature of the work, the skills required, and the collaboration demanded, and even the temperament appropriate to the task, are different. Indeed it was the shift that took place between two such economies that was at the center of attention of the Culture and Ecology in East Africa Project that I directed many years ago. And it was my examination of the shift from pastoralism to farming among the Sebei that led me to the recognition of the dynamic role of careers in the structuring of social change.

Earning a living is more than merely becoming competent with the bow or the hoe; it involves collaboration. It is no accident that the East African pastoralists almost always have some form or age-sets, for the age-set is a functionally efficient way of institutionalizing the collaboration required for handling and protecting the animals and for putting these dangerous and physically demanding tasks upon the young men. Nor is it an accident that these young men are inducted into their enforced collaboration through an elaborate hazing ritual of initiation. (It is worthwhile to note that the Plains Indians, who were essentially pastoralists caring for their large herds of horses, developed military societies that were very much like age-grades.) Nor is it surprising that the role and force of the age-set are diminished and the initiatory ritual given less attention when pastoral people turn to farming, as they frequently did. Age-sets have no function among farmers; they are no longer a useful institution and may become positively *dys*functional. My work among the Sebei has shown how institutions altered in response to the changed career demands as a result of this shift. Among these changes were land ownership shifting from communal to private: settlement patterns changing from widely separated, concentrated, and enclosed camps to the dispersal of homesteads over the land; reconstituted military action from cattle raiding to territorial expansion and the concomitant shift from young age-set raider-warriors to territorial defense by all able-bodied men; the declining political function of the older age-sets to an abortive effort to establish some kind of community law to replace the settlement of legal conflict by clan confrontations and feud; and the application of legal definitions of livestock ownership to the legal definition of land rights. These are the kinds of changes I have in mind when I say that task performance as an aspect of career is a dynamic force for social change, that institutions are derivative from individual actions.

Our work in East Africa involved not only temporal changes; we studied peoples who had sectors devoted primarily to pastoralism and other sectors to farming, so that we could examine contemporary variations in social behavior. We found that the shift brought about characterological changes. Robert Edgerton (1971) showed that the personality of the farmers was measurably different from those of the pastoralists, differences that were consistent over the four tribes we examined. Pastoralists showed more emotional liability than the farmers, who were more closed and restrained in their expression of affect; that the openness of the former gave way to the deviousness of the latter; that depression was more frequent among pastoralists, hostility and paranoid tendencies among the farmers.

TASK PERFORMANCE AND PEASANTRY

When Evalyn (Kunkel) Michaelson and I examined a sample of peasant societies, defined for our purposes as communities of agricultural producers operating within the context of nation states, we found that almost all had three-generation family systems as an ideal (Goldschmidt and Kunkel 1971), that family solidarity and the ownership of land were central cultural values (Michaelson and Goldschmidt 1971), and that whatever Great Tradition religion was adhered to, local ritual and belief strongly and consistently reinforced the values of home, landholding, and family solidarity (Michaelson and Goldschmidt 1976). Peasant village societies tended to have certain recurrent cultural patterns and social organization whether they were found in China, Japan, Southeast Asia, Egypt, India, Europe, or Latin America because the ecological circumstances demanded similar kinds of task performance and collaborative endeavor. (Peasantry is not the only possible forms of agricultural production; in America and increasingly elsewhere, farming is a commercial enterprise; elsewhere it has been based on slavery or indentured labor. In tribal societies it is quite different and most often the farm work is largely done by women.) The peasantry, as we examined it, involved a strong sense of local community, largely autonomous in its social interactions but subordinated to the centralized political and economic power of the state and where the individual farmers had either ownership or other established rights to land.

The efficient exploitation of peasant land requires a team of men and women working together; that is, the institutional form of the three-generation family was responsive to the task demands of farming under peasant conditions. We found that almost all these communities were patrilineal and that men were in active control of the farm enterprise. This stands in contrast to the situation of horticultural growers not under the control of a centralized government, where farming is often under the control of women and where most of the known matrilineal societies are found. Thus this recurrent patriliny is not a self-evident finding and deserves some explanation.

The most facile explanation is that peasant cultivation utilizes the plow and hence involves the control of large draft animals, which, in turn, requires the heavier musculature of the men. This notion gets some support from the fact that among pastoralists the large animals are always tended by the men and they, too, are almost always patrilineal. I do not think that this is the correct answer; for one thing, not all peasants use large draft animals and, for another, when they do, young boys often take care of them.

I see the explanation in terms of careers in the ecological context of peasantry. A central ecological fact of life among these societies is that they are part of a state system, and this means that the masculine carer activities characteristic of tribal societies— hunting, politics, and warfare—are not available to men. Especially warfare. Since these sources of personal achievement are consistently denied to the men, they turn to the one avenue of personal satisfaction that remains open: control of the agricultural enterprise. Peasant men derive their social gratification from maintaining a household, and this means trying to keep together a three-generation family, controlling the labor of their sons, whose marriages they closely supervise by bringing their wives into the household from outside.

This solution is not without its own problems; the young men are repeatedly found to chafe at the control of their elders, while their wives suffer even more under the often hard and demeaning control of their mothers-in-law (Michaelson and Goldschmidt 1971). (We also found that the ideal of three generations was not universally followed, suggesting that it was not an easy value to achieve.) But it is an effective means for exploiting land under conditions of limited resources and high labor demand. The prestigious persons in peasant villages—the ones with successful careers—are the men and women who have well-knit households with loyal and cooperative sons, together with their wives and children.

TASK PERFORMANCE AND DIFFERENTIATION

I must make explicit one aspect of careers that has so far only been implicit. While the shape of careers tends to be uniform within any social system, career *performance* varies. This is a most important matter. It points up two facts of social life: first, the universality of social differentiation (Jean Briggs describes a winter village of three igloos where two of the families looked down and virtually ostracized the third) and, second, that there is an inherent rivalry for social standing among the personnel of all societies. For whatever reasons—energy, skills, ambition, intelligence, strength, social advantage, personality—some men and women are more successful than others. We saw this at the outset among the Cheju diving women and the Mbuti hunters. It also means that individuals have to cope with the potential disruptive results of failure and that a healthy society will provide institutions for such coping. We cannot here develop this aspect of the thesis but will merely note that among the coping institutions are curing rites and shamanism, witchcraft, rituals of reenforcement, and techniques for projecting blame on others for one's own failures.

Whenever we look at curing rites, for instance, we find that, whatever hocus-pocus may be involved, they are dealing with the somaticization of maladies that are wholly or partly psychological in nature, and when we look at the etiology of such malaise, we find that it derives from some kind of ego impairment, from some failure of personal aspirations. Witchcraft is one means of projecting failure on others, as I learned when a girl, who cried as she was being circumcised (a terrible Sebei gaffe), explained it away as the action of a rejected suitor who caused her failure by means of black magic and, again, when a barren wife found the cause of her infertility in the magic of a jealous co-wife.

TASK PERFORMANCE AND OURSELVES

In this brief presentation I have tried to put what we call work into the context of a dynamic theory of human careers. The point that should be emphasized is that work is more than labor. However irksome or exhausting, it is a source of gratification; it is often *the* most important source of self-definition. Task performance is not only a major source of such gratification but, along with reproduction and the nurturance of children, one that *must* be engaged in in every society, and one that, because of this centrality, usually shapes the essential social institutions.

It is no different with us. Go back to Studs Terkel's *Working* (1972) and you will see the leitmotif of the role of work as the source of gratification—whether it is the poor garbageman who takes pride in his socially useful endeavors or the rich stockbroker who is disgusted with the little social value of his. We are really not so different from the Mbuti or the Korean diving women.

I want finally to exemplify briefly the viewpoint developed here with an examination of the most important event that took place with respect to the labor market in the latter half of the twentieth century: the entry of women into what we call the "work force." The work force is made up of those people who are (or who are seeking) "gainful employment." What a revealing phrase this is! People are gainfully employed when they are working for money, either as wages or as profit. This means that those who make and deliver your pizza are gainfully employed, while the person who makes a pie for the family is not; that the doctor who delivers a baby is gainfully employed while the woman who is in labor, ironically, is not. Tens of millions of women have entered the work force in the past three decades, mostly in the middle and upper ranks of business and the professions. Women had, of course, been part of the work force all along; on the farm they were regularly part of a team, much as in peasant societies; they also worked in factories in order to help support their families or supplement the wages of their underpaid husbands; they had engaged in "women's work," such as teaching and social work, and, of course, had worked as homemakers. But now they were entering areas from which they had largely been excluded; work that offered social standing.

This change was responsive to the changing ecology of social life and cultural values. As is always the case with such matters, there is a circularity between cause and effect and women's entry into this work force reinforced these social changes. Social life had in the past centered on the household, the neighborhood, and the local community: now it shifted to the workplace. Large families gave way to the small families of planned parenting; the domestic technology that removed the irksomeness of housework also removed its challenge to women's housekeeping talents. These and other changes all combined to make women, who had long demonstrated their intellectual equality with men in high school and college, understandably go to where the action is. What they wanted was not work, but the social rewards of being employed: the social life of the workplace in contrast to the increased isolation of the middle-class home; the independence provided by having their own income, the opportunity to demonstrate their competence in task performance and, above all, the sense of social worth that derives from being "gainfully employed" and to have others recognize and reward the display of their abilities. They bought into the values that had dominated their middle-class husbands and denied those of their mothers, who had found their gratification in child-rearing and homemaking (with the stretching of budgets and the children's birthday parties and all that) and the "standing behind their man." In my terms, women did not begin to *have* careers, they *changed* careers. They were doing in reverse exactly what I believe peasant men have repeatedly done. They changed careers in keeping with altered values and altered ecology: they illustrate the relationship between the workaday world, cultural values, social structure, and the sense of self.

ANTHROPOLOGY AND WORK

The most important thing that anthropology has to contribute to the sociology of work is to reshape the semantic domain of the concept itself. However necessary work may be, when not enforced or physically coerced it is not something onerous and irksome but a source of personal gratification. The very difficulties that work entails enhance the magnitude of such social reward. It is the universal means by which each person defines himself—paints his own portrait, as Samuel Butler said.

REFERENCES

Cho, Haejoang
1979   An ethnographic study of a female diver's village in Korea: Focused on the sexual division of labor. Ph.D. dissertation, Department of Anthropology, UCLA.

Edgerton, Robert
1971   *The Individual in Cultural Adaptation: A Study of Four East African Peoples.* Berkeley and Los Angeles: University of California Press.

Goldschmidt, Walter
1976   *The Culture and Behavior of the Sebei.* Berkeley and Los Angeles: University of California Press.

1990   *The Human Career.* Cambridge, MA, and Oxford, UK: Basil Blackwell.

Goldschmidt, Walter and Evalyn Jacobson Kunkel
1971   The structure of the peasant family. *American Anthropologist*, vol. 73, pp. 1058–76.

Harako, Reizo
1976   The Mbuti as Hunters: A Study of Ecological Anthropology of the Mbuti Pygmies (I). *Kyoto University African Studies*, vol. 10.

Michaelson, Evalyn and Walter Goldschmidt
1971   Female roles and male dominance among peasants. *Southwestern Journal of Anthropology*, vol. 27, pp. 330-52.

1976 Family and land in peasant ritual. *American Ethnologist*, vol. 3, pp. 87-96.

Radcliffe-Brown A. R.
1933 *The Andaman Islanders*. Cambridge: Cambridge University Press.

Terkel, Studs
1972 *Working*, New York: Avon.

Turnbull, Colin
1961 *The Forest People*, New York: Simon and Schuster.

1965a *Wayward Servants: The Two Worlds of the African Pygmies*, New York: Natural History Press.

1965b *The Mbuti Pygmies: An Ethnographic Survey*. Anthropological Papers of The American Museum of Natural History vol. 50, Part 3.

IVAR BERG

4

Theories and Meanings of Work: Toward Syntheses

INTRODUCTION

In this paper I will assay several sets of issues emerging from a literature reporting upon many decades of research on work that a productive theory of work would do well to join. An effort to deal with the different meanings of work, meantime, would be better informed if it were harnessed to the theories that have emerged in the work of researchers who have reported on the forces shaping the experiences of different workes in a variety of work settings.

In the opening section I address the first of these sets of issues, the "webs of rules" that underlie virtually all of the macro, messo, and micro structures in a society, to which we will then turn.

The distinctions, macro, messo, and micro, are analytical ones; they refer to levels of generality reflecting what one sees, for example, from the highest to the lowest peaks in a mountain range; as one descends to ground level the middle-altitude and lower-level peaks become more evident to the observer.

The rest of our intellectual apparatus, in these pages, are (1) social controls and (2) "natural" and "rational" systems of thought about social organization.

WEBS OF RULES

Workers in any society, from preliterate to industrial, are affected, directly impacted upon—even "shaped" by—an extraordinarily large and intricate "web of rules," a concept first developed by John Dunlop (1958). "The rules . . . evolve in gradually institutionalized relationships among managers, workers, and the representatives of political states, affecting job classifications, compensation, and the relative rights and duties of the three 'actors'" (Berg 1979). The webs characters and contents of these webs are, for example, affected directly and indirectly by macroscopic (international, national, and cultural) forces, microscopic (organizational) forces, and by "messo" forces at layers in between these macro and micro layers (Kerr and Siegel 1955). The messo forces are generated principally by the ways and means of the leaders of industries, of national and international unions, of industries' regulators, and, in the United States, by state laws and state courts.

Among the first of the three levels there are national/tribal laws and regulations together with varieties of (sometimes conflicting) culturally given and widely recognized norms arising from historical-traditional, religious, intellectual, political, and ideological thrusts. These forces can impact both directly and indirectly, for example, on childrearing patterns, education, and *rites de passage*, otherwise, in accord with widely shared (national) norms that leave whole populations with shared dispositions, most especially toward authority relationships; these forces also act upon legal principles, at the distant, or micro level.

In recent times, for another example, we have observed Iranian religious fundamentalists seeking to combine 'modern' systems of production with a social order organized around age-old Koranic prescriptions and proscriptions. In American society we are the heirs of ideas from the Enlightenment, especially concerning property rights, costs and benefits of market transactions, ideas about equity, equality and due process of law, and desirable circumscriptions on the central state.

Work, dispositions toward work, work relationships, and work processes, in short, are shaped in very considerable ways by rules coupled with normative imperatives in a particular enterprise, but they are shaped also by macro forces, forces that lie very distant from specific work sites, distant in time and in location. Workers and foremen in American steel mills engaged in even the most quotidian exchanges are empowered and limited at least as much by federal laws as by the terms of agreements stretching over many decades, with revisions and elaborations between a worker's local of the United Steel Workers union and the owners and managers of a given mill.

A theory of work, in short, must take account of pertinent historical developments at the macro level that help shape and otherwise inform actors who participate in plant-level developments. Consider that many industries' larger firms and their unions' national leaders lobby for national programs that will arguably favor them and their work forces over shorter runs. And member firms and their unions can seek to play their antagonists off, one against others. The rights of industry members to act collectively are sometimes treated as acceptable exceptions by national laws in the United States; in Germany, England, and Scandinavia, where local bargaining occurs less frequently, industrywide "web spinning" is a way of industrial life.

Among the messoscopic forces are those (generally slowly) changing forces arising from a society's division(s) of labor; most economies have differentiated social strata, sectors, industries, occupations, and large metropolitan communities. And they may have fairly widely differentiated proliferations of large associations, political jurisdictions (like America's fifty states), national unions, and political parties.

In each of these particulars one will find rules governing economic sectors, occupations, communities, labor organizations, and political activities. These rules in turn will influence the governance systems at the macro level "upwards" and the micro levels "downwards" as when, for example, industries lobby for what they consider valuable national programs such as tariffs, at the same time several companies will seek to secure industrywide employer agreements that may, in turn, evoke "whipsaw" bargaining tactics by local unions. These tactics, taken on behalf of thousands of workers in diverse employment settings, play one employer against others in an industry, as the United Auto Workers locals did very profitably for years against Americas three major auto manufacturers. In recent times we see the reverse, corporations securing advantages from some local unions at the expense of others by threats to relocate one or more operations to plants with more vulnerable or compliant local union chapters.

At the microscopic level, and among the most widely studied forces impacting upon work and workers by far, are economic organizations, from partnerships and franchises to large bureaucratic corporate enterprises. Within the corporations there will be an almost endless list of subsets—informal organizations, craft groups, grievance committees, subsidiary organizations, boards of directors, friendship cliques, product divisions, branch establishments, and departments (e.g., marketing, finance), to name a few.

Again, each of these economic organizations, and not a few of their subsets, are productive of reporting and operating procedures, entry requirements and allowances, and, more indirectly, of constraints charted in public ordinances and regulations like "OSHA." And these organizations may well be differentially impacted upon by statutory boundaries, defined in the United States by Congress, through executive departments and independent commissions that have separate industrial jurisdictions (the Interstate Commerce Commission, the Federal Aviation Agency, the Federal Communication Commission, the Railway Labor Board, for example).

A given group of workers (or employers) accordingly finds itself to be both victim and beneficiary of the contributions of many social actors to the webs of rules that cross-cut the aforementioned macro, messo, and micro levels of analyses. These webs are spun by citizens' representatives, legislators, public officials, and regulators at the macro level and judges, stockholders (including individuals, clusters of individuals, and large pension funds), and interest groups (retirees, free traders, and national organizations aspiring to aid what have recently come to be known collectively as protected groups, women and minorities among them) at the messo level.

Indeed a great many social actors have, as their principal chores, at all three analytical levels the making and changing of rules that will affect work and workers. As a matter of fact, in conventional enumerations of major occupations, "managers, professionals, and technicians," together with "supervisors," constitute well over one quarter of all employed workers and are among the largest numbers of "exempt workers," i.e. exempted from laws affecting workers who are paid wages. To put it more crisply, one in four employed Americans spends many working hours circumscribing job descriptions, writing "SOPs," and designing, redesigning, and implementing formal rules; if we add rule-writing bureaucrats in federal, state, and municipal agencies, we add millions more to the ranks of those who spend virtually all their time spinning threads in webs of rules. Many of the remaining three quarters contribute strands to the web of rules, informally, in give-and-take exchanges over hosts of issues—quids and quos—from "coffee breaks" to significant amendments to formal work assignments, as when professors stipulate class enrollments and course requirements that shape their department's obligations with consequences that generally lie beyond the reach of university managers.

Like spider webs, the strands of rules in a society's web of rules are connected to each other such that a tug on any one of them—large numbers of layoffs in the finance sector, a shift in fundamental legal perspectives regarding the replacement of striking workers, a fresh piece of "landmark" legislation like the Civil Rights Act of 1964, periodic changes in depreciation rates in tax regulations, or new collective bargaining agreements (or contracts, as they have now become)—will cause reverberations of varying magnitudes in the other lines of the web.

Significant rending of the web's threads, meantime, can cause the web's very character to change. Thus, a bargaining relationship after a 116-day steel strike in 1959 yielded to a bipartisan Human Relations Committee that settled work rules disputes for nearly thirty strike-free years. The actions at global levels (otherwise ignored in these pages) of an international cartel, like OPEC in 1973 and NAFTA and GATT in 1993-94, can substantially alter the way of life in a collection of national economies. Freezes on prices and wages, as in WWII America and during a brief period in the Nixon administration, effectively reduced the play of market forces. Path-breaking decisions by the Supreme Court, such as declaring the rights of women in their childbearing years to work with toxic materials, a case between the United Auto Workers and Johnson Controls Company in March 1991, can change significantly the reach of an employer's (and union's) unilateral exercise of traditional rights. Current efforts to prohibit sexist, homophobic, and racist slurs in business organizations not any less than on university campuses have sparked very lively debates over the balance between "politically correct" behavior and freedom of speech claims.

For most of us, most of the time, the more palpable tugs—because they are immediate—are those within an organization's web of rules. These tugs only rarely send strong distant "vibes"—a firm's or a government agency's technical judgment in an affirmative action or tax case; the movement of some of a company's activities to another plant; a new plant superintendent; a downsizing wave in one or more branch plants; a successful contract negotiation with a government client; a merger or acquisition; a landmark grievance over a key work rule, in an auto plant, over crew size, or, in 1994, involving the weight of boxes to be lifted by truckers in a large shipping organization. These tugs are immediately both palpable and often consequential to many of an organization's members.

The foregoing paragraphs will serve as a stage-setting device, especially for later references to the macro-micro continuum, and thus help to suggest that given the inter-connectedness of all these rules, the would-be "grand theorist" of work faces the formidable challenge of selecting or developing a conceptual apparatus, delineating applicable concepts and terms, and otherwise specifying commonalities in the phenomena among the levels of analysis, with a meta-theoretical eye to the research variables pursued in a vast literature. All of these challenges are generally referred to as "obstacles to specification of theory" (Gibbs 1989; 1990a; 1990b; 1990c). To put it a little differently, if theorists of work (and phenomena related to work) wish to deal directly with only a single analytical level—the micro level, for example—they had better attend to relevant findings relating to the two other levels or risk endorsements of simplifications resulting in formulations that are contradicted by the evidence mobilized by theorists who focus on the two other levels, a caution urged by Kalleberg and Berg (1987).

In the following pages I will develop further the idea of macro, messo, and micro levels of analysis. Then, I will cross-tabulate materials within these three levels, matrix fashion, with a pair of analytical persuasions or schools of thought that we may, after Alvin Gouldner (1959), call "naturalistic" and "rationalistic." Thereafter, I will return to ideas about the "webs" of rules, noted above, and to social control "as a central notion," in efforts to study work and workers. In the concluding section I will attempt to draw these several themes together.

MACRO, MESSO, AND MICRO ANALYSES

Those who study work in macro perspectives come closest to developing specifications relevant to theory construction and that appear to encompass a good many of the phenomena at the messo level and related phenomena at the micro level. They generally do so, however, without a great deal of conscious concern with theory construction as such. One could at least derive from the outlines of topics in their writings, however, a sense of the inventory of propositions that could be specified from the theoretic issues treated by those who do have a theoretical bent: bureaucracy, authority, division of labor, prices and costs (including opportunity costs), and legal and regulatory structures; bargaining processes; matters related to information costs and modes of acquisition; labor markets and labor forces, interest groups, stratification systems, national governmental forms, industrial relations systems, and cultural and historical traditions (cf. Stinchcombe 1990; Moore 1965; Form and Miller 1960; Williamson 1985; Dunlop 1958, Kerr and Siegel 1955; Coleman 1990; Dunlop et al 1975; Berg 1979; Kalleberg and Berg 1987; Bakke, Kerr, and Anrod 1967; Mills 1951; Bluestone and Harrison 1982; Parsons and Smelser, 1956).

"Macro" scholars, only briefly sampled here, often dip down to one or both of the other analytical levels—Stinchcombe's analysis (1990) is ostensibly about organizations not macro structures, for example, but he offers many insights into macro and messo forces by following his acutely sensitive nose. James Coleman's most recent writings aspire to lead us to a so-called grand theory; almost in reverse of Stinchcombe, Coleman's focus is upon the "cranied wall," in Alfred Lord Tennyson's transcendentalist passage in whose crevices he observes a large number of "little flowers" built around a theory of rational choices constructed by economists.

For the most part, though, macro-oriented writers tend to focus most systematically on structures, roles, organizations, persons (legal and natural), and groups, and upon the interests, rights, privileges, and immunities attached there to.

When they do focus on natural (as compared to corporate) persons they tend not to deal with an individual's motives or sentiments, per se. And when they treat attitudes, they aggregate them in percentage terms or in terms of rates, in categorical fashion, and make them out to be attributes of classes, groups, strata, and industry and skill groups, as well as to gender, age, ethnic, and "racial" subsets among larger samples of persons. Structures and roles can shape behavior but they are not, in any useful sense, anthropomorphic agents with wills or motives. When macro-centered thinkers do make references to individuals per se they tend to be key individuals with strategic places in larger systems and structures— elites with influence—in companies, unions, and public offices, who are "embodiments," (a term used frequently by Phillip Selznick in lectures), of their organization's missions and purposes and who have leave, within bounds, to act or speak legitimately for constituents.

The dependent variables under study by these macro scholars, include conflict; productivity; grievance patterns; mental health scores for occupations; corporative industry strike rates; mobility rates, and employment and unemployment rates; and aggregated and disaggregated statistics describing absenteeism, turnover, voting patterns, corporate allocations of expenditures, and union constitutions.

If macro writers turn to other studies of individual persons, they tend to be from reports of the employed person's self-perceptions, work experiences, and behavior, rather than on their attitudes. Only rarely do these writers juxtapose *job*-related personal reports to reports about *non-work*-related phenomena, though there are exceptions. I have reported, using other people's data, that workers' satisfactions with their current jobs and their current employers' ways vary quite systematically with these workers' attitudes toward the pattern of distribution *nationally* and of income among their occupations. Employers, it would seem, are held by respondents to be less responsible for a worker's economic circumstance than is the larger (national) system of values in accord with which occupations are perceived to be rewarded (Berg 1978: 63-74). But employers may well suffer, themselves, from a worker's discontent that is sparked by stratifying forces far beyond a manager's control; Americans, at least, appear to take out their indignation over perceived inequities on employers, even as municipal taxpayers punish school budgets for the sins of remote federal tax law architects.

And worker respondents to the well-known "Quality of Working Life" surveys can be (and have been) addressed in both macro and messo perspectives (in industry terms, Quinn and Shepherd 1974), but virtually all resulting prescriptions of the investigators' focus on an employer's intra-organizational options, not on an industry's prospects for organizing workaday life or on the central government's not inconsiderable capacity for improving "the quality of working life" by equal opportunity initiatives, safety regulations, or fair labor standards.

It should be added that macro- and to some degree messo-directed investigators tend to be far more interested in the rights and "economic interests" of the working population—managers' and workers' rights, privileges, and immunities—than in the aforementioned sentiments and feelings of workers. Among the thousands of shorter and longer strands in the webs of rules of great significance to macro and messo writers on work are laws (and their effects) in the areas of property rights, competition, fair employment practices, collective bargaining, occupational safety, and equal opportunity and affirmative action regulations. Not a few of these writers also work with "class" and imputed "class interests," construed in a Marxist or neo-Marxist fashion, as research variables. Generally the most operative conceptions of class ultimately involve groupings of occupations that are, individually, something substantially less than internally homogeneous (Kalleberg and Berg 1987).

The works of messo-level enthusiasts thus overlap significantly with macro-level studies, but messo-oriented investigators deal essentially with work and workers at what we may call the middle range; the interests of these investigators' are grouped into occupations—industries; labor markets (desegregated); interlocking corporate directorates; national and international unions; large economic subsectors—manufacturing or services—and large social groupings—gender, age, and ethnic background; blue-and white-collar workers; the professions; and communities (urban and otherwise, in the classic sociological tradition of so-called community power studies). Dependent variables of interest to these researchers are in line with those of macro-oriented researchers already noted.

The macro and messo groups do not deny the importance of psychological approaches to the phenomena under examination but focus on them only in marginal ways. These investigators' interests in motives simply give way to their larger concerns about (a) the socioeconomic interests of one or another population subset in the data they collect; (b) the interests of workers and managers in rights—civil and personal; and (c) the interests of contending groups in "distributive justice."

At the micro-analytical level, finally, the interests of investigators have largely been in what are termed the social-psychological "dynamics" of groups and the responses of respondents or subsets of respondents to a group's norms, rewards, and punishments. The ultimate concerns of micro writers are typically about individuals; theories concerning individuals within organizational settings (Barnard, 1938; Mayo 1933; 1935); and "antidotes" to an individual's stresses and strains (cf. Tannenbaum 1951). Extensive reviews have been published by Perrow (1986), Meyer (1978), Hall (1991), Berg (1979), and Etzioni (1975); critical overviews by the author (1978), together with blistering critiques of "plant sociology" by Baritz (1974) and by Kerr and Fisher (1957) that elaborate on others' reviews and question the legitimacy of social-psychological reductionism. One special case is George Homans, a major figure in micro-industrial sociology, who lauded the psychologizing of social phenomena in his presidential address to the American Sociological Association in 1965; earlier, in *The Human*

Group (1950) he generalized, in strictly social-psychological terms, from the celebrated plant-level Hawthorne studies to whole societies.

We need not rehearse here all the micro-level studies of "satisfaction, productivity, and morale" that borrowed and have continued to borrow from the micro "human relations tradition" founded at the Harvard Business School in the late 1930s. It is sufficient to say that the work in this tradition has been exceedingly influential in studies of work but that a considerable discount should be applied to it as a foundation for a theory of work because of its psychological reductionism and its neglect of forces suggested, in myriad inquiries, about the effects of the attributes of the larger (macro and messo) contexts of organizations.

The first conclusion in this paper is accordingly that the macro-, messo-, and micro-level literature dealing with work and workers (including managers) have not yet yielded to distillations or syntheses; each analytical level is visited by many theorists, but these students of work have not, between or among them, produced a general theory, a theory whose propositions and theorems on work at different levels are at least not contradictory of one another. As with much of social science theory, moreover, theorems outnumber axioms by large multiples.

The author's own efforts, though essentially not theoretical in either character or intent, have ordered studies into a scaffolding, macro to micro (Berg and Freedman 1978) and micro to macro (1979); the latter volume also leans heavily on the concept of the web of rules. In a later effort with Kalleberg (1987) I attempted to cross-classify a number of these materials on levels into a matrix in which the macro-micro continuum (a decidedly unequal interval scale) was on the axis, and five different markets (labor, resource, capital, product, and "political," again in no way a scale) were on the abscissa. Our purpose was to encourage scholars essentially interested in studies in a given cell, a cluster of cells, a row, or a column to consider the possibilities of tracking down related studies in other cell clusters that offer explanations of variance that are observed to be residual or unexplained, in the statistical sense, in their own work. Again, these exercises did not take specific sight on either would-be macro-messo-, or micro-interested readers bent on theory construction; rather we were urging readers to build research designs suggested by their own applications and specification of our "three-by-five" overall matrix design to the problems they are studying. A would-be theorist might, however, find the specifications and applications suggestive. A summary appears in Farkas and England (1988:

3-17); Table 4.1 is taken from Kalleberg and Berg (1987) complete with chapter reference to the text.

The points to be inferred so far:

(1) The single most frequently echoed subjects in macro-, messo- and micro-level studies of work and workers, whether explicitly or implicitly, are control and authority. While Gibbs does not reduce all the social sciences to control matters, his suggestion that it is at the center of social relations is especially well taken in connection with every study cited herein; nary a one of them omits controls, those who exercise them, and those whose behavioral options are fixed by them.

(2) The three scholars who have sought most consciously to elaborate in theoretical terms on these transcendent topics are Max Weber in his treatments of traditional, charismatic, and legal-rational authority in conjunction with national, institutional economic historical developments; John Dunlop in his and his colleagues treatment of webs of rules, at our three levels, in comparisons of national industrial relations systems (1975); and Jack Gibbs in his aforementioned volume on social control. Aristotle, quoting a proverb, remarked in Book I of his *Politics*, that "well begun is half done." By Aristotle's lights, a work theorist's work is thus halfway home, given the rich apperception in the many works by Weber, by Dunlop and his associates, and especially by Gibbs. And, if we are to move from theory to the meaning of work, we will need to attend to questions about the who's, what's, when's, why's—and how's—of control. In the process we can benefit from treatments of controls in politics, family, and religious settings. Elton Mayo, for example compared workers and managers with preadolescents and parents!

In the next section we urge that many students of work and workers may also be classified, after Alvin Gouldner, as rationalists or naturalists, depending upon whether they are looking essentially at macro- and messo-levels or micro- and messo-level phenomena.

NATURAL AND RATIONAL SYSTEMS
APPROACHES TO WORK

As we have noted, there are overlaps among a few scholars' works when one breaks the phenomena under examination down into the three analytical levels, especially macro with messo and messo with micro. It is reasonable, for example, to look at industries, national unions, or regional labor markets (all messoscopic phenomena) in conjunction with national (macro) or organizational phenomena (micro), given the postulate that many rulemakers' doings at each level are interactive with each other, reflective of each other, argumentive of each other, and, sometimes in "catch-22" fashion, contradictory of each other. Consider that America's anti-trusters worry about powerful companies setting prices that are "unfairly high," while fair trade law enthusiasts focus on prices being "unfairly low"!

But specialists focused on organizational, or micro, levels are generally disposed to factor out the forces external—exogenous in economese—to employment settings. These specialists tend to exemplify two analytically different tendencies in their approaches to micro phenomena, however, a pair of approaches that, like the different lenses in bifocals, allow for different micro-observations (Gouldner 1959). Gouldner identifies one group's approach as "rational system thinking" (rationalists hereafter), because of their emphases on organizations as structures with attributes shaped by their designers' faith in scientific and economic rationality and by their faith in planning, social engineering, "legitimate" bureaucratic divisions of labor, procedures, S.O.P.s, and so on.

The other group's approach Gouldner conceives as "natural system thinking" (naturalists hereafter), a system of thought that assigns less emphasis to the design of structures that reduce the play of individuals' and their groups' whims, and a great deal more emphasis to an organization's members as social-psychological actors, actors whose "sentiments" govern their actions and lead them to elaborate voluntarily (and often inventively) on the social or work structures and webs of rules, designed by employers, in which they find themselves. These strands in the webs of rules are functionally equivalent to the dotted lines customarily found in organization charts.

Pioneers in the naturalist tradition included Elton Mayo, Chester Barnard, Fritz Roethlisberger, and W. J. Dickson (Berg 1978). Natural system thinkers observe that workers invent methods to gain some control over their circumstances, circumstances that employers could exploit such that workers could turn their own efforts from a subversive to a more productive account; these investigators make essentially no room for there being fundamental conflicts of interest between workers and employers; they urge, instead, that workers can be helped by group dynamics, sensitivity training, and related interventions to see the world as managers see it and to recognize that as the economic pie grows

TABLE 4.1 Relations between (Disaggregated Markets and Work Structures: Macro-to-Micro-Analyses)

	State	Class	Occupation	Industry	Business Organization	Union
Product Markets						
Industrial	Tariffs					
Consumer				Consumers and the oil crisis		
Capital Markets						
Industrial	Impacts of public policies on Investments		Impacts of public policies on investments	Impacts of public policies on investments	Impacts of public policies on investments	Impact of public policies on investments
Investment	Conglomeration	Economic concentration			Conglomeration	
Consumer	Deductible interest payments					
Resource Markets						
Raw Materials	Oil crisis	Oil crisis	Oil crisis	Oil crisis	Oil crisis	Oil crisis
Processed materials						
Labor Markets (demand)						
Industrial			Within and between differences in occupations' members' capabilities to control their circumstances		Strikes and grievance behavior	Strikes and grievance behavior

Retail and service		Franchising		Franchising
Government/public service		Government bureaucracy at work structure	Government bureaucracy at work structure	
Internal (intrafirm)				
Labor Markets (supply)				
Skills, human capital Cohort sizes; ti..tx	Public policies and the labor force	Public policies and the labor force		
Gender, race, age		Sex and race/ethnic income differences	Sex and race/ethnic income differences	Sex and race/ethnic income differences
Political Markets				
Agencies				
Appointments				
Policies	General policies and discrete programs			
Programs				

through productivity, workers will gain even if shares of the pie remain the same. Conflicts between workers and managers are thus gainsaid.

One popular version of the contrarion rationalist school derives directly from the 1790s writings of St. Simon, "the last of the aristocrats and the first of the socialists." The Naturalist school derives from the ideas of St. Simon's student, August Comte, many years later. The former emphasizes planning in accord with scientific principles; the latter emphasizes voluntarism and spontaneity; one stresses methodical reasoning and cold logic, the other psychologically complex sentiments; one bureaucracy and roles, the other informal groups and the importance of secure social status to individuals; one the economic interests of organizational members and the utility of incentives, the other the social-psychological rewards of group membership.

Gouldner urges that Weber, in his treatment of the three systems, "legal rational," "charismatic," and "traditional" by which authority is taken to be legitimate in the eyes of beholders, came very close to a synthesis of the two micro perspectives, as did Durkheim's treatment of the "noncontractual elements of contract" and of social norms. In the more recent literature, Scott (1992) offers an inventive and prospectful scheme for balancing the social-psychological with the more structuralist approach.

The core issues dividing the "purer" rational and natural system writers concern the exercise of authority in social systems in essentially democratic societies. For rationalists the only satisfactory compromise rulers can reach with democratic-egalitarian values is to rule (1) by virtue of their certifiable merit and their technical virtuosity; (2) by their stresses upon published procedures and rules— bureaucratic rather than ad-hocratic—and essentially predictable actions; (3) by their objectivity and their dedication to reason, evidence, and experimentation; and (4) by their emphases on due process and the "rule of law." Rationalists thus tend to take conflict in stride and search for mechanisms for managing it. Owners, with authority in other times, claimed legitimacy essentially by appeals to their property rights. As Berle (1932) showed Americans, ownership became separated rather dramatically from the control of corporate enterprises as owners yielded to the professional managers of modern times from the 1890s to the 1920s. The claims of a manager's legitimacy accordingly shifted from property-based to competency-based logics. Inegalitariaism is essentially acceptable in a democracy, in principle, only if those with authority are meritorious. We could tolerate aristocracy in America, Jefferson noted, if it were "an aristocracy of talent."

For naturalists, in a republic democratic values are secondary to values derived from property rights, but owners had best appoint able people to manage; had better use some proto-democratic means, such as "worker participation"; and had best recognize that managers must lead followers whose actions reflect at least some rational concerns (maximizing income) along with many more of what they called nonlogical sentiments, that is, sentiments that are informed less by economic interests than by psychological urges that may be traced back to experiences with parental authority.

In their practical effects rationalists' conceptions of democracy lead them to recognize conflicts of interest, at all the analytical levels, between authority figures and their human charges and therefore to seek to identify and cultivate arrangements for augmenting rational bureaucratic structures with formal mechanisms for accommodating the conflicting interests of superordinates and subordinates. Generally these accommodations take the form of institutionalized bargaining mechanisms; industrial democracy, for rationalists, is best realized through the representation of employees by elected leaders who serve in a relatively constrained structure of industrial relations systems that include grievance procedures (day-to-day), arbitration (when necessary), and contract negotiations (periodically); strikes are, in legal terms, generally viewed as last (but legal) extensions of bargaining in most industries. It is, in a sense, a limitation of the rationalists' position, by 1994, that fewer and fewer American job-related interests are expressed in settings governed by collective bargaining. Nearly 80 percent of employed Americans work in settings in which the micro-level strands in webs of rules are under an employer's unilateral control and, even in many unionized firms, the union's capacities to influence the rules has become significantly weakened by union avoidance/human relations initiatives by managers, draconic downsizing efforts, high unemployment levels, "supply side" economic policies, and trade imbalances.

In their practical effects the naturalist's conceptions of employees as carriers of both some rational and many sentimental dispositions, meantime, lead them to postulate a harmony of interests in the workplace and a need to increase this harmony by being sensitive to all employee's need for self-actualization. Naturalists assume that subordinates bring "zones of acceptance" or "zones of indifference" toward the initiatives of superordinates to their work settings and that social scientists can help managers to broaden these zones, thereby broadening the scope of their authority.

If these positions, in which there are some overlapping perceptions of superordinates and subordinates, were consistently defended in terms of their basic principles, the would-be theorist might be able to identify a peaceable synthesis—as some have—through profit-sharing arrangements or employee stock-ownership plans, for example. The fact of the matter, however, is that the resulting theory would be most readily applicable to micro-social systems that are self-sufficient, "autarchic," and invulnerable to extra-organizational forces; it would not be so readily applicable to most microsystems simply because they are so rarely "self standing"; indeed most microsystems are not even the beneficiaries of protections against a variety of market forces afforded, for example, by oligopolistic or monopolistic status. Nor are most microsystems able to shelter themselves very effectively from laws, regulations, cyclical economic changes, or the vagaries in habits of the consumers, though very small enterprises, the most vulnerable to market forces, are exempted from many public regulations.

Now it is the case that most naturalists do not even venture, in systematic ways, into the messo- and macro-level phenomena that impact on the organizations on which they accord the lion's share of their attentions. When they do so, however, they tend, somewhat ironically, to take laissez-faire structures of the wider social system as desirable 'givens'! Central governments, for example, should play only limited parts for naturalists in directing economic society; central planning, so necessary to firms, should be limited to a very few matters, especially the maintenance of law and order, in the larger social system. And the *fewer* messo structures designed to impact on firms (for regulatory purposes or, more generally, for the assurance of practicable adjustments among parties with conflicting interests) the better. Employers, properly trained, can lead rationally planned enterprises effectively by being psychologically sensitive; rational political leaders cannot and should not do so by intrusive public policies.

Rational systems writers take a very different view: authority problems for them are less relevantly psychological than they are political in the workaday world as well as in the macro and messo spheres of human affairs. This being the case the theoretical and empirical issues become issues of political economy (i.e. "governance" of the enterprise), in the interest of balancing the (now competing, now complementary) goals of equity and efficiency. To put it another way, the problems for rationalists lie in discovering workable "constitutions" for the governance of firms, of a flock of messoscopic structures, and in understanding macro public policy effects.

It is when naturalists move from the micro to the national, or macro, level that they part in most significant ways with their naturalist colleague-antagonists. While naturalists seek to limit laissez-faire in the workplace—Elton Mayo called it "the rabble hypothesis" of economists—they tend to have considerable (but by no means unlimited) faith in laissez-faire as a macroeconomic philosophy! The economic interests of individuals, in accord with their own readings of Adam Smith, are best pursued by an employer's efforts to accomplish the corporate aims and thus to produce the greatest good for the greatest number in an unfettered economy. The worker's needs in the workplace for reassuring affiliations with workmates, in an effort to temper the effects of anomie, meanwhile, and the endowment of managers with subtle social psychological— perhaps even paternalistic—sensitivities toward employees thus gives way among naturalists to a ruggedly individualistic, laissez-faire philosophy of economics when the larger economy is under discussion!

Rationalists, meantime, view macroeconomic phenomena as being a bland of highly competitive persons, corporate and natural, untempered by conscience or cooperative spirit, with innumerable anticompetitive consolidations of economic and thus political power, which include large corporations, unions, industry trade groups, and anti-social and even criminal conspiracies. (In 1954 the sixteen largest U.S. firms shipped over 80 percent of the products of 120 industries.) The rationalist's prescription for macro governance are, well, rationalistic—a blend of "full employment" programs coupled with regulatory measures targeted on oligopolistic economic agents and agencies who practice "administered prices." In these events, rationalists urge, we should take conflict as a given and strive to design mechanisms for tempering conflicting interests.

American rationalists, beyond St. Simon, derive intellectually in a straight line from American institutionalists, from John R. Commons and the "Wisconsin School," most particularly. Before modern econometrics and mathematical economics there was the marginalist school; prior to these paradigmatic approaches, rooted in price theory, there were the institutionalists who contested Marshallian or neo-orthodox, marginalist simplifications and reductions in favor of assessments of the richer textures of economic transactions. The textures are reflections and refractions of social, political, and legal arrangements that enable key economic actors, corporate persons in particular, to talk neo-orthodox economics, with stress on competition, as they adapt to price competition by developing non-price-competitive strategies and, not uncommonly, even anticompetitive methods (Wright 1904; Commons, et al. 1926, 1932, 1935, 1936; Arnold 1937). I have highlighted the macro and micro perspectives regarding naturalistic and rationalistic approaches in Table 4.2, metaphorically, as liberals and conservatives exchange places.

TABLE 4.2. Theory in Macro- to Micro-Analyses

	Macroscopic Level Analyses	*Microscopic Level Analyses*
Rational Systems Approach	(1) J.K. Galbraith, et al. [Liberals]	(2) Milton Freedman, et al. [Conservatives]
Natural Systems Approach	(3) Milton Freedman, et al. [Conservatives]	(4) J.K. Galbraith, et al. [Liberals]

The economists who later split off from neo-orthodox "reductionism" were industrial relations writers, labor law specialists, and labor economists in the 1930s and 1940s. They saw both employers and employees as parties to both market-type exchanges, as reductionists see them, and to political-power exchanges, at all three of our analytical levels; they regarded the needs for bargaining processes and shifting compromises to be endemic to production relationships. The differences in interests between the principal groups in the workplace were not those between "capital" and "labor" but between managers who, like workers, were organized (as companies and unions, respectively), restricted output, and engaged in wasteful as well as productive behavior. In common with rationalists, the industrial relations profession and many labor economists urged that both workers and managers have rationally conceived interests and psychological sentiments; but the interests take precedence over sentiments in the rationalist's agenda of significant issues as well as in the prescription for joining them.

The natural system writers also split off from the views of mainstream economists essentially only at the micro level where, they argue, the individual-based theory of the economist leaves far too little room for other social science views—anthropological, sociological, and social-psychological. Managers with training could apply these human relations techniques—predicated on Freudian psychoanalytic conceptions, anthropological conceptions of a preliterate society's tribal life, and sociopsychological conceptions of group dynamics. We thus have had several "theories" of work: mainline economic, industrial relations, and institutionalist-labor economics on the one side and economic/institutionalist and group dynamic on the other.

Practicing managers, as I have argued elsewhere (Berg and Freedman 1978), have been attentive to reforms, urged in an evolving literature on human relations in the workplace, essentially only when labor markets have been tight enough to prod managers into dealing with the independence of spirit that tight labor markets encourage among workers. These periods have often coincided with energetic union organizing efforts—a circumstance that adds to reform-bent managers' hopes to "head 'em off at the pass." Indeed, not a few academic social scientists have recently packaged naturalist ideas about worker participation, work restructuring, quality circles, and self-actualization under the label of union avoidance programs (Berg and Freeman 1978). These packages are the stock-in-trade among most sociologists, social psychologists, and anthropologists in elite M.B.A. programs in which courses on organizational behavior, the human relations tradition in its newest incarnation, is a substantial cottage industry. By the 1990s these reformist efforts are visited upon the survivors of draconian downsizing decisions: "we will have teamwork—or else. . . ."

Industrial relationists (and institutionalists) meantime have continued to pursue concerns about conflict and industrial democracy at all of our analytical levels while naturalists leave off at micro levels, tending to be more sympathetic, as noted above, to the mainline economist's conception of the structures and functions of messo and macro realities.

One of the main points: natural systems and rational systems writers agree, at the level of the firms, that local (micro) webs of rules ought to make room for a worker's motives, sentiments, and needs, as well as rights and interests (beyond those assured by natural and statutory law), respectively. The writers part company when they approach events at the two higher levels. The closest to a synthesis of all of these materials currently available is by Oliver Williamson (1985), an economist in control of all of the other relevant social science materials, but he acknowledges the legitimacy of a few thoughtful critics of his "transaction cost" model among the rationalists, the most articulate of whom are Mark Granovetter

(1988), and Charles Perrow (1986); these two critics focus on his reluctance to back away from the sovereignty of price theory and of "atomized" individuals, as units of analysis, in his transaction cost analyses. Naturalists break off from the cash nexus at the micro level, while rationalists treat economic changes in institutional terms.

In the next section we comment on the "common denominators" in the foregoing sections and endorse a recent argument that "social control" is a candidate to be treated as the central notion in anthropological, sociological, and social-psychological analysis. It is my position that this argument is especially strong in relation to researches into industry and into "economy and society," because the writers focus on power relations by either dealing directly with conflict or by adroitly recasting conflicts among interests into psychological motivational terms.

SOME ADDITIONAL THOUGHTS ON THE WEB OF RULES

I have indicated that the key concerns of both rationalists and naturalists are with authority, superordination and subordination, and hierarchy (i.e., with control).

For the pure naturalists (Mayo and Barnard, among the moderns) management's authority flows directly from the "votes" of worker-followers whose "zones of acceptance" (or indifference) are generally wide and vulnerable to expansion; they can be broadened by sensitive leaders who recognize the norms of work groups and help workers to turn these norms in the direction of supportiveness when they appear (as when workers restrict output) to be unsupportive. For Barnard, the Army was the epitome of democracy (Barnard 1938) because, in accord with his logic, he perceived that soldiers have the option of rejecting orders if they deem them illegitimate! This only one year before Hitler's soldiers and airmen slaughtered noncombatants and a scant two years before the first of 13 million American soldiers could be governed by a system of military 'justice' that allowed service personnel to be accorded up to three days confinement and one daily meal of bread and water for looking at an officer in a fashion that the officer considered to be "silent contempt."

Whatever the explicit concerns—the ultimate concerns are very clearly with the "hows" of the exercise of authority. For naturalists, the legitimacy of an employer's authority is essentially an unexamined given; for rationalists, this legitimacy is problematic. For naturalists, management's rights are directly derivative of the rights of property owners while workers per se have second-order rights; for rationalists, managers and workers both have rights, both should thus have remedies, and both may turn to the law in quest of justice and equity.

For the pure naturalist the emphasis is on preemptive initiatives that will minimize legalistic recourses by workers in favor of therapeutic interventions by managers targeted on mutual understanding. These interventions included counseling individual employees who needed help to recognize that their nonrational (*not* irrational) sentiments are born of a worker's nonwork experiences, especially with their parents in their formative years. A group's sentiments are also candidates for revisions into constructive norms; managers, can help individuals for whom group membership is of putatively great value. And the vast group dynamics literature, both experimental and descriptive, does appear to leave little doubt that most individuals are disinclined to be labeled a deviant, (i.e., a loner), unless autonomous behavior affords gratifications or rewards that significantly outweigh the benefits of conformity, as matters of "high principle" sometimes can for a given individual. The space between conformity and the assertion of dissent is, of course, Chester Barnard's famous zone of acceptance and zone of indifference, zones whose dimensions any decent (and observant) employer can generally gauge, albeit only with the help of trained observers.

For the rationalist, the margin for managers to err is wide, a judgment informed in no small degree from the reading of the large numbers of nonfrivolous grievances filed in work settings in which formal grievance procedures have been codesigned by workers and employers. The interests represented by these grievances may well gain no productively systematic expression; in most workplaces there are no formal venues for their expression. While there is no need to gainsay the existence of zones of acceptance, it is demonstrable that managers far more often lose arbitration awards when they fail to live by whatever system of due process the parties have agreed to (Berg and Freedman 1978: 171–84). It would be very difficult, by the way, to prove that most such grievances are filed simply because there is an agreement to cosponsor a grievance system; the availability of venues does not explain their utilization, just as their absence is no assurance that working Americans have no serious misgivings about their treatments.

Indeed arbitration, typically the venue to which parties to a labor-management agreement repair when grievances have not been agreeably settled at earlier stages, became a strategically significant strand in the Republic's web of rules when the Supreme Court held that grievance procedures, arbitration, and the documents enabling them in a work setting are collectively, in constitutional terms, a system of "industrial common law unto itself" (Trilogy case 1960). If enabled to do so in a bipartisan agreement, arbitrators will produce holdings that may not be taken by the losing parties to the courts, as they could prior to 1959. Labor management agreements have generally contained a "reserved rights" clause denying workers a capacity to claim rights to contest managers on matters not stipulated to be "bargainable" in the agreement. Balancing such clauses are clauses ensuring that workers can grieve a manager's interpretation of one or another term in the document, an opening for unions. The latter clause, as managers and their protagonists viewed matters, was fine if, after arbitration, managers could seek to undo holdings favoring unions by recourse to the courts as they could prior to Trilogy. By the late 1970s employers' lawyers, (with unions weakened by market forces) essentially persuaded the courts to nullify the 1959 decision. Since the 1970s, managers have won longer and longer agreements containing more and more manager-friendly stipulations, contract-style; the term labor management "agreement" is now an anachronism.

CONCLUSION

The point is that authority, hierarchy, and control are ultimately *the* central notions, whether implicitly or explicitly so identified, in all but a minority of studies reported in the literature relevant to would-be work theorists; the only correlatively significant concepts are comprehended by the notion of the "web of rules" that encompasses both public laws and regulations and private systems of jurisprudence; "S.O.P.S"; hierarchial charts of *all* employees' ('not just managers') authority and responsibilities; and all manner of directives, plans, schedules, and procedures. Again, each of these types of webs of rules are essentially about controls.

It is accordingly my suggestion that problems of superordination and subordination; hierarchies (whether in crude, macro, society-wide, or in micro, corporate bureaucratic terms); and control and authority are, explicitly or implicitly, the most central ones in the bulk of studies of work and workers.

It is my further suggestion that these problems have been addressed generally in accord with rational system or natural system perspectives; rarely are these emphases on impersonal structures or on social psychological phenomena, respectively, brought simultaneously to bear; separate weights are assigned to the roles of the forces stressed in each of these two sets of emphases.

It is my suggestion, next, that we can never escape the rationalist's concerns; even the authors of an extensive literature on small groups and "group dynamics," though significantly (and constructively) social psychological in character, admit of power relations starting with simple but notoriously unstable "triads." By like token, it is virtually impossible to invest enormous theoretical interest in studies, conducted in the tradition of Chester Barnard, when their authors stick with narrowly social-psychological diagnoses regarding workers' groups, relations among workers and first-line supervisors, and regarding middle managers and upper-level managers, despite abundant scholarly evidence on conflicts over rights and interest among these populations in the workplace.

If readers do not agree with this judgment about the limits to doctrinaire human relations I would invite their attention to the character of recent equal opportunity and affirmative action cases, for example: sexual and racial harassment charges, even involving peers, focus on the theoretical advantages of dominant—a revealing term—over minority and other protected persons. These cases, the newest of evolving developments in the American workplace, deserve brief discussion here by way of illustrating this paper's central theses.

The charges in these harassment cases typically involve (senior) perpetrators and (junior) victims; defendants are almost always cast in terms of superiors using their positions to extract favors or otherwise to abuse protected group members. No doubt the alleged perpetrators (or many of them) are "acting out"—sadists, bigots, exploiters, victimizers, and so on. But it is their role-driven behavior that is justiciable; their psychological states—their intentions—are not, in the first instance, evidence of illicit behavior but, conceivably (and slightly less significantly), of psychopathology.

Defendants' defenses, meantime, often tend to include claims that there have been misunderstandings, that there is an opportunistic quality in the arguments of insincere plaintiffs with personal axes to grind, and that they are entirely innocent (or that they were provoked). Typically, defenses do not include claims of psychological illnesses, perversions, or pathologies, otherwise. Whether one is cynical about or entirely supportive of a plaintiff's harassment charges, we can thank protected group members' leaders and many of their members, sincere or opportunist, for highlighting social rather than psychological phenonema and for forcing our attention, whether intentionally so or not, to procedures.

I would, of course, for reasons too complex to review here, grant that some segments of the *remedies* in these cases are palpably social-psychological: it is a rare affirmative action/EEOC program in an employment setting that does not make room for sensitivity training programs, of some type, for alleged perpetrators, even if formal charges are never registered. "Diversity consulting" has become a good deal more than a cottage industry, and the intra-corporate agencies that process changes have every incentive to encourage charges.

Not uncommonly relevant interventions are accepted by protected groups' members as constructive attacks on the "institutionally unacceptable" (racist, sexist, or homophobic) behavior of victimizers. Indeed, it is not at all uncommon to discover that formal procedures, (i.e., "due process" that might serve defendants), are prefunctorally suspended—the Bill of Rights is not applicable to private organizations—while putative miscreants are treated. But the suspicious plaintiffs, in many settings, have the reserved right, later, to bring formal legal complaints against even those who are in or have completed their sensitization exposures, up to five years or more *after* they were named by putative victims. In that event, defendants may, finally, repossess relevant claims under the Bill of Rights (to be confronted by their accusers, for example, or to be informed of charges and to review the alleged evidence against them) if the EEOC or courts are introduced. Defendants, however, benefit not at all from justice thus delayed. And the innocent ones among them tend to look upon the prolonged "treatments" as gratuitously slanderous insults!

I have intended in these equal opportunity and affirmative action cases to dramatize the point that controls—authority—are at stake, at the beginning and at the end, though there may be (for good and for ill) a considerable amount of psychologizing in between.

CODA

About our main points: the "down from up" or "up from down" perspectives implied by the macro to micro levels of analyses can be defended more exactingly than my adumbration here suggests, were space unlimited. I will not argue, however, that the theorist will have a correspondingly easy time in efforts to deduce, in accord with the law suggested by the tale of Occam's Razor, an uncomplicated, parsimonious, theory.

My only hints inhere (1) in my urgings, following Gibbs, to make control the theory's starting point; (2) in my urgings that we identify the several webs of rules and the procedures they contemplate, at successive approximations from macro to micro and micro to macro levels, that govern work and workers; and (3) that we seek to strike balances between naturalists and rationalists emphases.

One possibility for the specification of productive and legitimate simplifications: focus, *at each level*, on *key* rules, such as those dealing with competition, property, legitimacy, common law and constitutional rights of persons (legal or natural) per se, and the procedures (where they exist) for rulemaking, for example, at the micro level. I note these areas because I doubt that a serviceable theory can be constructed without attention to the controls we employ at macro levels in search of cooperation, efficiency, due process, and personal well-being in a society that tries (1) to "empower" different persons and different groups differently; (2) to admire both equity and efficiency; (3) and to value both equality and merit. The names of Max Weber, Emile Durkheim, J. R. Commons, Clark Kerr, Sen. Herbert Lehman, Sen. Paul Douglas, John Dunlop, Neil Chamberlain, Frank Tannenbaum and, most recently, Jack Gibbs are among those, meantime, who have laid theorists' groundwork for them.

I would add, finally, that one of the "hottest" set of issues—the current debates over the rights and entitlements of individual persons, including the natural and corporate versions (Coleman 1982), on one side, and of persons as members-of-groups, on another side—involve the introduction of only a few truly novel dimensions to studies of work and workers. Group rights may seem new to those focused upon current demands of gays and protected groups, but they borrow from the logic of corporations seeking limited liabilities for owners and from unions seeking to bargain collectively.

We may wish to curse or thank the newer social movements' leaders for their sharpening of control issue but, either way, their and their critics' arguments have a long history in studies of work since Adam Smith. Smith wrote in 1776 of people, after all, as the real wealth of nations and offered embellishments on older (generally religious) writings about work, in his treatment of control, especially in his metaphor for the division of labor, his pin factory. There is indeed little in the chapters of *The Wealth of Nations* that does not bear on the matter of control. And even when he "psychologizes" the control-authority issues in firms, Chester Barnard writes purely (if neither simply, explicitly, or ingenuously) about control. An examination of key topics in the literature on work will thus reveal much material about control: organizations, the division of labor, collective bargaining, bureaucracy, markets, regulations, wage administration(!), stratification, income distribution, "supervision, productivity, and morale," and much more.

To put it another way, theorists of work may want to start at the beginning by making intellectual room, for example, for Adam Smith's apprehensions about the likely conspiracies to subvert the efficiencies of markets' controls that are born when two or more men of commerce meet. He wrote, twelve years earlier, of "moral sentiments" as social controls over economic and other factors. Smith dealt ultimately with factories as rational systems and with natural, emergent systems (markets), with macro to micro phenomena, and with controls in dozens of contexts, otherwise.

Theorizers may be ever-so-gently reminded that they will also find Plato, Aristotle, Locke, Bentham, Mill, St. Simon, Marx, Durkheim, and Weber, among many others, helpful in their enterprises. Gibbs, however, has tied the matter to one large and relevant theme; theories of work will be far more than meta-theoretic exercises if they contain well-documented and well-reasoned arguments by the authors that their theories are special cases of a general theory of control. In the meantime, Scott (1992) offers the best assessments about the exchanges between many consequential forces external to organizations and, in reverse, of many of the forces impacting on an organization's environment that are generated by the organization's own policies and practices, in what he calls "an open systems" perspective.

REFERENCES

Arnold, Thurman W.
1937   *The Folklore of Capitalism.* New Haven: Yale University Press.

Bakke, Wight, Clark Kerr and Charles W. Anrod, eds.
1967   *Unions, Management and the Public.* New York: Hancourt, Brace and World.

Baritz, Loren
1974   *The Servants of Power.* Westport, CT: Greenwood Press.

Barnard, Chester
1938   *The Functions of the Executive.* Cambridge, MA: Harvard University Press.

Berg, Ivar
1979   *Industrial Sociology.* Englewood Cliffs, NJ: Prentice-Hall.

Berg, Ivar, and Marcia K. Freedman
1978   *Managers and Work Reforms.* New York: Free Press.

Berle, Adolph A.
1932   *The Modern Corporation and Private Property.* New York: MacMillian.

Bluestone, Barry, and Bennet Harrison
1982   *The Deindustrialization of America.* New York: Basic Books.

Coleman, James S.
1982   *The Asymmetric Society.* Syracuse, NY: Syracuse University Press.

1990   *Foundations of Social Theory.* Cambridge, MA: Harvard University Press.

Commons, John R. et al.
1926; 1932; 1935; 1936 *History of Labor in the United States*, vols. 1–4. New York: Macmillan.

Dunlop, John
1958   *Industrial Relations Systems.* New York: Holt, Rinehart and Winston.

Dunlop, John, Frederick H. Harbison, Clark Kerr, and Charles Myers
1975   *Industrialization and Industrial Man Reconsidered.* Princeton, NJ: The Inter-University Study of Human Resource in National Development.

Etzioni, Amitai
1975   *A Comparative Analysis of Complex Organizations*, rev. ed. New York: Free Press.

Farkas, George, and Paula England, eds.
1988   *Industries, Firms and Jobs.* New York: Plenum.

Form, William H., and Delbert C. Miller
1960   *Industry, Labor, and Community.* New York: Harper & Row.

Gibbs, Jack P.
1989   *Control: Sociology's Central Notion.* Urbana: University of Illinois Press.

1990a Control: sociology's central notion. *American Journal of Sociology.* 27:1–27.

1990b Still another mercifully better grand theory. *Social Forces.* 69: 625–633.

1990c The notion of a theory in sociology. *American Journal of Sociology.* 4:129–158.

Gouldner, Alvin
1959   Organizational analysis in *Sociology Today.* Merton, Robert K., et al., eds. New York: Basic Books, pp. 400–428.

Granovetter, Mark
1988   The sociological and economic approaches to labor market analysis
in *Industries, Firms and Jobs.* Farkas, George and Paula England, eds.
New York: Plenum.

Hall, Richard
1991   *Organizations: Structures, Processes, and Outcomes,* 5th ed. Englewood Cliffs,
NJ: Prentice-Hall.

Homans, George
1950   *The Human Group.* New York: Harcourt Brace Jovanovich.

Kalleberg, Arne, and Ivar Berg
1987   *Work and Industry.* New York: Plenum.

Kerr, Clark, and Lloyd H. Fisher
1957   Plant sociology: The elite and the aborigines in *Common Frontiers of
the Social Sciences.* Komarovsky, M. ed. New York: Free Press, pp. 281–
309.

Kerr, Clark and Abraham Siegel
1955   The structuring of the labor force in industrial society. *Industrial and
Labor Relations Review* 8:151–168.

Mayo, Elton
1933   *The Human Problems of an Industrial Civilization.* New York: Macmillan.

Meyer, Marshall, and M. C. Brown
1978   The process of bureaucratization. *American Journal of Sociology* 83:364–
385.

Mills, C. Wright
1951   *White Collar.* New York: Oxford University Press.

Moore, Wilbert E.
1965   *The Impact of Industry.* Englewood Cliffs, NJ: Prentice-Hall.

Parsons, Talcott, and Neil Smelzer
1956   *Economy and Society.* New York: Free Press.

Perrow, Charles
1986   *Complex Organizations: A Critical Essay,* 3rd ed. New York: McGraw-
Hill.

Quinn, Robert P., and Linda J. Shepherd
1974   *The 1972–73 Quality of Employment Survey.* Ann Arbor: Institute of Social
Research, University of Michigan.

Scott, Richard W.
1992   *Organizations: Rational, Natural, and Open Systems.* Englewood Cliffs, NJ:
Prentice-Hall.

Stinchcombe, Arthur L.
1990   *Information and Organizations.* Berkeley: University of California Press.

Tannenbaum, Frank
1921   *The Labor Movement: Its Conservative Functions and Social Consequences.* New York: G.P. Putnam's Sons.

Trilogy Cases
1960   *United Steel Workers of America v. American Manufacturing Co.,* 363 U.S. 564; *United Steelworkers of America v. Warrior and Gulf Navigation Co.,* 303 U.S. 574; and *United Steelworkers of America v. Enterprise Wheel and Car Corp.,* 303 U.S. 593.

Williamson, Oliver
1985   *The Economic Institutions of Capitalism.* New York: Free Press.

Wright, Carroll D.
1904   *Regulation and Restriction of Output: Eleventh Annual Report of the Commissioner of Labor.* Washington, DC: U.S. Government Printing Office.

5

Work and Technology in Modern Industry: The Creative Frontier [1]

INTRODUCTION

Work and technology are closely related, both as intellectual constructs and as empirical phenomena. The interrelationship of these concepts may be illustrated by examining their formal definitions.[2] Charles Perrow's (1967:49) widely accepted definition of organizational technology, for example, holds that technology is "the actions that an individual performs on an object, with or without the aid of tools or mechanical devices, in order to make some change in that object."[3] Another more general definition conceives of technology as "tools and tool systems by which we transform our environment, derived from human knowledge, to be used for human purposes" (Tornatzky and Fleischer 1990:10). Both of these definitions agree upon the ends toward which technology is directed (i.e., change or transformation) but disagree somewhat concerning the means by which these ends are achieved (i.e., whether or not "tools" must be involved).

Work, on the other hand, has been defined by Herbert Applebaum (1984:2) as "productive activity which alters the physical environment to meet human needs. . . . "As in the definitions of technology presented above, the end or function of work is alteration of something in the human environment. And, as in the first definition, the means are basically unspecified (i.e., work is "productive activity"). Thus, both technology and work may be defined as actions (possibly aided by tools) or activities that alter or transform aspects of the environment. The conceptual cores of these definitions are so similar that it is difficult to distinguish between them.

In many cases, it is also difficult to separate work and technology empirically. If one observes the operation of a CAD (computer-aided design) workstation, for example, it is nearly impossible to untangle the being and actions of the CAD operator from the existence and performance of the machine. The CAD operator possesses within her body and mind the knowledge and skill that are needed to operate the CAD machine. Without such knowledge and skill, the operator would have a different conceptualization of the world and a different life; she would not be an operator and might have no work at all. The machine, on the other hand, cannot function without constant physical manipulation initiated by its operator. Each function of the machine requires a specific set of actions by the operator. When no work is being performed, the technology lapses into a nonfunctioning state—it is lifeless, powerless. Under such conditions, a tool is not technology at all (as technology is defined above) but inert matter. Thus, the operator and her machine interpenetrate one another; technology in its empirical form merges with an almost invisible seam into human work activity.

The close relationship of work and technology is not serendipitous, nor does it necessarily reflect construct confusion. Rather, the connections between the concepts of work and technology are purposeful and significant; that is, they reflect the fact that technology often has been designed and built to support, augment, and finally act as a substitute for work activity. This functional relationship between work and technology appears to be panhuman, being displayed in both preindustrial and industrial societies. Indeed, from the invention of the first human tools, technology has extended the human capacity to do work (i.e., "to alter the physical environment to meet human needs" in Applebaum's words). In preindustrial societies, technology's support of work is achieved through its action as a multiplier of human effort (e.g., a hoe multiplies the effort of human hands, while a draft animal and plow enhance the multiplier effect). In industrial societies, technology goes beyond the extension of human effort and begins to take over work tasks that initially were performed by humans. The technological takeover in modern industry is accomplished by breaking work down into smaller and smaller component tasks and applying specific domains of knowledge to do each of these small tasks and to fit the tasks together in an appropriate sequence. Through this process, industrial technology (i.e., capital) evolves to become a nearly perfect substitute for work activity (i.e., labor), so that such technology resembles work in its action and its output. The principal purpose toward which much of industrial technology has been directed explains why the formal definitions of organizational technology and work are virtually indistinguishable; that is, both technology and work are intended generally to perform many of the same basic functions.

The interrelationship of work and technology, and the process underlying this association, clearly have theoretical (and political) implications. Although work and technology are inextricably connected, they are not the same thing, and some distinction between them is necessary for theory-building purposes. Some writers have argued that, if we cannot distinguish between work and technology, then statements regarding causal relationships between these phenomena may become tautological (e.g., see Bernard and Pelto 1986). Further, the fact that industrial technology may serve as a substitute for human work activity suggests the possibility of tension and conflict between the two. As Harry Braverman (1974) has demonstrated, the evolution of industrial technology not only has broken down craft work into ever smaller components but also has tended to encroach upon and dismantle skill-based occupations in the process. Such encroachment has not taken place in a contextual vacuum but has been shaped and guided by sociocultural forces that pit elites (the creators and controllers of formal technology in modern industrial organizations) against those who do work. Within this context, there is an ongoing debate regarding the relative dominance of technology and work in modern industrial organizations. Elites often argue (or assume) that industrial technology is dominant over work because technology forces work into an ever-narrowing sphere of activity and because it also has the capability to break down, take over, and replace human labor. Workers and their advocates, on the other hand, argue that technology actually represents the elite's interest in dominating, controlling, and minimizing the work force; thus, it is not technology that is dominant but the interests of elites.

For both theoretical and political reasons, therefore, it may be useful to gain a better understanding of the distinctions and interrelationships between technology and work, especially in industrial contexts. In this paper, we will explore hypotheses that have been advanced to explain the differences between technology and work in modern industry and the nature of causal connections between these phenomena and their cultural contexts. Further, drawing on ethnographic data pertaining to the relationship of work and technology in modern industrial organizations, we will present a revised schema for conceptualizing the relationships among work, technology, and cultural context. The new schema will suggest the following: (1) work and technology act upon one another as mutually shaping causal forces; (2) work differs from technology primarily in its dynamic, creative, and problem-solving potential; and (3) the nature of the causal connection between work and technology varies over time and across sociocultural contexts. For purposes of this chapter, we will limit the applicability of these three propositions to modern industrial organizations; their generalization to other contexts remains a subject for future research.

CONCEPTUALIZING THE WORK-TECHNOLOGY INTERFACE

A careful examination of the constituent elements of work and technology reveals the basis for interlinkage between these two constructs. Work (both in preindustrial and industrial societies) has been conceptualized as a complex construct containing several dimensions. These dimensions—or universal features that characterize work in all cultural contexts—include a knowledge base, communality, allocation of time, rules and norms, reciprocity and exchange, incentives and motivations, organization, leadership, controls and spurs to effort, prestige, interaction with nature, expenditure of energy, concept of value, and localization (Applebaum 1984).

A review of the literature on technology suggests that several of these dimensions, or universal features of work, also have been conceived as fundamental elements or characteristics of industrial technology. Congruent elements across the two domains include a base of knowledge (Tornatzky and Fleischer 1990); allocation of time (Dubinskas 1988); rules and norms pertaining to techniques, tools, and materials (Kusterer 1978); reciprocity and exchange (Orr 1986); organization and coordination of tasks (Galbraith 1967); prestige (Thomas 1993); interaction with environment (Bernard and Pelto 1986); expenditure of energy (White 1949); and localization of effort (Baba 1990). Since technology is so often a substitute for human work activity, and thus often fills a social space once made and filled by human beings, it is not surprising that technology's mode of action, and many of its social effects, resemble so closely those of human labor.

In spite of these similarities, however, it is clear to members of our society that work and technology are not the same thing. The fact that they have been assigned separate semantic handles is one indication of their distinction. More importantly, however, is the general use of the term work to mean productive *human* activity, while the term technology more often refers to *nonhuman* tools or devices, which often are the products or by-products of work. Although as intellectual constructs work and technology are difficult to separate, we seldom confuse the two in everyday life. Work is something that people *do*, while technology is something that people *make* (often as a product of doing). The difference between living behavior and the product of such behavior is a real, hard difference that makes us keep our theoretical feet on the ground. Thus, while work and technology share many core features, they also are distinctive phenomena.

Some writers have argued that the apparent linkage or overlap between the two constructs creates certain theoretical problems. For example:

> We all recognize that the use of machines and their products requires "knowledge," "skills," "capital investment" . . . and many other less tangible entities. This is not technology per se but we can readily include these factors in the expression, "techno-social system." If we were to include all those other cultural features in the definition of technology, most of our resulting theoretical statements would be tautological. For example, if we were to include human technical skill as part of the definition of technology, then a statement such as "technological change modifies the hierarchy of skills of workers" becomes circular (Bernard and Pelto 1986:360).

These scholars have endeavored to resolve the theoretical problem of separating work activity (or behavior) and technology by formalizing the distinction between them which is reflected in common usage of the two terms. Thus, Bernard and Pelto (1986) suggest that:

> . . . technology consists of individual, particular things, physical observables. Since the general meaning has always focused on human products, we therefore define technology

as "all those machines, devices, and other physical apparatuses made and used by humans for instrumental purposes, and the physical products of those machines and devices."

While this definition is intuitively appealing, a problem arises when one enters the domain of modern industrial organization. Here we find what are referred to as "soft" or social technologies, complex and formalized processes, procedures, methodologies, and systems designed specifically to accomplish the functions of traditional technology (i.e., effect an action which changes an object), yet with little or no use of material tools or devices. Louis Tornatzky and Mitchell Fleischer (1990) define social technology as "tools characterized more by replicable procedures and behavior patterns than by hardware." Examples of prominent social technologies in industry are quality methodologies, "just-in-time" production techniques, and design for manufacturability programs. To these examples may be added many others, including human factors, engineering methods, and training curricula (Tornatzky et al. 1983). Most of these social tools are founded on a base of knowledge that includes information from the social or operating sciences, and they all involve ways of organizing and processing information and/or other resources in order to effect the transformation of physical objects.

To limit our conception of technology only to material tools and devices would exclude from consideration as technology many of the methods used in industry to effect change. Some would argue, no doubt, that social technologies such as those mentioned above should properly be considered part of organizational structure (i.e., part of the apparatus of coordination and control) and not part of an organization's technological base. While such a materialist argument supports Bernard and Pelto's (1986) distinction between work behavior and technology, it overlooks the fact that social technologies may function as both structure and as technology simultaneously. That is, many of these methods and procedures both organize the work force *and* are involved directly in the transformation of objects in the production process. Quality-oriented technologies such as the Taguchi method (Taguchi and Clausing 1990), for example, embody formal procedures for identifying and solving product quality problems; the output of these methods may concretely alter both the production process (e.g., modifying the assembly line) and/or the things being produced (e.g., improving the quality of manufactured articles). Quality methods thus are pieces of the organizational apparatus that are functioning as part of the technology (i.e., a "social" or organizational technology).

In our view, it is not productive theoretically to completely separate work behavior and technology. While such complete separation may be forced (e.g., as in Bernard and Pelto), it does not add to our understanding of the relationship between these constructs, but rather creates an artificially restricted view of technology (a view which, ironically, is held by many engineers).

Work and technology are, in fact, interlinked constructs—two phenomena that overlap on certain dimensions. The most important areas of overlap are those related to (1) technical knowledge and behavioral techniques, both of which are simultaneously embodied in the physical and mental being of the worker and embedded in the functional requirements of the machine and (2) "social" technologies that are encoded formally in written texts and provide a template that organizes information and orchestrates the activity of human work groups as an integral part of the production process. Interlinkage on these dimensions does not mean, however, that work and technology are the same thing; each continues to display dimensions of distinction. Work, as a human activity, is characterized by several features that are not shared with technology (e.g., its communal nature, the need for incentives and motivation, leadership). Industrial technology, on the other hand, often includes some form of material hardware, which, when not linked with behavior, is in fact inert matter and thus not part of work. Also, modern industrial technology frequently is founded on a base of formal scientific knowledge that is not necessarily required for successful work activity.

If we conceptualize work and technology as distinct, yet interlinked constructs, what becomes of Bernard and Pelto's (1986) theoretical problem (i.e., that interlinkage will create tautological statements regarding the relationship between work and technology)? It is proposed here that the threat of tautology is not so great as Bernard and Pelto suggest. This latter statement rests on three arguments.

First, as indicated earlier, interlinkage does not mean exact sameness. Even if interlinked, work and technology continue to possess distinctive characteristics that should allow specified changes in certain dimensions of either construct to occur independently of change in the other construct. For example, it is possible to change the hardware in an engineering workstation without changing the software. Such a change in the hardware component of the technology may have little significant impact on the behavioral component of work activity.

Second, even if the workstation hardware mentioned above had changed with respect to human factors characteristics (thereby requiring behavioral change), it still would be possible to trace such change in behavior directly to changes in hardware. Here, we see that the ability to conceive of technology as a system comprised of several distinctive components, including a knowledge base, methodological requirements (i.e., the behavioral interface), and a physical presence, allows us to trace paths of change among system components, and between systems, without creating tautologies.

Third, there is empirical evidence for the existence of an interlinked work-technology domain. Ethnographic research on the introduction of automated production systems in manufacturing settings shows that informal working knowledge and techniques—developed by the work force and embodied only in their individual and collective memories—often add a missing component to formal automated systems, a component without which the formal systems could not function properly (see for examples Orr 1986; Howard and Schneider 1988; Scribner and Sachs 1989). The fact that many automated systems, initially developed without the benefit of informal knowledge and techniques, failed during their introduction to the work environment suggests that work and technology are intertwined in practice. The depiction of interlinkage does not equate with the creation of tautologies; rather, it serves to create a model of reality that is more accurate than that portrayed by work and technology constructs that are separated completely.

CAUSAL RELATIONS BETWEEN WORK AND TECHNOLOGY

The close relationship between work and technology creates additional theoretical problems, one of the most important being the conceptualization of causal relations between the two constructs. Whether technology determines and drives work activity, or whether technology is itself determined by other forces has been a matter of debate for some time. Three different models of causal relationship between work and technology have been advanced, including (a) technological determinism; (b) sociotechnical systems theory; and (c) cultural construction of technology. We examine each of these models below.

Technological Determinism

Technological determinism is a theoretical orientation that views the causal arrow as moving from technology to work; that is, technology is seen as the primary force that shapes and directs the nature and substance of work. This viewpoint has been influential in modern industry since the industrial revolution and still is the dominant mode of managerial thinking about the relationship between technology and work. Many modern industrial managers believe that it is their prerogative (and indeed, their responsibility) to select the most appropriate technology for their industry and firm and that human workers must adapt and conform their behavior to technological requirements. This viewpoint often portrays technology as a preexisting, autonomous thing that is value-free, reflecting purely technical considerations and performing purely instrumental functions. In other words, technology is seen as divorced from social or cultural influence, and determinative with respect to the behavior of the work force.

The determinist point of view is reflected in the scientific management movement founded by Frederick Winslow Taylor and his associates in the early decades of the twentieth century. Taylor attempted to formulate principles and methods that would enable workers to turn out as much work as possible, given the technology in question. Taylor's methods required workers to conform bodily movements exactly to the technological requirements of a job and to continue this conformity for as long as physically possible, all without thinking (see Taylor 1947). Taylor was not interested in technology per se, but his methods introduced the idea that it is possible to "scientifically" select individuals who are best suited to the technological requirements of a particular job and train them to meet those requirements exactly. Thus, as in the viewpoint of modern management, technology is viewed as a managerial given and as largely determinative of work activity.

Technological determinism (or the technological imperative, as it is sometimes called) is a pervasive concept throughout the managerial and social sciences.[4] In organizational theory, for example, a technological imperative that links technology with organizational structure in a deterministic relationship was the concept that launched modern contingency theory in the 1960s (Tosi 1984). This imperative has been reconfirmed more recently in methodologically sophisticated re-studies (e.g., see Fry 1982).

The technological imperative means that managers and industrial engineers should design whatever form of work organization the technology in question seems to require. The human costs of such an imperative are treated generally as necessary outcomes of efficiency but are not viewed as reason to influence technological or organizational design.

Socio-Technical Systems Theory

Socio-technical systems theory arose from a research program conducted by the British Tavistock Institute in the late 1940s and early 1950s. The concept of socio-technical systems originated when researchers discovered a novel form of work organization that had emerged spontaneously in the South Yorkshire coalfields and apparently resulted in greater personal commitment, lower absenteeism, fewer accidents, and higher productivity that was normal for this industry. The new form of work organization responsible for these improvements was one in which semiautonomous work groups interchanged roles and shifts, regulated their own affairs, and participated in decisions concerning their work arrangements (Trist 1981:8).

From the discovery of semiautonomous work groups there emerged a paradigm shift concerning the nature of work organization. This new paradigm was first conceptualized in the following way:

> Work organizations exist to do work—which involves people using technological artifacts (whether hard or soft) to carry out sets of tasks related to specified overall purposes. Accordingly, a conceptual reframing was proposed in which work organizations were envisaged as socio-technical systems rather than simply as social systems. . . . The social and technical systems were the substantive factors—the people and the equipment. Economic performance and job satisfaction were the outcomes, the level of which depended on the goodness of fit between the substantive factors (Trist 1981:10).

In theoretical work on the socio-technical systems concept, F. E. Emery identified the dimensions of the social and technical subsystems (e.g., on the social side, occupational roles and structure, methods of payment, the supervisory relationship, and work culture; on the technical side, level of mechanization/automation, unit operations, temporal-spatial scale of production process). Emery believed that the social and technical subsystems were *independent* of one another, in that the former follow the laws of the human sciences while the latter follow the laws of the natural sciences. Yet, as Trist notes, "they are *correlative* in that one requires the other for the *transformation* of an input into an output, which comprises the functional task of a work system" (1981:24; emphasis in the original). In other words, the social and technical components of the system are independent in terms of original causation, but each depends on the other to generate output (i.e., work). Thus, work activity is not an independent but a dependent variable, its character determined by the interaction of human beings and their sociocultural requirements on the one hand and technical elements of the workplace on the other.

Viewed in systems terms, the coupling of two dissimilar entities requires *joint optimization*; the optimization of only one subsystem may result in suboptimization of the socio-technical system as a whole. Indeed, joint optimization may require suboptimization of *individual* system components to ensure the best overall fit. Thus, from a socio-technical systems perspective, it may be necessary to suboptimize the social organization of the work force and/or the design and operation of the technology in order to achieve the most effective combination of the two.

As in the technological determinist model, socio-technical systems thinkers conceive of technology as an independent variable. This latter approach differs, however, from that of the technological imperative in two important respects: (1) technology is not strictly determinative of work but holds co-determinative status together with human beings and their social requirements; and (2) work is not viewed only as human activity but as a product of human-technical interaction.

Socio-technical systems theory thus radically alters the determinist paradigm by recognizing human factors as a causal force in the emergence of work organization. Like the determinists, however, socio-technical systems thinkers still view technology as a force of nature, more or less independent of social action and control. The perceived autonomy of technology may be an important factor underlying the failure of socio-technical systems theory to explicate clearly (i.e., in operational terms) a systematic means by which technical and social subsystems can be jointly optimized. After all, if technology is truly independent of human social systems, then we have no theoretical machinery that will allow us to join the two parts into a coherent whole. It is this independence of technology that becomes the central point of contention for the cultural constructionists, whose theoretical arguments we examine next.

Cultural Construction of Technology

Within the last several decades, a third conception of work-technology relations has emerged whose roots may be traced, at least in part, to Marxist theory. This third approach—called cultural (or sometimes, social) construction of technology—admits the existence of a larger social order surrounding both technology and work, a social order that shapes both of these phenomena and their interaction.

Some have interpreted Karl Marx's emphasis on the material powers of production as reflecting a basically technologically determinist perspective. In fact, however, Marx's Hegelian orientation required a dialectical interplay between technology and the social relations of production. This means, among other things, that social class relations will be reflected within a society's technological apparatus. It is this idea—that social relations are reflected in technology—that provides a theoretical foundation for the argument that technology is culturally (or socially) constructed.

The cultural construction argument holds that the physical form of technology and its functional characteristics are determined by sociocultural factors (not solely, or even primarily, by engineering or technical considerations). That is, what technology looks like, what it can do, and what kinds of inputs it requires are properties shaped by economic and social relationships, as well as beliefs and values that originate through the historical process of sociocultural development. Cultural construction also implies that technology may serve functions other than those suggested by its utilitarian capabilities and that these nonutilitarian functions (i.e., symbolic or expressive) also are culturally determined.

An example of cultural construction is provided by Marxist Harry Braverman (1974), whose work illustrates the ways in which the form and function of technology may reflect social relationships. Braverman (1974) asserts that the technology of the assembly line found in Western societies, for example, is both a construction and a symbolic reflection of class relations in capitalist societies.[5] Assembly lines in the West traditionally have divided labor into small and menial tasks and also typically have separated the planning or control of job tasks (assigning these to managers) from the execution of such tasks (which is assigned to workers). According to Braverman, these special characteristics of assembly lines optimize productivity for the owners and managers of an enterprise but at the expense of the craft-related knowledge, technical skills, and job satisfaction of the work force. Braverman (1974) argues forcefully that the features of an assembly line (i.e., its technical structure and functions) cannot be understood solely on the basis of technical needs and requirements but must be viewed within a larger social, political, and economic context:

> It is . . . (the) "master" standing behind the machine, who dominates, pumps dry, the living labor power; it is not the productive strength of machinery that weakens the human race, but the manner in which it is employed in capitalist social relations. . . . Acting for the master in a way which he plans with inexhaustible care and precision, machines seem in human eyes to act for themselves and out of their own necessities. These necessities are called "technical needs," "the requirement of efficiency," but by and large they are the exigencies of capital and not of technique. For the machine, they are only the expression of that side of its possibilities which capital tends to develop most energetically; the technical ability to separate control from execution.[6]

For Braverman, the effect of modern industrial technology on the human work force is a representation of worker domination and control by a more powerful class. That is, technology (and its consequences) is constructed by, and symbolizes, social relationships.

The view that technology is culturally constructed is significant in that it suggests that there is not "one best way" to design technology. Rather, there are a multiplicity of ways, each of them reflecting varying social and cultural imperatives (Nobel 1984; Pfaffenberger 1989). This latter point is highly relevant to industrial applications of technology, since it means that technology designers, engineers, and managers should have considerable flexibility in creating and choosing among a range of possible technological designs that ultimately will affect people in the workplace and the marketplace.

In comparison with other models, cultural construction provides a fuller and more accurate representation of reality because this model includes the larger context in which technology and work unfold. The constructionist point of view sees technology not as an autonomous, value-free thing (as in technological determinism) nor as a purely physical phenomenon strictly obeying the laws of natural science (as in socio-technical systems theory). Rather, technology is viewed as a value-laden proxy for a powerful set of social actors, a proxy constructed through the dynamic interplay between technological possibilities that exist at any given point in time and the social context in which technological choices are made.

The cultural construction model also suggests that work is not necessarily determined by technology but is affected both by technology and culture. The effect of technology on work, however, often is portrayed in a rather deterministic manner; that is, once technological choices have been made, technology exerts a controlling and dominating influence over work. This form of technological determinism is frequently emphasized in the writings of cultural constructionists. The controlling and dominating influence of technology is expressed both directly and indirectly.

According to the cultural constructionist argument, the direct effects of technology on human work activity unfold through the evolution of technology over time, a process that results in the gradual restriction, abridgement, and destruction of human effort and skill. Braverman explains the negative effects of technology on work in the context of his deskilling argument. According to Braverman (1974), industrial technology facilitates and abridges work activity by taking over part of the work that originally was performed by human craftsmen. As such, technology evolves over time, embedding even larger quantities of knowledge and possessing even greater functional capabilities, it gradually takes over more and more of the detailed labor process. At first (as in preindustrial societies), simple tools are used to add greater strength and precision to human muscle power. Later, machines emerge that provide not only strength and precision but also a supply of energy that eliminates some or all of the need for human muscle. Following the development of machines, technology evolves in the direction of greater automation, and additional aspects of the work process— including conveyance between machines, holding and turning materials, packaging, and inspection—all are performed by machines, often with little or no help from humans. At this relatively advanced stage, the machine is partly controlled by the feedback of information from its own operations. Finally, the ultimate in automation is achieved by the "lights out" factory (unknown to Braverman, but predictable by his theory) in which totally automated control systems and robotic devices build automobiles or other goods completely in the dark—lights are not needed because humans are not present.

What is happening to the human role in the workplace as technology evolves toward total automation? According to Braverman (and also to Bright [1958a, b], the Harvard Business

School scholar from whom Braverman derived much of his data), technology takes on greater powers at the expense of human skill. The evolution of technology controls and dominates work directly through the degradation of skill, a process that Braverman called *deskilling*. Braverman argues that, through the process of deskilling, the human work force has come to possess fewer and less sophisticated skills over time, until finally this process "creates that mass of simple labor which is the primary feature of populations in developed capitalistic countries" (Braverman 1974:83).

In the cultural construction paradigm, technology also controls and dominates work indirectly. Indirect control and domination is exercised through a process in which existing social class relations not only are reflected in technology but also are created, maintained, and reinforced (or, reproduced) through technology. The construction of class relations through technology occurs when technology exerts pressure and stress on the work force (for example, the mind-numbing and alienating monotony of assembly line work, the fatigue and physical debilitation resulting from such work), which serves both to reinforce (and remind them of) their social status and to eliminate or reduce any opportunity they may have to enhance that status.

Thus, in the cultural construction model of work-technology relations, we find the theoretical possibility of technological choice and the constructive role of the surrounding sociocultural context. In spite of these enhancements, however, the causal chain still bears significant resemblance to that of the technological determinists; i.e., technology still seems to dominate and control human work activity, albeit for reasons different than the determinists would propose. Although choice is a theoretical possibility in the constructivist approach, many scholars in this tradition have emphasized choices made by managerial elites in which technology was employed consciously as an instrument of power, one designed (or selected) specifically to enable surveillance, subjugation, and/ or diminution of the human factor in the work process (see for examples Zuboff 1982, Nobel 1984, Hirschorn 1984). Thus, although the three models of work-technology interface examined thus far vary in several significant ways, all of them view work as subordinate to technology in certain respects. Only in the emergent model of work-technology relations that we examine next do we find the possibility that industrial work might hold some directive influence over technology.

WORK ACTIVITY: THE CREATIVE FRONTIER
OF TECHNOLOGY

Since the Hawthorne studies of the early 1930s, field research in industry has documented various dimensions of work activity that are not under the strict control of technology (or management). Among these dimensions are the informal technical know-how and related illicit procedures used by workers to speed the rate of production (see Roethlisberger and Dickson, 1939; Roy 1952, 1954, 1958). In the early literature, informal know-how and illicit procedures were associated primarily with the practice of "making out" on piecework; i.e., controlling the rate and yield of production to ensure stabilization of piece rates. Workers were known to develop such know-how and procedures on their own, and to pass it along to other workers via informal communication channels.

In the late 1970s, Kenneth Kusterer (1978) expanded our understanding of informal technical know-how. He showed that such "working knowledge" (as he called it) was designed not only to enhance workers' control over the rate and yield of production but also to enable achievement of several other goals (for example, the repair of malfunctioning equipment, the solution of production problems). Kusterer's work suggested that informal know-how and illicit procedures were widespread in industry and were not limited to piecework conditions. His work also was significant in that it demonstrated that work activity spontaneously creates an *informal dimension of technology* (that is, physical modifications of equipment, methods, and procedures that are not officially designed, documented, or sanctioned but are developed spontaneously by the work force). These changes made by the work force in the physical condition and operation of technology must be considered part of the technology itself, for without them, the technology simply would not be able to operate under actual (and often adverse) conditions of work.

Over the past decade, industrial anthropologists and others have learned a great deal more about informal working knowledge (see for discussion Baba 1990) and the informal dimension of technology. Ethnographic studies of work in advanced technology settings (that is, where new forms of technologies are being introduced) have shown that workers continuously create solutions for technological problems that arise when new technology is implemented. Confronted with difficult technological problems or breakdowns, workers use a wide range of informal behavioral techniques to encourage effective problem solving. Informal techniques documented in the ethnographic literature include sharing of war stories about machine repair (which allows informal communication of successful diagnostic and repair operations; Orr 1986), troubleshooting sessions in which workers debug failed computer systems by comparing system rules with the real logic of production (Scribner and Sachs 1989), and doing "end-runs" around computer bottlenecks, sometimes feeding the computer false information deliberately in order to make it do what workers know it should do (but cannot because of system rigidity; Howard and Schneider 1988).

Patricia Sachs and Sylvia Scribner (1990) provide a detailed illustration of the creative role played by work in supporting technological and organizational systems that are less than perfect. The example is drawn from their ethnographic work at Kemps, an electronic components manufacturing firm in New England, where management recently installed an automated inventory planning and control system (MRP). At Kemps, workers in the production planning department are responsible for coordinating the production of finished goods. These workers must check their computer screens to find out whether all components needed for final assembly on a job have been machined and passed inspection. If so, the computer signals the workers to "release" an order for production (i.e., allow final assembly to begin).

One of the production planning workers at Kemps, however, does not accept the computer screen's information as final. This worker (named Fay) understands that the computer's records are usually three to four days late in documenting the exact status of components coming out of the machine shop. The delay results from a bottleneck in the flow of information from the machine shop to the automated system. To alleviate this bottleneck, Fay takes a walk around the machine shop twice a day in order to memorize the part numbers on all of the new components that are ready to go into production. Then, she overrides the computer record (which indicates that these parts are not yet ready) and releases the job for production three to four days early. In this example, Fay is using her initiative and problem-solving creativity to supply additional knowledge that the automated production planning system was not able to capture on its own. Fay's creative behavior, which speeds the production process, also defies the technological determinist conception of work. A Tayloristic view of Fay's job most likely would have required her to follow the computer's instructions, thereby delaying production.

In all of the cases cited above, spontaneous and informal work activity had a profound influence on technology (and production) by creatively solving problems that were not soluble within the formal domain of technological knowledge (as represented within the automated system). Indeed, at advanced technology sites such as those studied by Julian Orr (1986), Robert Howard and Leslie Schneider (1988), and Sylvia Scribner and Patricia Sachs (1989) it is clear that work activity begins to constitute a *creative frontier* for new technology. By creative frontier is meant a domain of application (that is, a time and place where technology is used) in which new technology and its organizational/behavioral interfaces are further developed and refined in a dynamic manner by spontaneous problem-solving activity. At the frontier, workers discover the actual capabilities and limitations of the technology, and they spontaneously generate coping strategies and tactics that maximize technology's inherent capabilities and compensate for its limitations. This frontier is only penetrable by the work force, since the actual capabilities and limitations of technology can be discovered only under real conditions of work.

Oftentimes, workers and other users of technology develop innovative solutions for, and improvements to, technology at this frontier that can serve as templates for new technology innovation (see for example von Hipple 1976). In other cases, such as that represented by Fay's walkabout ritual, work embeds potential improvements to the interface between technology and work organization. Indeed, Japanese manufacturing systems have discovered and institutionalized the creative frontier as a means to generate continuous improvement in manufacturing processes and products (see Shimada and MacDuffie 1986; Nonaka 1992). In Japanese organizations, the application of work activity to the continuous improvement of technology is one of the key mechanisms through which workers participate actively in the production process.

The conceptualization of work activity as a creative frontier of technology suggests a new model of work-technology relations. In this new configuration, technology confronts work with problems, failures, and opportunities, while work responds by generating solutions, improvements, and innovations. Work and technology thus become a mutually interactive complex, each affecting the other in a dynamic manner. Since work-based solutions and improvements can become part of the technology itself and are absolutely essential if technology is to operate effectively, we again must conclude that work and technology are interlinked constructs; the substance of work becomes the fabric of technology. Both of these constructs, in turn, exist within a cultural context that molds each of them in equally complex ways.

In the new configuration, the concept of cultural construction is extended and strengthened. Technology is constructed not only be social relations (in which elites dominate) but also through work activity (in which nonelites are a dominant force). Technology is thus doubly constructed, once by the elite, and once again by the work force. While the relative influence of these two forces is heavily context-dependent, the new model does not assume that elites always have the upper hand in technological choice and that work therefore is universally dominated by technology. Rather the emergent model acknowledges that technology choice—because of its serious implications for power relations within the organization—often opens onto a political battleground in which divergent interests struggle to sway decisions toward their own ends. Recent ethnographic case studies by Thomas (1993) show that elites are not always successful in this battle and may not always be able to force their technological choices onto the work force. To the extent that work groups learn to exercise political clout in the workplace, they will gain greater opportunities to choose technological configurations that enable work activity to make creative contributions to future generations of new technology.

THE EVOLUTION OF THE
WORK-TECHNOLOGY RELATIONSHIP

In James Bright's (1958a) classic analysis of the work-technology relationship (used extensively by Braverman [1974] as grounds for his deskilling hypothesis), industrial technology was found to evolve through a series of levels, each representing higher degrees of automatic control. Bright (1958b) summarized this evolutionary process as follows:

First, there is the substitution of mechanical power for manual effort, which takes some burden from the worker (after Level 2). . . . Then, as increasing degrees of fixed control yield the desired machine action, the worker does less and less guidance of the tools (Levels 5-8). . . . As the ability to measure is added to the machine, a portion of the control decision information is mechanically obtained for the operator (after Level 8). . . . As the machine is given still higher degrees of automaticity, more and more of the decision-making and appropriate follow-up action is performed mechanically (i.e., by the mechanisms). For instance, as the selection of necessary machine speeds, feeds, temperature control, and so on is mechanized, further "decision-making," "judgment," "experience," and even "alertness" demands are lifted from the worker (Levels 12–14). . . . Finally, the machine is given the power of "self-correction" to a minor, and then to a greater degree (Levels 15–17), until the need to adjust the machine has been completely removed from the worker.

Bright found that human physical and mental effort *increase* during the early evolution of technology. Both types of effort and skill, however, begin to *decrease* after the emergence of higher levels of automatic control.

Although Bright's influential analysis, conducted more than thirty years ago, undoubtedly was accurate in its time, evidence is mounting that the conclusions he reached are now obsolete. When Bright conducted his analysis, there were very few examples of advanced industrial automation available for study. In fact, Bright's (1958a) work included only one example of automated production at a refinery. In the 1950s, industrial automation had barely advanced beyond the stage of conveyorization (Adler 1983).

The continuing development of technology since the late 1950s suggests that Bright did not anticipate accurately the nature of work-technology relations that would emerge following the evolution of higher levels of industrial automation. For example, Bright did not (and could not) consider fully the emergence of large-scale computer-aided information technologies that automate an entire sequence of production-related tasks (such as automated inventory planning and control systems). Recent ethnographic research following the introduction of such systems shows that these complex, automated processes often do not operate smoothly or effectively without intensive worker involvement and interaction, especially when the systems are newly installed or otherwise untried (Howard and Schneider 1988, Scribner and Sachs 1989). Further, such systems often require new and higher levels of skill for normal operation, even of workers who are relatively low in the organizational hierarchy (e.g., see Adler 1986).

A thorough discussion of the reasons why modern information-based technologies often fail without intensive worker involvement and skill upgrading are beyond the scope of this paper. However, it should be noted briefly that these new work requirements relate in part to the enormous complexity of advanced automation systems and to the fact that such systems may not include all of the local knowledge (or, informal information) that is critical to actual operation (see Baba 1990). Indeed, the more sophisticated the technology, the greater the possibility of failure. Although information-based technologies may be planned by designers and engineers to be fully automated and foolproof, very complex production technologies rarely work as planned under real operating conditions. Variances in raw materials, temperature or humidity, operator behavior, as well as operator error and defects caused by normal wear and tear all combine to culminate in malfunction and defects, especially in new systems that have had little prior use outside the engineering laboratory. Further, the interconnected nature of such systems, and the speed with which they operate, often mean that un undetected error will have far-reaching and disastrous consequences, with little opportunity for rectification. Automated systems do not yet (and may never) possess the capabilities necessary to detect and correct all of their potential failures and the hazards that arise through failure. Such detection and correction requires the intervention of human workers, especially workers that are guided by sufficient conceptual knowledge and technical skill.

Larry Hirschorn (1984) has described the near catastrophe that occurred at the Three Mile Island nuclear reactor as an example of insufficient work input and skill that nearly ended in a national tragedy. Maintenance workers and reactor operators in this case did not command sufficient knowledge of the reactor plant to recognize or diagnose multiple warning signs that pointed to a failure in the plant's water cooling system. Multiple errors and misdiagnoses by plant personnel compounded an initially minor problem many times over and almost generated a meltdown of the reactor. Hirschorn argues that complex technology, no matter how sophisticated, will never reach the state of perfection imagined by Bright and Braverman. The more complex the technology, the more it requires human work interaction and continuous learning in order to perform properly under real conditions of work.

The foregoing discussion suggests that the relationship between work and technology is a dynamic one that changes across cultures and over time. Before the industrial revolution, craft production allowed workers to wield tools under conditions that they (the workers) largely controlled. At that time, work activity controlled the use of technology. Following Taylor's scientific management movement, however, industrial technologies became rigid, mechanical, and largely determinative of the form and substance of work. During this period, technology appeared to control work activity (although it never was able to achieve complete control).

The rigid control of work by technology was allowable in mass production markets that were not subject to international competition. In the modern age, however, rapid technological change and intensive international competition have created a situation in which Tayloristic production systems must compete with those that have evolved differently in other cultures. The lean production systems of Japan, for example, do not employ a strictly deterministic philosophy in conceptualizing the relationship between technology and work. In Japan, human workers actively engage the technological system, constantly challenging and changing those systems as they invent new ways to improve production processes (see Womack et al. 1990). Such lean production systems have proven more efficient and competitive than those invented on the other side of the Pacific, which have depended upon rigid technological control of work to ensure productivity objectives. The current effort by Japanese industry to move beyond lean production toward flexible production systems is anticipated to bring with it an even greater need for worker involvement and discretion at the local level (Iwata et al. 1990). If the Japanese are successful in this effort, then the technology-work relationship in that nation may be evolving toward an even higher level of influence and control by work activity over technology.

The foregoing discussion suggests that causal relations between work and technology are contingent on sociocultural context. These culturally conditioned relationships are, however, more dynamic and variable than previously envisioned in traditional models of cultural construction.

CONCLUSION

This paper began by questioning the distinction between work and technology, noting that although these constructs are similar, they are not the same. Work is basically human activity, while technology generally is comprised of the products of human activity; i.e., tools and techniques. The interlinkage of these constructs is most noticeable under conditions in which human work activity functions as a tool or technique. In spite of this interlinkage, however, there are still various dimensions of difference between the two constructs.

Ethnographic research on situations in which work activity is engaged in the process of *becoming* a tool or technique (i.e., in response to technology's limitations and challenges) suggests another dimension of difference beyond those listed in Table 1. That is, work may be viewed as a creative and dynamic force with the power to modify and improve technology, while technology represents the static or frozen knowledge of past work efforts (including the work of scientists and engineers). Once technology is created, it cannot evolve further without work effort.

While conventional wisdom tells us that such evolution is primarily the province of scientists and engineers, work ethnography demonstrates that the continuous evolution of technology (including its ongoing evaluation and improvement) also is dependent on the efforts of the work force. This knowledge—that work creates technology—must be understood if production is to achieve the goals of quality and competitiveness set by many industrial organizations.

NOTES

1. An earlier version of this paper was presented at the 1990 Annual Meeting of the American Anthropological Association as part of an invited session titled "Toward a Theory of Work."

2. Although there is no agreement within or between disciplines concerning the definition of technology, most scholars agree that technology includes more than material tools and devices (see Baba 1990). The inclusion of knowledge, skill, plans, and behavioral techniques in the definition of technology is especially likely in the social sciences, including anthropology (e.g., see Bock 1974).

3. The formal definition of *organizational* technology is presented here, rather than numerous other ones that are available, because of this chapter's intended focus on forms of work and technology found in modern industrial organizations. Clearly, the conceptualization of technology from an organizational standpoint creates a rather specialized definition, one that may not accommodate all of the uses of technology that can occur outside the bounds of industrial organization.

4. In anthropology, certain materialist paradigms (i.e., general evolutionism) are founded on a basically deterministic view of technology. Leslie White, for example, believed that the evolution of culture in general (but not necessarily in all specific instances) proceeded through a sequence of stages that were driven by technological innovations, each of which

permitted human populations to capture and expend greater amounts of energy (see Harris 1968). According to White, technology determines both the amount of energy captured and the efficiency with which it is used. In turn, the amount of energy available per capita and the efficiency of its use determine the complexity and elaboration of social organization and ideology. In other words, White postulated a technological imperative in cultural evolution. It should be noted, however, that White's theory is not strictly deterministic, since he allowed for limited feedback from social organization and/or ideology to condition the evolution of technology.

5. A technological determinist might argue against Braverman that the organization of work in the formerly socialist states of Eastern Europe and the Soviet Union (prior to the late 1980s) was a near replica of that found in capitalist systems. Thus, the determinist would assert, it is not social class relations that shape work organization but the requirements of industrial technology at its then-current level of development (which were basically the same under socialism and capitalism). A counter-argument to the technological determinist perspective would emphasize that the previously socialist states of Eastern Europe and the Soviet Union essentially borrowed their form of industrial work organization from the West without bothering to explore alternative methods of production (such as those discovered by socio-technical systems researchers, or those developed in modern Japanese industry). This counter-argument would suggest that capitalist class relations also were reflected in the industrial work organization of pre-1990 socialist societies, albeit indirectly.

6. The mind-numbing repetition of much industrial work encourages many industrial workers in the United States to save their mental energy and creativity for work efforts outside the industrial organization (in avocations or family businesses, for example). Western industrial workers endure the drudgery of repetitive work (such as that found in the automobile industry) because of the relatively high wages that traditionally have been paid for such labor.

REFERENCES

Adler, Paul
1983 Rethinking the skill requirements of new technologies. Working Paper. Graduate School of Business Administration. Harvard University, unpublished manuscript.

1986 New technologies, new skills. *California Management Review*. Fall, 1986: 9–28.

Applebaum, Herbert
1984 *Work in Market and Industrial Societies*. Albany: State University of New York Press.

Baba, Marietta L.
1990   Local knowledge systems in advanced technology organizations. In *Strategic Management in High Technology Firms*. L. Gomez-Mejia and M. Lawless, eds., pp. 57–75. JAI Press.

Bernard, H. R., and P. Pelto
1986   *Technology and Social Change*. 2nd ed. Prospect Heights, IL: Waveland Press.

Bock, Phillip K.
1974   *Modern Cultural Anthropology*. New York: Alfred A. Knopf.

Braverman, Harry
1974   *Labor and Monopoly Capital*. New York: Monthly Review Press.

Bright, James R.
1958   (a) *Automation and Management*. Norwood, MA: The Plimpton Press.

1958   (b) Does automation raise skill requirements? *Harvard Business Review*, July-August.

Dubinskas, Frank A.
1988   *Making Time: Ethnographies of High-Technology Organizations*. Philadelphia, PA: Temple University Press.

Emery, Frederick E.
1959   Characteristics of socio-technical systems. London: Tavistock Documents #527. Abridged in F. E. Emery, *The Emergence of a New Paradigm of Work*. Canberra: Centre for Continuing Education.

Fry, Louis W.
1982   Technology-structure research: three critical issues. *Academy of Management Journal*. 25(3):532–52.

Galbraith, John K.
1969   *The Affluent Society*, 2nd ed. Boston: Houghton Mifflin.

Harris, Marvin
1968   *The Rise of Anthropological Theory*. New York: Thomas Y. Crowell.

Hirschorn, Larry
1984   *Beyond Mechanization*. Cambridge, MA: MIT Press.

Howard, R., and Schneider, L.
1988   Technological change as a social process: A case study of office automation in a manufacturing plant. *Central Issues in Anthropology*. 7(2):79–84.

Iwata, M., A. Makashima, A. Otani, J. Nakane, S. Kurosu, and T. Takahashi.
1990   *Manufacturing 21 Report: The Future of Japanese Manufacturing*. Wheeling, IL: Association for Manufacturing Excellence.

Kusterer, K. C.
1978   *Know-How on the Job: The Important Working Knowledge of "Unskilled" Workers.*
Boulder, CO: Westview Press.

Nobel, David
1984   *Forces of Production.* New York: Knopf.

Nonaka, I.
1992   The knowledge creating company. *Harvard Business Review.* Nov.-
Dec.:96–104.

Orr, Julian
1986   Narratives at Work: Story Telling as Cooperative Diagnostic Activity.
Proceedings of the Conference on Computer Supported Cooperative Work, Austin,
Texas, December 3–5, 1986.

Perrow, Charles
1967   A framework for the comparative analysis of organizations. *American
Sociological Review.* 32(April):194–208.

Pfaffenberger, Brian
1989   Artifacts as Signs, Technology as Ritual. A Paper Presented at the
1989 Annual Meeting of the American Anthropological Association,
Washington, D.C., November, 1989.

Roethlisberger, F. J., and W. J. Dickson
1939   *Management and the Worker.* Cambridge, MA: Harvard University
Press.

Roy, Donald
1952   Quota restriction and goldbricking in a machine shop. *American Journal
of Sociology.* 57(May):427–52.

1954   Efficiency and the fix: Informal group relations in a machine shop.
American Journal of Sociology. 60:255–66.

1958   Banana time: Job satisfaction and informal interaction. *Human
Organization.* 18(Winter):158–68.

Sachs, P., and S. Scribner
1990   Work Practices, Knowledge, and Culture: Organizational Confusion.
A Paper Presented at the 1990 Annual Meetings of the Society for
Applied Anthropology. York, England.

Scribner, S., and P. Sachs
1989   A Study of On-the-Job Training. Laboratory for Cognitive Studies
of Work. The Graduate School and University Center of the City
University of New York. Unpublished Manuscript.

Shimada, H., and J. P. MacDuffie
1986   Industrial Relations and "Humanware": Japanese Investments in Automobile Manufacturing in the United States. Unpublished Manuscript.

Taguchi, Genichi and Don Clausing
1990   Robust quality. *Harvard Business Review*. Jan.-Feb.:65–75.

Taylor, Frederick W.
1947   *Principles of Scientific Management.* New York: Norton & Co.

Thomas, Robert
1993   *What Machines Can't Do.* Berkeley: University of California Press.

Tornatzky, Louis G., J. D. Eveland, M. G. Boylan, W. A. Hetzner, E. C. Johnson, D. Roitman, and J. Schneider
1983   *The Process of Technological Innovation: Reviewing the Literature.* Washington, D.C.: National Science Foundation.

Tornatzky, L. G., and M. Fleischer
1990   *The Processes of Technological Innovation.* Lexington, MA: Lexington Books.

Tosi, Henry L.
1984   *Theories of Organization.* 2nd ed. New York: John Wiley & Sons.

Trist, Eric L.
       The Evolution of Socio-Technical Systems. Occasional Paper No. 2. Ontario, Canada: Ontario Quality of Work Like Center.

von Hipple, Eric
1976   The dominant role of users in the scientific instrument innovation process. *Research Policy.* 5(3):212–39.

White, Leslie
1949   *The Science of Culture.* New York: Grove Press.

Womack, J. P., D. T. Jones, and D. Roos
1990   *The Machine that Changed the World.* New York: Rawson Associates.

Zuboff, Shoshana
1982   New worlds of computer mediated work. *Harvard Business Review.* Sept.-Oct.:142–52.

FREDERICK C. GAMST

6

The Web of Rules in Comparative Work Relations Systems

THE WEB OF RULES FOR WORK

Today, the world is in a state of momentous flux of economic development, especially regarding industrialization and the creating of a global market. This flux drastically affects the lives of every human. The United States, Canada, and much of northwestern Europe are deindustrializing and downsizing older heavy industries. In a quest for inexpensive work relations, the United States is further industrializing Mexico. The nations of the Pacific Rim are well into a period of rampant industrialization and of expanding of global market shares of many kinds. The countries of central and eastern Europe and the former Soviet Union are in various stages of attempting to reorganize their bases of economic exchange in a decaying industrialism. China is departing from some of the fetters and social stabilizers of the central planning of industrialization. Various states of the Third World are attempting to modernize their economies and industrialize in sundry directions but with inadequate capital resources. These developing states still have many remainders from their traditional, that is, preindustrial, modes of production. Such traditional modes must still be reckoned with in considerations of economic development.

The idea of a "web of rules" guiding each society's gainful work provides a fruitful way of bringing some degree of commonality in all of these seemingly divergent kinds of flux in economic development. Through this idea of the "web," the differentiated but necessarily interrelated components of industrial and industrializing societies are fitted to one another (Berg 1979:82–6). Use of the web of rules has been especially fruitful in investigating large-scale modern organizations and their members.[1] Such organizations are the substance of industrial societies (see Gross and Etzioni 1985; Coleman 1990). But the utility of the web is not limited to modern societies. This idea of a web may also be extended from the industrialized and industrializing to preindustrial societies, and thus form one theoretical construct for examining all human work.

As Clark Kerr and Abraham Siegel, the originators of the idea of the web, envisioned, its study involves both a historical depth and a broad spanning of sociocultural phenomena, all not traditionally part of the research domains of economics and industrial relations. These originators note that study of a web enters "the traditional preserves of the anthropologist, the sociologist, the psychologist, and the political scientist" (Kerr and Siegel 1955:151). The idea of a web, accordingly, is necessarily that of a network of formal and informal regulations of all kinds including practices and related ideology guiding the social relations of all work (Gamst 1984a, 1989:66–7). But, thus far, the web is usually applied to formal aspects of a society with modern industries. The idea of Clark Kerr and Siegel was greatly expanded by John T. Dunlop in his monumental *Industrial Relations Systems* (1970[1958], 1993).[2] Although Dunlop at first included, but did not emphasize in the web, informal rules and practices and other sociocultural dynamics—of interest to most students of human society and behavior—he later did so, to a greater extent (1970[1958]: 7–8, 1988).

Across the great range of cross-societal patterns of work, a common denominator exists in "the structuring of a web of rules relating the work force to the work process" (Kerr and Siegel 1955:64). In this chapter, as an anthropologist of work, I apply in three ways the conceptual framework of the web of rules for work relations. First, I use a general ethnological (sociocultural anthropological) formulation of the web for application cross-culturally, to all human societies. Second, related to this use, I examine a theoretical concept long of concern to ethnologists, property rights, in conjunction with the web and apply it to foraging, agrarian, and industrial democratic societies. Third, in the societal application necessarily having the greatest expository extent, I show the usefulness of the web for comprehending the many-stranded work relations of American society, as exemplified by railroaders.[3] In so doing, I build upon six decades of industrial and organizational studies originally conducted by ethnologists, sociologists, and psychologists during the early 1930s in the research project at Hawthorne. The ethnological study of modern industry and organizations is thus over six decades old (Gamst 1990a).

APPLYING THE IDEA OF THE WEB OF RULES

Human work cannot be understood merely in terms of efficiency of exchanges in the market. It must be comprehension as a sociocultural process encompassing organizations, laws, practices, and customs for work. Such understanding is central to economic anthropology and brings together market, polity, and society with its culture, including normative prescriptions (Polyani, Arensberg, and Pearson 1967; Dalton 1967; Sahlins 1972; Applebaum 1984; Plattner 1989). In its full range, the idea of the web allows an understanding of this kind.

The web has a range of forms, or "rules," including prescriptive regulations for doing work and interrelated procedures for conducting the power relations of work. These forms include contracts, laws, orders, decrees, awards, policies, customs, values, and formal and informal rules, practices, and procedures. The forms are dynamic and fluctuate with the abilities of the bodies of actors involved to exercise power. Necessarily, the web is more than just formal regulations and logic; it is also the social interactions of persons (Black 1989:vii, 3–8). The web fosters, among other things, "norms of output, pace, and performance" (Kerr et al. 1973:52). The central function of all webbed rules is to govern the relationships and behavior of all the bodies of actors interacting in the workplace and work community in reaching an accommodation between workers and controllers of their work.

Comprehension of the forms in the web allows the researcher of a single and comparative society to probe beyond the shaping of the work force by particular cultural configurations such as capitalism or socialism. Comprehension permits probing beyond the constraints of particular kinds of poliitical economic integration of society such as inndustrial democracy, the dually organized agrarian state (Gamst 1974), the redistributive cheifdom (Gamst 1988c), the egalitarian band (Gamst 1979), and so forth, to a systemic theory of the structuring of human labor. The idea of the web provides a way of integrating all the various patterns of guides to action relating to work, and it contributes to an understanding of the structure of labor and the form of work organizations.

Social interactions of "labor" relations exist in some form in all the levels of economic integration of societies from foraging through industrial (Dunlop 1993:44–5). For a comparative ethnological understanding of the entirety of the human social relations and cultural patterns of work, going beyond just the industrial, we must transcend the narrower conception of employer-employee connections. We must go to a broader comparative ethnological conception of *work relations*, in both traditional and modern settings, among those who in some way control an aspect of production and those who produce goods or provide services. Industrial relations, in other words, are a recent, modernized subset of an older, all-encompassing work relations. Work relations begin in the technologically simple societies of remote prehistory and continue into today's hyperindustrial ones.[4] Of course, in any society some gainful work, such as a person fishing, may occur without any work relations of control between controllers and producers.

All societies, however, have some form of a work relations system, concerning who does what work, under what social controls and constraints. This might be only a natural division of labor by age and sex resulting in mature, gender-separable Jacks and Jills of all trades. But in every society socioeconomic decisions are made. Which goods and services are created, when; Who furnishes leadership or at least stimulation for production; What are the social relations among those who lead or stimulate and those who produce; Who gains what from the production; and What standards of and discipline for work are applied, by whom, and under what circumstances? As a focus of these questions, and especially that of who gains, we examine the concept of ownership of work under a web in two preindustrial and one industrial societal settings.

THE WEB IN PREINDUSTRIAL SOCIETY

The Hunter-Gatherer Wayto

In the simplest of egalitarian foraging groups, all work relations might consist of reciprocities of exchange of goods and services within and among families related by kinship. For a few such peoples, consumption of goods and services is frequently of those produced by the immediate family, with little exchange outside of this group. But this is not usually the case among foragers, because wider cooperation and exchange is needed to survive in the habitat (Udy 1959).

The Semitic-speaking Wayto foragers, hunter-fisher-gatherers, dwell on the shores of Lake Tana the source of the Blue Nile in Ethiopia. Typically for such a society, they number some 2,000 in population. Among the patrilineally structured Wayto, work relations are highly complex. Hunting work group ranges from a few to a score of armed men. An older, more experienced male is allowed to assume leadership, because without direction a fatality could easily result among the hunters. Or a hunted hippopotamus could readily escape in the three-dimensional expanse of the lake's waters. No formal authority is part of the status of the hunt leader. He directs the others in their joint work only because of his age and experience. The latter quality is readily visible in a longish "bushy" head of hair, in what an American would call an Afro.[5] This is the symbol of a stalwart (*gwobuz*) hunter of large dangerous animals or armed men. A *gwobuz* leader never fails to have his directions heeded in the heat of the hunt itself. His older followers, however, might debate and, sometimes, even argue appropriate hunting tactics and techniques, before or after the hunt.

Decisions of when and what to hunt are reached through group consensus, but junior males have little say in this matter. Fishing, in contrast, is done on an individual or family basis, using family-owned lines, fish spears, and traps, and by groups using poisonous fish stuns. With one exception, gathering of wild plants for food or craft use is done by women and children in family or larger groups. The product of most fishing and gathering belongs entirely to the family doing the producing. Few formal or informal rules organize gathering.

The exception is that men slash and gather the tough papyrus reeds for making their boats, and this work is sometimes done in cooperative groups under informal direction of an elder. Reed boats, of one-person to several-person capacity, are sometimes used to ferry Muslim merchants and their wares to various lake short points. This transport labor is done in the market for a price paid in money or goods by the merchant. He organizes the work, sometimes with a senior Wayto supervising firsthand several fellow boatmen.

The Wayto's primary energy source is hippopotami. Hippos and crocodiles account for one-half of all human deaths by wild animals in Africa. Such a dangerous aquatic monster when downed by several men, from one or more families, is equitably shared among all in the village. Even those who did not take part in the hunt and those who could no longer or never could produce any wild animal or plant food receive a fair share, according to status criteria of age, sex, and number of dependents.

"Ownership" of game is given by formal rule to the hunter who lands the fatal blow to an aquatic beast. "Why the last of all the dangerously executed thrusts against the beast?" I once asked. "Would you want to go into a dense papyrus-reed thicket after a hippo who is wounded?" was the Socratic question that answered my query. I then understood the rule for "ownership" of game. An owner must distribute by formal rule one-half of the meat of the beast that he dispatched. The other half, however, he cannot keep and also distributes, because it is the informal custom for a *gwobuz* hunter to do so. Thus, in accord with the generalized system of reciprocal exchange dominant among the Wayto, the "owner" receives only an ordinary share of the meat from his game. But he keeps all of the hide, which is sold in the market for use in crafts. A *gwobuz* owner's main reciprocated compensation is positive affect from fellow members of his band. His praises are indeed sung, and he may wear his hair long.

The sedentary-band membership of each village, ascribed by birth and contracted between families by marriage, collectively owns and exploits a demarcated foraging territory, which they protect by force of arms against poaching from other Wayto band-villages. In the past, through negotiations among neighboring bands, elders constructed the formal regulations for demarcation of boundaries. All bands informally poach in the territories of other villages when not observed. Rather than fight when caught, poachers hand over game to the villagers having jurisdiction over the hunting in a particular location. Hunting tools, such as spears and papyrus-reed boats, are individually owned but, when not in use, according to custom, may be readily borrowed.

The Wayto as hunters and gatherers do not pay taxes of any kind to the encompassing, but not directly controlling agrarian state of the Amhara (Gamst 1979, 1984c). Should Wayto take up agriculture, agrarian statutes require them to pay taxes to the state. Thus the Ethiopic web of rules in the past helped keep the Wayto down on the swamps and discouraged their moving to firmer land to till with the plow.

The Agrarian Qemant

In socially stratified agrarian states, dually structured between a small number of elite and numerous near powerless peasants, work relations are far more complex than for foragers (Gamst 1974). The secular and clerical elites of the state and church extract some form of wealth from the peasants who are subordinated by law. This was so in the agrarian Ethiopia discussed here and extant before 1975. The relation of producers to the means of production is variously controlled (Gamst 1970, 1974).

The Qemant are a Central-Cushitic-speaking division of the remnant Agaw peoples and constitute an enclaved peasantry numbering some 25,000 to 35,000, surrounded by the Semitic-speaking, politically dominant Amhara with a population of some 5 to 8 million. Until the "creeping revolution" of 1974–1975, which deposed the last king of kings, Haile Sellassie I, most Amhara were peasants, a few agrarian elite, and some modernizing townspersons of an Ethiopian state in transition from a form of feudalism (Gamst 1988a). Among the Qemant, Amhara, and other peasantries of north-central Ethiopia, work relations consist of varying mixtures of feudal obligations payable mainly in kind, payments in money and service to the modernizing central state, free use of land from a kin group, rental of land, ownership of tools, rental of tools, and laboring for a possessor of land and owner of tools (Gamst 1988a, 1988b, 1991).

For the Qemant, large ambilineal kinship groups—with somewhat achieved memberships, through the choosing of the one ambilineage to which an adult desires to belong—own land, and most individuals receive usufruct for some share of a group's acreage (Gamst 1969, 1988b, 1994). Each ambilineage has the same formal regulations based on the ethic of kinship for allocation of land to its members and has informal practices for increasing previous allocations to individuals. Because land belongs to the ambilineage, no amassing of real property across generations is possible. Use rights to land are not heritable but must be claimed anew in each generation.

Almost all families own houses and most own all the capital equipage of agricultural production, such as oxen, plows, other tools of tillage, and seed stock. A few families having no usable or no claims to usufruct must rent land from a family that does. Similarly families with no or insufficient capital equipage either rent this too or become sharecroppers. The owners of capital equipage and the holders of use rights to land, within the local customary range of charges, set the rents and crop shares paid by agrarian proletarians. Some proletarians are former slaves.

The traditional legal code of the Ethiopia dominated by the Amhara is the *Fetha Nagast* (legislation of the kings), written in the dead language Ge'ez and introduced in the seventeenth century from a thirteenth-century compilation (Guidi 1897–99). A separate written canon exists for ecclesiastical matters. A modern code alleged for the sake of the fiction of continuity to be merely a "revision" of the traditional code was introduced in 1930–32. Until 1974, this modern code and still later ones were supplemented in the countryside by the *Fetha Nagast*, which had many conflicting localized interpretations (Sedler 1965). Customary local law was used in the main for civil matters. Its format is oral, varies regionally, and is little studied except in the north (Conti Rossini 1916).

Contracts regarding property are strictly observed, both in agrarian courts of written law and traditional councils of elders using customary law. Some of the secular tax assessments in Qemantland are through a form of feudal claim by a lord imposed on a piece of land cultivated by a peasant. Peasants are not bound to land by law. A part of a peasant's production on his ambilineal usufruct, however, is assigned, enfeoffed, by the state to a military or clerical overlord (Gamst 1988a). The superior claim of this kind to production is grounded in state law. Other tax assessments are paid directly to the treasury of the central government of the modernizing state.

During the last century, some secular elite and affluent peasants owned slaves. These legally fettered workers labored over their masters' crops and flocks in return for provision of food, shelter, clothing, and spouses. Here we find still another form of work relations in which the possessor of the agrarian means of production also owns the producers. All direct regulations for slave labor were unilaterally promulgated by the master, in accordance with local customs for such control and as sanctioned by the codified and customary laws.

Although a peasantry in the web of the feudal state of Ethiopia, the Qemant still preserve some of their earlier web of rules from their once autonomous chiefdom (Gamst 1988c). Now subordinated within Ethiopia, as a chiefdom, the Qemant constitute a commonplace polity existing organizationally between the familistic, egalitarian groupings of humans and the coercive state. The chiefdom is a centralized political organization of a territory. It is permanent, hierarchical, and hereditary. Legitimization is sacrosanct, thus, theocratically legal and based on religious ideology and related customs and etiquette. Power for a chief stems from a power-acknowledging group, all the Qemant. The Qemant's paramount chief is a *wambar* (from the word for *judge*) who mediates between the people and their great rule-making god, *Mezgana*, a variety of the common Bronze-Age sky father. One of Mezgana's cardinal rules guiding work is that the annual agricultural cycle may not begin until the rite of spring is first celebrated.

As with all classic chiefdoms, that of the Qemant is a stratified redistributive system of exchange. The chief collects some of the goods and services produced by all. A part of these goods and services are distributed to the people at large, but a good part of the collected wealth supports the chief and his administrators, subchiefs, and priests. All commoners must render three days of cultivating corvée to the paramount chief and, according to locality, to each area chief and community priest. In addition in a balanced reciprocity, Qemant leaders receive payment in kind from communities and individuals for their rendering of various ritual and judicial services. The two superior (regional) chiefs of the Qemant, of which one is paramount, receive tribute from the local (area) chiefs, and this is collected in local corvée and fees. In the web of the stratified society of the Qemant, the chiefs' collections are as sure as death.

THE WEB AND PROPERTY RIGHTS TO TRADITIONAL WORK

In traditional, that is, preindustrial, societies there usually existed some sort of property right to particular kinds of customary work. Cross-culturally viewed, property—which may be incorporeal or material, fixed or movable—is normative. Property fosters the unifying of people in collectivities with regard to a defining and limiting of the relations between persons and things (see Hoebel 1968:58–60; Lowie 1947[1920]:205–8, 235–43). Property consists of a thing for which some party has a normative right or interest regarding value of some kind. The thing alone is not property. It becomes such by virtue of an encompassing network of social relations. In the network, rules require a duty of members of a society to recognize the right of a party somewhat exclusively to possess, use, and dispose of the thing. The owning party with a right, such as that to (incorporeal) work could be an individual, a group within a society, or the entire society. As E. A. Hoebel and E. L. Frost note: " . . . the hereditary right to work is a traditional incorporeal property right for certain groups in India, and the available work is distributed accordingly." Among the Madiga caste of leather workers in Madras, the right to work is heritable as with any other property (Hoebel and Frost 1976:255). Common (nonartisan) laborers in agrarian towns do not ordinarily have property rights to work and are readily replaceable, unless the labor is organized into some form of a guild where a monopoly on certain tasks approaches closure (Sjoberg 1965:187–96).

The male hunters of village "A" of the Wayto own communally the right to hunt in the territory of this community. Qemant Agaw cultivators descended from apical ancestor "K" jointly have the right to till the acreage of their cognatic kin group, covering some small part of Qemantland. The neighboring and related Falasha Agaw have communal ownership, in the region, of the crafts of iron smelting and working for males and potting for females (Gamst and Baldia 1980; Gamst 1992a). The Qemant priest of community "X" cannot practice religion or collect wealth in community "Z," the worksite of another clergyman.

For the Qemant and Amhara peasant, all manual labor save for that connected with agriculture and the military is disdained. As these peasants say, literally translated, "Clever with hand, servant he is; clever with mouth, master he is." In part because of this low value in the web for most manual labor, particularly for the crafts,endogamous groups perform trades such as that of iron working, weaving, tanning, potting, and minstrel services (cf. Pankhurst 1968:256–79).

Premodern workers, in other words, usually have property rights of some kind to their work. They may gain these rights through ethnicity as among the Falasha, through kinship as among the Qemant and Wayto, through caste membership as in India and elsewhere, through a combination of kin ties and guild contracts as in medieval Europe. Such persons could not lose rights to work without some manner of culturally specific due process.

Industrialization destroyed the traditional property rights to work. Today, as E. Edward Herman and Alfred Kuhn explain: "The restoration of some kind of attachment to income is the persistent core around which much of labor's activity revolves." Such attachment they term "priorities to jobs" and consists of web mechanisms of work relations especially seniority systems (Herman and Kuhn 1981:441–2). To understand this quest for restoration of such attachment, we first discuss the nature of the web of rules in American society, then review the web and property rights to industrial work, next focus on the web in the American railroading, and finally analyze railroaders' economic security in the Interstate Commerce Commission's web.

THE WEB IN AMERICAN SOCIETY

It is to the work—or more specifically, its subset, industrial—relations of the United States that we focus the main part of this paper. Industrialization has engendered new rules for work and related corrective discipline.[6] The original rule-engendering process coincided with the introduction of the fuel-energized machine and the timepiece to production; increased exchange of goods, labor, and land through the price-making market; increased true division of labor, with its numerous specializations of occupation and worktask; and furthered new, profound kinds of distinctions between controllers of work (employers) and their workers (employees). Industrial society to a greater degree than agrarian society has specialized, interdependent components (usually, modern organizations). These components are each internally bonded and externally interrelated in the wider societal (and intersocietal) environment by what Kerr and Siegel call "an industrial texture of law, custom, and belief" (1955:162–3). The web of rules affects not only organized workers to whom these apply directly but also to unorganized workers, because the rules have a great multiplier affect (see Kerr and Staudohar 1986:6, 227–58).

For the creation of goods and services in American society, the web of work force regulations concern labor-management relations; recruitment; training in worktasks; broader enculturation in work life; locational patterns of dispersion by occupation and industry; processes of worktasks; standards of production and productivity; maintenance of the modern organization; and the all-important times, pacing tempo, and coordinating synchronization of work.

The Three Principal Bodies of Actors in the Web

Kerr and Siegel outline several general modes of distributing the essential power for making rules governing the work force among the three centrally concerned bodies of actors: employers, workers, and government regulators (1955). It should be noted that, in industrial society, workers, although capable of acting as individuals, ordinarily make rules through their collectivities. These include union organizations for dealing directly with the management of a business organization and nonorganizational coalitions of workers who, along with the organized workers, petition the state to legislate and administratively regulate that which they desire, for example increasing security and rights in jobs. Several organizations of workers, often self-employed, have some of the characteristics of a guild. Thus physicians, acting through their guildlike associations on several hierarchical levels, limit the size of their population of active practitioners and protect themselves with monopolistic work rules, for example, against the taking of their tasks by nurse practitioners, midwives, foreign-trained physicians, and others. Included in their web of rules are a confusing patchwork of state laws regulating labor in health care.

Other sources of rule making for the web exist beyond the three central bodies of actors. Political parties are important for rules in Communist party-states and less so in democratic states. Churches are of some influence, for example, in some of the Spanish-speaking world and Poland. The aggregated general public is powerful, through its public opinion and potential for political reaction against entire industries, particular organizations, and government. Smaller but influential bodies of actors include myriad single-interest associations. These sometimes form an unstable coalition to further their diverse special concerns against an antagonistic prerogative generally opposed in some degree to all the single interests.

As a great source of wealth and as a creator and enforcer of political power, government is the superior actor in the pluralistic, tripartite web (Adams 1992). At times its actions, however well-intended, are deemed an onerous regulatory burden by the nongovernmental actors and by individuals (U.S. Senate 1973; Kaufman 1977). Modern government furnishes all manner of direct and indirect things of value to individuals and organizations thereby making it powerful as an actor (Reich 1964). Government dispenses money and provides social and other insurance. It is a source of goods and services (including use of public resources), contracts, franchises, licenses, subsidies, and other benefits. In furnishing all of these things of value, government develops commensurate power in its relations with the other actors in the web. Beyond furnishing things of value, government creates and interprets laws and through law enforcement proscribes actions.

Whether regulations made by the state or by other actors, the bureaucratic nature of the web of rules fosters both alienation and integration of the worker into the work group and its community. Formal procedures and impartial, impersonal relations tend to maintain a social barrier between workers and the controllers of work. On the other hand, uniform treatment and rewards without arbitrariness tend to have a worker accept the control by management. Along a continuum between bureaucratic alienation from and integration into a work group, a worker is positioned by a number of factors including rewards; security; quality of work life and its social relations; positive affect from the wider community regarding tasks performed; the techniques, demands, and arrangements of worktasks and their connections to the encompassing procedures of the job; and background cultural factors such as values, lore, and symbols regarding work.

Each industrial relations systems has a set of ideologies, that is, socially learned and somewhat shared ways of thinking about conducting and controlling work and consisting of what could be termed *modalities* guiding behavior such as norms, ideals, standards, plans, values, and the prescriptive aspects of roles.[7] The idea of the web is not an exposition of static, totally prescriptive modalities for behavior, however. Instead, it is an analytic perspective allowing inspection of the dynamic power relations among concerned bodies of sometimes self-interested and self-serving actors, and individuals within these groupings. As Ivar Berg explains, in the United States, each of the three central bodies of web-enmeshed actors has a stewardship concerning a large part of the human and material resources in a society. Each body continuously attempts to have enforced its particular views of "efficiency, equity, justice, and opportunity" in a balance of its own interests against the other two sets (Berg 1979:124). In a single society, the ideologies of the three actors overlap but may not coincide in profound ways. In the United States and in Canada today, railroad managers do not see the legitimacy of or desire to interact with trade unions and have made broad, often successful, attacks on their existence and prerogatives. The volatility of the actors' relations thereby increases.

Industrial, and the broader work, relations do not treat as "given" but attempt to explain as systemic variables the various rules and the interrelated chains of rules in the web of a particular society such as that of the United States, Russia, the Czech Republic, Japan, the Zulu, or the Navajo. Beyond its bodies of actors, an industrial relations system has a number of environmental features such as technology, market or budgetary restraints, and the structures of social power in the larger society (cf. Dunlop 1993:12–21). These features must be studied in considerations of the web.

The web is not an ahistorical synchronic perspective; it is essentially diachronic. Ideas of, modern, industrial relations systems are used most heuristically as analytic tools "when a specific system is examined in its historical context, and changes in the system are studied through time" (Dunlop 1970:388). Especially, the relative positions of the various bodies of actors engendering and manipulating the rules and the somewhat shared ideologies of these bodies must be understood. Comprehended must be the historical exercises of power and establishments of privilege concerning the individuals represented by these bodies. Needed is a historical perspective so that we may examine how over time exercise of power builds or submerges equity. In the discussion, in following sections, of the web for property rights and other economic security of railroaders, such a historical perspective is necessarily developed.

In the United States, in keeping with the underlying logic of federal labor laws, government holds that the two parties to labor contracts (management and organized labor) normally should solve their particular problems within the broad web of steadily evolving public policies and statutory regulation (Berg 1979:123-4). Against this background, property rights to work have emerged under certain aspects of the web.

THE WEB AND PROPERTY RIGHTS TO INDUSTRIAL WORK

The Problem of Job Destruction in America

America has lost many millions of jobs having good pay and reasonable fringe benefits. Large corporate employers terminate thousands of loyal, long-time employees and their livelihoods, even when the firm is profitable. Government's intervention for the employee is often inept, to provide job retraining that is either not useful or for nonexistent work and does little to provide economic security. The attachments of a worker to the job are far less in the United States than in other industrialized countries, for example, Germany and the United Kingdom (Meyers 1964, Abraham and Houseman 1993; Daniel and Stilgoe 1978). Our discussion of the American web provides a comprehensive understanding of work apropos of economic security of workers. Economic security is the greatest work issue in industrialized countries (Gutchess 1985).

In the new, emerging industrial relations of the 1990s, with its international economy and globalizing labor market, labor unions may no longer be able to safeguard the interests of employees by removing their wages from the supply and demand competitions of the market. It is largely beyond the power of unions, without government help, to counter effectively and influence employer decisions made in a global setting, far transcending the web of rules of the country of the labor organizations (Kochan 1993:187-9). The

North American Free Trade Agreement will provide telling examples of harm to American and Canadian workers owing to lack of government protection from the forces of an extra-national labor market (McGaughey 1992; Bradsher 1992).

In the United States, within the arena of the web, a continuing power contest occurs, however uneven, between management and organized labor over economic security for workers and property rights in jobs.[8] To increase its competitive advantage, management creates, changes, or abolishes job descriptions, work positions, work sites, and processes of production. As soon as the new kinds of circumstances on the job obtain organized labor seeks new accommodations leading to economic security and property rights. This battle over security is also joined by unorganized labor through requests for legislation. Especially with the federal level of government, organized workers strive for enactment of statutes in Congress and interpretations in the courts in their own quests for definition of the web (see Northrup and Miscimarra 1989).

We now examine the web for the work relations, first, in the United States and, then, among American railroaders regarding property rights and other economic security of work. Because of the enormously lengthy and intricate statutory and judicial written constructions in the railroaders' web, and their considerable accretive interactions with these, any accurate presentation must necessarily be significantly longer than those for the preliterate Wayto foragers or illiterate Qemant peasants.

The Issue of Job Protection in America

Social reformers and trade unionists have long confronted the impregnable position of owners of material property under Anglo-Saxon law. Their quest was, In what ways could workers secure similar property rights to their own incorporeal work? In America, one goal was "to establish a structure of inalienable property rights in jobs and rights to income," notes Solomon Barkin of the Textile Workers Union of America (Barkin 1954:121). More specifically, it was through union controls on work that workers first sought a system of property rights in jobs similar to the legally entrenched individual rights to traditional property.[9] This, Barkin believes, has not been achieved. Economic well-being has been advanced, but the worker "has gained no vested rights in any particular job" (1954:130). True. Property rights in a job, however, are not an all or nothing characteristic and exist along a continuum of possibility from none to full.

In the United States, such a continuum concerns the *economic security of a worker* attempting to satisfy the material needs of his or her family, regarding the handling of the household income and expenditures. Included in the continuum, ranging from less to more freedom from economic danger, are: *income security*, the attempt to retain, over a specified period, all or some of one's income; *employment security*, the attempt to retain roughly comparable work with the employer; *job security*, the attempt to keep one's job with the employer; and *property right in a job*, an interest, justly claimed, to the benefits of value of a job.[10]

Federal regulation of the workplace is quite broad, protecting employees during their time of employment. As Sar A. Lavitan and others explain, a "web of federal workplace regulations. . . . has developed in response to changing labor market and social needs" (1986:225). Since the 1930s, this federal web facilitates equal access to jobs, guarantees a minimum (if inadequate) wage, requires a generally safe and healthful job setting, and provides rights to bargain collectively with employers. Furthermore, the web of federal and state regulations either provides directly or controls to some extent benefits outside of but consequent to work, in retirement, unemployment, injury, and other disability.

Despite these many job and job-related protections, in the United States the employment-at-will doctrine prevails under law, except where it is mitigated by specific rules. Under American case law, developed because of employer pressures, at will-employment has been customarily determinable at the will of either party: employment may be terminated by employer or by employee without cause. Thus a worker whose job security is not guarded by a collective agreement, tenure (assurance of employment after the passing of a probationary period and standards of performance), or civil service statute may be discharged at the employer's will.[11]

At times, workers not protected by one of these three mechanisms of security have successfully litigated in the courts in a challenge to the doctrine. Here the plaintiff maintains that an employment contract is implicit and cannot be broken without due process by the employer. Despite this kind of successful adjudication, the two-thirds, or so, of American workers not protected by unions, tenure, or civil service have no amount of job property under the web.

Property rights to jobs are not always sought directly as such. As William Gomberg writes, in our work-ethic society, management desires an amount of work producible at a point near the physiological and mental limits of human ability (1965). Trade unions do not always openly reject such an expectation; instead, they frequently counter the managerial desires by discussions of rules for health and safety. But, "In the back of the mind of the trade unionist is an emerging property right which he is attempting to assert" (Gomberg 1965:366). The central values and "staging" for the public of work relations in American society ordinarily do not allow direct grappling with the issues of restricting the output of workers. But demands concerning health and safety accord with societal conventions of behavior and, for this reason, are well accommodated in statutes.

The idea of property rights in jobs is often used in a general sense as an analog to the standard property rights in objects, Frederic Meyers explains. "Nevertheless, it implies a change in the system of rights and obligations surrounding employment and the relationship of employer to employee" (Meyers 1964:1). A job is an abstraction, both a folk and a legal convention for a kind of work. But "a job" is an abstraction becoming more concrete, just as with the abstractions concerning a firm's "good will" and equity in a brand name. All three incorporeal things can develop a monetary value and can become propertylike.

The essence of some kind of propertylike rights to a job under the web is security against at-will-dismissal and against other arbitrary employer interference in the connection between work and worker (for example, assigning a junior, favored person to the preferred task of a senior, unfavored employee). The contrary view of workers is that in a general contract for work, employment-at-will must be restricted. No longer should the employer be able to terminate freely the labor contract. Given some erosion of the at-will doctrine in the courts even in a conservative state such as Nevada, the high $80,000 average cost for an employer to defend against an unlawful-discharge case, and recent state employment termina-tions acts that provide a substantive right of good cause protections for employees (Aalberts and Seidman 1992), at will may eventually disappear as a barrier to the development of property in jobs. The Fifth Amendment to the U.S. Constitution characterizes property as a thing having secure possession, according to law: "No person shall . . . be deprived of life, liberty, or property, without due process of law. . . ."[12] If employment becomes some kind of property or analog to it, then employment is a right the continuation of which is unilaterally at the will of an employee (see Meyers 1964:1–2).

An originally watered down Worker Adjustment and Retraining Notification (Warn) Act of 1988 requires an employer to give employees and local and state government sixty days notice prior to a mass layoff or plant closure but affords no employment protection. This act was further weakened in 1992 by a court (Adelson 1992), and it still has almost no beneficial impact for workers (Nasar 1993). It could, however, yet be the beginning for further legislation of rights in jobs.

In all, a collective bargaining agreement results in some job security—that is, an equity with a firm—in accordance with the contract's provisions (and until it can be shown the worker is either not competent on the job or has engaged in a significant illegal conduct on or off the job). The classical liberal doctrine of employment at will, regarding action by the employer, is blocked in such an agreement. The broad exception is that an employer's reduction in (employee) forces is generally allowable when it is caused by ordinary seasonal fluctuations; business cycle downturns; reduction in customer demand, for other reasons; or uncontrollable stoppage of production.[13]

THE WEB IN AMERICAN RAILROADING

The Web in a Mature Industry

For a focused examining of a mature development of economic security, including property rights to jobs, we now turn to the American railroad industry. In the United States and other countries such as France, the railroad industry was the locus of the web's development for employment security. A job existed in a less abstract, more objective sense in this industry in part because of the interrelated division of labor so vital for continuous production. If one specialized job was not performed properly, the trains stopped running in their linear space (Meyers 1964:3).

Specifically, we examine the ways in which the provisions of the web gradually allowed an American railroader to develop in his or her job economic security including some amount of an equity, that is, a property of value (see Ables 1962:Kozak 1989). To achieve some degree of property rights in jobs, railroaders have had a long, highly antagonistic struggle with their employers (e.g., see Keating 1953). This adversarial interaction between the two bodies of actors may be viewed in work relations as an attempt of employees to increase their control over managers while, reciprocally, reducing the latter's control (see Gibbs 1989:304-9).

Some degree of economic security in jobs develops in industrial democracies because the public feels there is more to a job than just the cost-benefit trade-off for the employer. This kind of reasoning was at the base of the pioneering ruling in 1934 of the Interstate Commerce Commission (ICC), providing a limited security to railroad employees in the case *St. Paul Bridge and Terminal* in a combination of railroads. Because the ICC found a "public interest in the broad sense" in providing such security, the employees of the small terminal railroad absorbed into another railroad kept their own separate craft seniority lists and were given a pro rata share of extant work (199 I.C.C. 588, 1934).

Jobs became more economically secure on railroads when encompassed by seniority systems for particular crafts. As Gomberg writes, the jurisdictional claim (over an extent of territory and a range of tasks) of a switchman to marshall freight cars of a train in a yard and a parallel claim of a brakeman to handle the same cars out on the road come from emerging craft property rights to work. Instead of a property deed to rights in real property, a collective labor agreement exists for rights in such incorporeal property (1965:366). Gomberg concludes: "In a sense, the labor movement embodies the development of a new set of property rights. . . . " For example, "[m]any of the work rules define an emerging property right of the worker in his job" (1961:120).[14]

The Special Place of Railroaders under the Federal Web

Under the federal part of the web, both railroads and labor unions representing their employees have been viewed by government as vested with the public interest. Accordingly, Congress legislated, the President administered, and the Supreme Court interpreted and upheld an evolving separate tradition of laws regulating labor-management relations on railroads. Developing out of a series of preceding federal legislation solely for rail labor relations beginning with the Arbitration Act of 1888, the current Railway Labor Act was enacted in 1926 (Ellingwood 1928).[15]

The U.S. Supreme Court holds that employees of railroads are subject to the federal Railway Labor Act (RLA) of 1926 (45 U.S.C. § 151, et seq.), as amended, to the exclusion of other conflicting law. Explaining that "[t]he Railway Labor Act is essentially an instrument of industry-wide government," in *California v. Taylor*, 353 U.S. 553 (1957), the Court held that the web of federal labor law for railroads under the RLA is a "state within a state." For labor relations, Congress "has provided, by the Railway Labor Act, techniques peculiar to that industry" (353 U.S. 553, 565–6, 1957). Under the RLA, agreements made with management by a bargaining unit of employees have the full force of federal law behind them, backed by the Constitution. As the Court ruled: "A union agreement made pursuant to the Railway Labor Act has, therefore, the imprimatur of the federal law upon it and the force of the Supremacy Clause of Article VI of the Constitution. . . ." (*California v. Taylor*, 353 U.S. 553, 561, 1957).

The statutes as such regarding rail labor are of limited effect in the web. For the past century or so, legislated statutes provide most of the new business law. The meaning of a provision of a statute and the kinds of instances the provision covers, however, are concerns determined by the courts.[16] It is the interpretation of these laws in the courts (and to a lesser extent in arbitration), then, that defines the relative powers of the three principle bodies of actors in American work relations. Many statutes are intentionally lacking in detailed instruction because of conflicting pressures, or, at times, inexpert drafting by legislators. Officers of administrative agencies, judges, and arbitrators are, accordingly, delegated authority to interpret statutes. The RLA is an example of such an intentionally general statute. A great number of laws in the web enacted to safeguard not only the labor and human relations features but also the environmental health and safety aspects of employment are weak in the legislative intent. Not enough personnel and other resources are provided for the administrative agencies to more that just begin to see that these laws are followed. Accordingly, whatever property rights in work emerge, these are little protected under law in sharp contrast to the more traditional property rights.

Economic Security for Railroaders in the Web of Seniority

It is an American view that the longer the service on a job, the greater the amount of personal investment in it. Thus, apart from its security under law, a seniority system is favored in popular opinion. With a developed seniority system as part of the language of the labor agreement, management's rights to dismiss or reassign employees becomes restricted. Some economic security is thereby provided the worker, and property rights to a job emerge further.

As E. Edward Herman and Alfred Kuhn explain, a major form of economic security for a worker is in a seniority system (1981:443). Seniority, they say, may be considered a kind of property right involving priorities to jobs and job privileges. "American unions, especially craft ones, traditionally attempted to establish their 'ownership,' or 'property rights,' in jobs much as did the guilds before them. In its most complete form, this would mean that the job could not be abolished without union consent and that the union could establish the rules under which 'ownership' would transfer to a particular person who filled the job" (1981:442).

Seniority systems for railroaders evolved in the web prior to the first federal laws of 1888 for rail labor relations. Originally, seniority was a unilateral grant by management surrendering this principle to employees as part of a railroad's policies. Seniority was at first an informal localized practice on a railroad. By 1870, the unilateral principle of seniority was well-developed and made formal on the Erie Railroad (e.g., Gould 1870). Apart from seniority, the written labor "schedules," as they are still called on railroads, listing rates of pay and some of the formal conditions of employment (work rules) were drafted unilaterally and signed only by management (e.g., CB&Q 1878). Gradually, seniority evolved into a right under law, encompassed in a lawful bilateral schedule. Schedules thus increasingly became bilaterally negotiated agreements, between a railroad company and a union local serving as a bargaining unit and representing in a geographical area the collective interests of a craft or class of employees. As 1875 began, the first rail labor contract, or bilateral schedule, and seniority provisions were implemented (NYC&HR 1875). For the (on-train) operating crafts, by the end of the 1880s, the seniority right had become widespread and by 1914 virtually universal. During federal operation and control of the railroads from 1917 to 1920, under the United States Railroad Administration (USRA), labor agreements and seniority provisions modeled on those of the operating crafts were negotiated for almost all other railroad employees (USRA 1919).[17] All this was in place in the web, before rail management and labor agreed upon the rules that *they* would have Congress legislate as *their* Railway Labor Act. With the passage of the RLA in 1926, workers' connection with "property rights in their jobs received its first quasi-legal sanction" (Gomberg 1961:122).

As it evolved on the nation's railroads and became fixed essentially into its present form by the federal USRA, seniority may be viewed as a mechanism of work relations, governed by length of service in a unit of work, for allocation of scarce opportunities among employees in the unit and for protection of these advantages against all nonunit members. Because seniority right is bilaterally, contractually, based, it can only be modified by agreement. Only in accordance with the terms of the agreement is the right enforceable. Furloughed employees have seniority rights only as provided by this contract. When time is not contractually limited, furloughed workers retain rights so long as they are both available and able to work. Whatever the union bargaining agent agrees to in good faith regarding the nature of seniority, all the contractually covered employees, whether or not a member of the union, must abide by—absent unlawful provisions in this agreement. The seniority provisions are subject to a modification originating in the internal appeals process within the labor organization.

Resulting from union action, agreement seniority by right was further constructed in 1937 by the federal National Railroad Adjustment Board's (NRAB) First Division (Awards No. 1842:132, *Caldwell Case*; and 1843:147, *Haileyville Case*) as follows: "Seniority, in railway service, is a preferential right to perform a certain class of work to the exclusion of all others not holding such seniority in that service. Once established, it cannot be arbitrarily destroyed." Accordingly, the NRAB added to the web of law the railroaders' premise that agreement seniority right includes a monopoly on the performance of the worktasks of a particular craft by its members upon a seniority territory. Neither management nor another party can abrogate seniority right or give part of it to those not on the governing seniority roster of holders of the right. Thus excluded from the right is a universal class of all the world's people not included in the roster group.

In all, on railroads, through seniority an employee's connection to his job has evolved toward some manner of property right.[18] Economic security for railroaders involves not only seniority systems protected by the RLA but also includes economic security under another federal act.

ECONOMIC SECURITY FOR RAILROADERS IN THE WEB OF THE INTERSTATE COMMERCE COMMISSION

The ICC Job Protective Conditions

To begin, it should be noted what is called job protection in the railroad industry, as in the private Washington Job Protection Agreement of 1936, is really any of the forms of economic security. The protection usually is income security for a specified period but ranges to some form of property right in a job.

Because of actions by rail labor during the Depression, permanent economic security has also been constructed in the web of the Interstate Commerce Act (ICA) of 1887, as amended by the Transportation Act of 1940. In its 1940 amendment, the ICA requires the Interstate Commerce Commission (ICC), to encourage "fair and equitable" working conditions related to the transactions it approves regarding railroads. With this law added to the web, the Commission became directly involved in rail labor relations. Under the 1940 amendments to the ICA, the ICC was allowed by Congress considerable freedom in handling the economic security provisions of Section 5(2) (f) of the act. Over the years, the ICC constructed a succession of standard *conditions* increasingly more protective for railroaders in the combinations, particular kinds of abandonments, and certain other ICC-approved transactions regarding railroads. These conditions gradually added to the web of rules. ICC conditions are of two fundamentally different kinds: (1) *imposed* on the railroads and unions, and (2) collectively bargained under the provisions of the RLA by the two parties and merely *approved* by the Commission in its order authorizing a combination or other transaction.

Once the ICC has approved what it considers a new standard case with changed protective conditions for labor (such as those labeled as *Oklahoma* or as *N.Y. Dock*, discussed in a following subsection), the Commission generally applies these latest conditions, until it orders subsequent changes in a future standard case. As empowered under the ICA, the ICC, among other matters, must consider in its approval of transactions among railroads, the adverse affect upon employees of the lines involved. At first, transactions were defined as limited to combinations or abandonments among railroads, but this coverage gradually expanded, as will be explained. *Adversely affected* refers to a railroader's termination of employment, displacement to a lesser-paying job, or forced movement to another town as a result of a transaction among railroads.

Not Commission or Congressional benevolence but constant union activity and exercise of power are the basis of the formerly continuously expanded economic security for railroaders under ICC conditions. Unions request legislation from Congress and test in the courts the ICC interpretations of its conditions. In such actions, serious setbacks for railroaders occurred beginning in 1986. Selected highlights illustrative of the development and operation of the web are discussed in the following sections.

Establishment and Limits of ICC Economic Security for Railroaders

Rail employee protection under the ICC-imposed conditions has, in the main, consisted of some variety of monetary compensation to offset an employee's lost income from a Commission-approved transaction among railroads. For example, in the ICC's first comprehensive, imposed conditions (labeled *Oklahoma*), of 1944, affected railroaders would receive 100 percent of former earnings for up to 4 years consequent to a combination or abandonment involving two or more railroads (*Oklahoma Ry. Trustees—Abandonment*, 257 I.C.C. 177, 1944). Sometimes, in private agreements among railroads and unions, the actual job or at least employment is preserved, as in the *Norfolk and Western* conditions approved by the ICC (307 I.C.C. 401, 1959).

In the combination of the Erie and the Delaware, Lackawanna and Western in 1960 (312 I.C.C. 195, 1960), the unions challenged the ICC's position that it should protect displaced railroaders by means of monetary compensation and not by guaranteed employment. Accordingly, in 1961, the Supreme Court ruled on whether Section 5(2) (f) of the ICA required a job freeze. The model of intent favored by the unions, Section 7(b) of the expired Emergency Transportation Act of 1933, had required such a freeze. In *Brotherhood of Maintenance of Way Employees, et al. v. U.S., et al.,* 366 U.S. 175 (1961), the Court found that the legislative history of ICA Section 5(2) (f) did not support an interpretation requiring employee protection in the form of a job freeze or of an employment guarantee. The *B.M.W.E.* case of 1961 was a landmark decision. It derailed the steady striving by unions toward property rights in jobs under the web of the ICA.

Although private agreements under the RLA negotiated between a railroad and a union and approved by the ICC might result in actual job property rights, or, at least, employment security, the ICC's *imposed* conditions would now be limited to some form of income security. As is evidenced by *B.M.W.E.*, the web also consists of the legislative history of a law.

The Telegraphers' Further Attainments in Job Security under the RLA

Despite the *B.M.W.E.* setback for railroaders, other gains continued to be made in the movement toward their goal of job property rights. Under the web, the principle of economic security was extended to adverse effects upon rail employment owing to technological change and to reorganization, that is, rationalization, of the work process. This extended economic protection was through the medium of collective bargaining under the RLA, as reviewed by the courts.

Under the web of the RLA, rail labor agreements never expire but are continuously in effect. Unlike in other industries, railroaders thus never work "without a contract."[19] The provisions of a particular labor agreement limit the date before which negotiations may be reopened unilaterally by either party. Bargaining may begin after this specified date, with the serving by either party of a "Section-6 notice" on the other, in compliance with the directives of this section of the RLA. In 1958, in accordance with Section 6, the Order of Railroad Telegraphers (ORT) filed separate notices with the Chicago & Northwestern (C&NW) and with the Southern Pacific regarding this small union's desire to bargain collectively with each railroad.

Facing technological change in evolving electronic communications, the ORT wanted from each railroad an agreement for an added work rule in the web. This rule would prohibit the elimination of any job covered by an ORT contract then extant. The C&NW held that this matter was not bargainable under the RLA or under the terms of the agreement between it and the ORT. The issue of being bargainable was then litigated by the ORT in the courts. A lower court upheld the position of the ORT, but the Seventh Circuit Court of Appeals reversed the lower court. In 1960, the Supreme Court reversed the appeals court, finding that the matter was bargainable under the RLA (*O.R.T. v. C.&N.W. Ry. Co.*, 362 U.S. 330, 1960). Because the regulations of the web are ever subject to litigation and potential reinterpretation or further interpretation by the courts, workers and managers tend to "buy into" this generally equitable system of work relations.

Mandatory bargaining under the RLA on the matter of extending job security for rail telegraphers occurred first with the Southern Pacific but reached an impasse. Thus, under the provisions of the RLA, a Presidential Emergency Board (PEB) was specially created by the President of the United States. PEB No. 138, in 1961, adopted the principles of income security for adverse effect from combinations of railroads that had been developed in and since the private Washington Job Protection Agreement (WJPA) of 1936 between the nation's railroads and rail unions.[20] The PEB recommended that WJPA principles be extended to employment made worse by technological change and by the reorganization of work.

As championed by the quite small ORT, in a number of subsequent bilateral agreements under the RLA and as further recommended on the matter by additional PEBs, most railroads agreed either to elements of the WJPA or to greater job protection. ORT-covered employees facing technological disruption of customary jobs were thereby protected in the face of the early revolution in electronic communications. Some railroads agreed to a guarantee of employment at no loss in compensation or else a severance allowance. Only natural attrition of an employee in the affected craft would eliminate a protected job. Thus by use of the normal processes under the railroads' webbed work relations, the principle of employment security was firmly established for *intra*-company jobs threatened by managerial rationalization. Property right to a job had certainly been obtained in the web for telegraphers.

Railroaders' Increased Economic Security during the 1970s

In a 1971 case, important in railroaders' development of economic security, the Supreme Court ruled as follows. If a collective agreement exists for implementation of a railroad combination "and the Commission, as here, adopts or approves it," then, this labor contract has the same legal power as a condition for economic protection *imposed* by the ICC in an order. In *N.&W.RR. Co. v. Nemitz, et al.*, 404 U.S. 37 (1971), the Court decided that a subsequent labor agreement could not supersede the terms and conditions of a prior implementing labor agreement in a combination of railroads.

One more example of the many milestones in the expansion of railroaders' security is the ICC's conditions established in its *N.Y. Dock* case, 360 I.C.C. 60, (1979). In these *N.Y. Dock II* conditions, included were the Railway Labor Executives' Association's (RLEA)[21] request for a substitution of an ICC-approved (broader) "transaction" for the older (narrower) "coordination" among railroads. Since the 1930s, the ICC had used this circumstance of "coordination" in determining adverse effects to employees. The more inclusive "transactions" comprise merger of railroads, sale of lines between railroads, abandonment of lines, leasing of lines to other railroads, and granting of trackage rights for the movement of another railroad's trains. *N.Y. Dock* conditions established a regulatory floor of economic security in the web. Upon this floor, increased benefits of protection could be developed by the actors labor and government vis-à-vis the actor railroads. Rail unions could accept this floor level, now increased to up to six years with a guarantee of 100 percent of income. Or else the unions could bargain collectively with the railroad or petition government for yet more generous provisions. For certain railroads, employee security more liberal than *N.Y. Dock* was enacted into law by Congress at union request.

The Reversal of the Expansion of Railroaders' Economic Security

In 1986, the ICC exempted a particular kind of sale of a rail line from its formerly expanding conditions of economic security for railroaders. Such transactions involved unprofitable or little profitable lines that railroads desired to sell to nonrailroad firms. The determining characteristic of the ICC's pivotal exemption was sale of a line to a nonrailroad. Such an exemption from requiring income security, the ICC held, was at its discretion under a revision of ICA (49 U.S.C. § 10901) by the Staggers Rail Act of 1980. Only in transactions such as a line's abandonment or acquisition *by another railroad* must it impose income security (under 49 U.S.C. §§ 19003, 11343) reasoned the Commission (ICC 1987:35–36). The ICC also argued that if the lines were offered for sale with the financial encumbrance of up to six years of payments of income security for each adversely affected railroader, then the trackage would not be salable and would simply be abandoned.[22]

The Staggers Act of 1980, made a slight change in Congressional intent regarding railroaders' security under the ICC. Far more important, the Republicans, taking control of the presidency in that year made great ideological changes in appointments to the ICC by that party. Political parties thus are potent actors in the web. With a change in the ICC's political direction, the web would now begin to provide increasingly less protection to railroaders. The movement toward property rights to railroaders' jobs now began to wane, after waxing for sixty years or more. The rail unions litigated in the courts the ICC decision to construct an expandable loophole, large enough to run a train through, in the web of protective conditions, and lost (888 F.2d 1227, 8th Cir.; 1989; 110 S. Ct. 1808, 1990).

If the web of the ICA provided decreased support for railroaders, perhaps the web of the RLA could replace the lost security. Accordingly, the rail unions argued that the sales of lines to nonrailroad firms were violations of Sections 2 and 6 of the RLA, because, without negotiations, the transactions changed the terms and conditions of employment. A conflict between two codes in the web, the RLA and the ICA, was evident. This was a problem for the courts.

A further reversal of railroaders' fortunes occurred in 1989 when the Supreme Court ruled that the Pittsburgh & Lake Erie (the firm) could sell its entire railroad property to a specially established nonrail subsidiary of a railroad company. The P&LE was not required to bargain with its employees regarding this sale, ruled the Court. The P&LE was, however, required to bargain about the effects of this transaction on its employees, but it had to do so only through the date it completed its proposed sale (*P.&L.E.R.R. Co. v. R.L.E.A.*, 105 L. Ed. 2d 415, 1989). This last requirement imposed on management was a somewhat empty victory for labor. The ICA, the Supreme Court seemed to imply, does not supersede the RLA; management must negotiate with labor regarding the effects of the sale of its railroad to a nonrailroad firm. But, having a limited impact, this requirement under the RLA is only until the completion of the sale. In all, the Court did not give clear guidance for application of the web it had cut apart in this matter. The railroads had a narrowly circumscribed and ill-defined obligation to bargain with their employees. The protective web of economic security for railroaders was unraveling rapidly.

Under the RLA, when all of the procedures to settle a *major* management-labor dispute (defined as concerning pay and conditions of employment) are unsuccessfully exhausted, either side may exercise economic self-help. For example, a union would be free to strike the employer and a railroad to lock out its employees. A dispute that is *minor* (defined as an interpretation of an extant agreement), under the RLA, is a matter for settlement through arbitration, by the National Railroad Adjustment Board and special (public law) boards with similar powers. A union or railroad may not exercise self-help in a minor dispute. If the sale of a railroad's property to a nonrailroad firm led to a major dispute under the RLA, the unions would be able to use a powerful mechanism of the web. Railroaders could ultimately strike the railroad and bring their strategic economic power to bear; trains would be stopped on their tracks. The railroaders' strategy now was to have the labor disputes in question regarding line sales judged major ones under the RLA.

The Third Circuit Court of Appeals, however, in 1990 found that a labor dispute issuing from such a sale of a line to be "minor" (*G.C.A., U.T.U. v. C.S.X. Corp.*, 893 F. 2d 594, 3rd Cir., 1990). Thus railroaders do not have a right to strike under the web to prevent loss of economic security when a line or an entire railroad is sold to a nonrailroad, even when specially created to circumvent the rules of the web. After decades of strife in the web over economic security, with an ally in the governmental actor, the employer actor had decisively defeated the employee actor.[23] Government, after all, is not neutral but continually reconstructed as a result of numerous partisan contests. The question remains, Do the defeats for railroaders amount to a mortal blow under the web of rules?

CONCLUSIONS

As in the discussions of control of the work force for the Wayto foragers and the Qemant peasants, we see that the idea of the web of rules is useful for including all manner of traditional work relations in a theory of work. A general theory of work relations, designed by its originators with the anthropologist, among others, in mind, is heuristically applicable to human work of all societies. As in the discussions of property rights in work among the Wayto, Qemant, and modern American railroaders, particular kinds of theories and analyses of work relations can be conducted under the rubric of the broad general theory of the web.

With the idea of the web of rules, a researcher of work avoids ethnocentrisms. These include seeking a labor movement and finding none as in contemporary China or Ethiopia of the Communist period from 1975 through 1991. And these involve using a classic capitalistic model of modernization and development as the yardstick for cross-societal comparisons, thereby regarding some circumstances as not "measuring up" or in some way abnormal. Thus, as Kerr and Siegel originally posited, the broad subjects of both monocultural and cross-cultural study of industrialization and industrialism are not the labor movement in capitalism but the work force in socioeconomic development. The broad focus in studies of development is the particular nature of the universal work relations of humans.

In the realm of industrial work, the idea of the web enables us to concentrate on the nature of the essential conditions and forces affecting which single one, or which combinations, of the three central bodies of actors can assume power for rule making regarding the work force. Through the use of the web as a framework for analysis, we can focus closely on the ways in which the three central, and other, actors attempt to maximize their rule-making and rule-manipulating empowerments. Consider, for example, the power contests depicted in the railroad industry, among the employer, the employees, and the concerned members of government. With guidance from analyses using the idea of the web, we can study more precisely the historically pertinent paths and directions of actors' empowerment for the construction and use of rules to achieve control of or influence particular aspects of work forces. Our discussions of the evolution to date of the web in the railroad industry demonstrate that the historical changes of the web must be known for an understanding of the current relations among and attainments possible for the actors in the web.

The web enables us to investigate systemically the salient aspects of the relationships of industrial work. For example, how do the various bodies of actors attempt to influence the interaction of workers with the productive process? If "industrial democracy" involves the workers' effective participation in making and enforcing the rules, what are the conditions for and implications of its counterpart, which is some form of "industrial autocracy"? Must a relatively free market inevitably lead to free politics? To what extent is industrial democracy practicable outside of wealthy countries in the Western tradition? Can it succeed in Poland; could it flourish in Mexico; might it take root in Ethiopia; will it ever be found in Singapore; and is it a Chimera in Russia? How do different environments, for example, of national material resource scarcity or of global worker abundance impinge on the kind of rule-making relationship that obtains? How is the rule-making relationship affected by different patterns of initial industrialization; such as, into primitive smokestack industries of manufacturing or into modern electronic-based industries of information processing? How do different circumstances of production affect the kind of rule-making relationship, for example, production in large part for the military, for developing the infrastructure, or for consumer demands? Are some rule-making relationships transitional and others more stable as eventual stages of attainment? And, finally, with what criteria does one evaluate each of the various kinds of rule-making relationships? Ethnologically, that is cross-culturally viewed, what and from which ethnocentric viewpoint are "good" work relations?

NOTES

Acknowledgment

Support for various periods of field research providing data for this paper was provided in part by grants from the Foreign Area Fellowships of the Social Science Research Council and American Council of Learned Societies, National Science Foundation, National Institute of Mental Health, and German Marshall Fund. I thank Miriam Lee Kaprow and Ivar Berg for perceptive comments on aspects of this paper. And I am grateful to Robert S. Bogason for almost two decades of highly informing exchanges about railroad industrial relations and for provision of opportunities for research on railroads.

1. Emile Durkheim, the rules "fixed the respective duties of employers and workmen" (1947 [1893]:13).

2. The idea of the web was augmented by Kerr, Dunlop, Harbison, and Myers (1973), Dunlop and others (1975), Berg (1979), Schuster (1984), Perrow (1986), Kerr and Staudohar (1986:1–10, 154–97), Kochan, Katz, and McKersie (1986), Kalleberg and Berg (1987), Meltz (1991), and Kaufman (1993). Dunlop's book has been appropriately characterized as "perhaps the most influential book in . . . industrial relations since the Second World War" (Meltz 1991:10) and the "most notable attempt at theorizing in industrial relations" before the 1980s (Kaufman 1993:148). For a bibliography of uses of this book see Meltz 1991:18–9. In my own writing and teaching, I find the idea of the web quite fruitful as a conceptual frame for the study of work (Gamst 1987, 1989).

3. Empirical data and insights for this chapter come from field research in the Horn of Africa since 1964 and from firsthand contact with the railroad industry (companies, labor unions, and governmental agencies) since 1955 as an operating railroader, university researcher, and professional consultant. For investigation of work in industrial society, the ethnologist must do more than conduct fieldwork through participant observation and other field techniques. For the necessary understanding of the organizational and legal context of the work, this researcher must also be abundantly conversant with its web of rules.

4. Rather than a "postindustrial" society emerging from an industrial one (Bell 1973), some ethnologists, and others, maintain that we are evolving into an intensified or hyperindustrial era (Braverman 1974:313–5; Harris 1982:46–9). In fact, the modern office or fast food franchise, as with Adam Smith's factory manufacturing pins, has a minute division of labor and use of effort-multiplying and time-saving machines in the providing of services, such as communications, or products, such as mass-produced burgers. Dull, routinized, and simplified work performed in the office, hospital, testing laboratory, computer data entry facility, and other sites result in the same kind of apathy and alienation as found on the assembly line. In both reactions, the paramount interests of workers are often verbalized as being in "quitting time and payday."

5. Varieties of this symbolically valorous hairstyle are not pan-African but restricted to the Horn of Africa and adjacent Beja areas of Sudan. The hairstyle gave rise to Rudyard Kipling's entirely laudatory "Fuzzy Wuzzy" verses, in which the Beja armed with spears and sticks were the only thing not giving a damn for a regiment of heavily armed British infantry (Gamst 1984b:132–3). Part of the reward for the lethal work of defeating and ridding their land of these economy-controlling foreigners was public display of the huge crown of hair.

6. For this historical development in the Anglo-American railroad industry during the past 150 years see Gamst 1983, 1986a, 1992b, 1993:110–12.

7. For discussion of the modalities for behavior in the web, see Gamst's previous chapter, note 3.

8. John R. Commons was a pioneering reflector on what he saw as "working rules" broadening the concept of private property to include incorporeal property such as rights to jobs (1957 [1924]). His student, Selig R. Perlman, held, "the safest way to assure group control over opportunity . . . was for the union . . . to become the virtual owner and administrator of the jobs" (1928:199).

9. Carl Gersuny holds that only the self-employed have property rights in jobs. Further, employees are analogous to tenants, however secure their union-effected tenancy in the job, and thus merely the authorized possessor of a job (1984:52–4).

10. It should be noted that, until recently, the web in Japan provides a considerable amount of employment rather than job security, in which a veteran employee is guaranteed some job rather than his or her particular job (see Marshall 1986:140–8; Beck and Beck 1993). Employment security rather than job security has been a goal of some industrial unions such as the United Auto Workers, United Steelworkers, and Communications Workers of America. Such a policy includes demands for retraining for changing jobs (Shostak 1991:13–6).

11. A constitutionally secured property right, to some extent, for public employees was constructed by the U.S. Supreme Court in 1972, with dismissal for cause permitted only after due process (*Perry v. Sindermann* 408 U.S. 593, 1972).

12. Although the Constitution did not establish property rights in work, reflecting the relative power of actors, in several provisions it entrenched the property rights of owners of slave workers.

13. Of course, in the private sector (and to some extent in the public sector, as public employees are experiencing in the 1990s), no job security exists if an organization is not economically viable (Trowbridge 1986:410–1; Dunlop 1990:126–35).

14. The rail web contains not just a lengthy code of "work rules" governing conditions of employment but also of "operating rules" guiding work and thereby entering into these conditions of employment. Relevant, then, but outside of the scope of this chapter are the operating, air brake, safety, personal deportment on and off the job, and other related rules on railroads unilaterally promulgated by management until 1970, when the federal government also became involved in their construction. These formal rules and the related practices of management promulgated for controlling in all of its aspects the work on their lines of rails began in embryonic form at least by the late 1700s and continue to evolve (Gamst 1980, 1983, 1986a, 1989, 1990b, 1992b). As every railroader is instructed and experiences,

the two complex codeas are intertwined at work. Railroading is conducted on the job and managed with reference to the intertwinings.

15. For the legislative history of the RLA, see U.S. Senate 1974. The RLA handles labor-management disputes by mediation and voluntary and mandatory arbitration and has provisions for procedures in national emergencies. Developed in part from the RLA was the National Labor Relations (Wagner-Connery) Act of 1935 (29 U.S.C. § 151, et seq.) covering the labor-management relations of most nonagricultural and nongovernmental organizations aside from the railroad and airline industries. Owing to successful lobbying of Congress by the Air Line Pilots' Association, the airline industry was covered by the rail web with a 1936 amendment of the Railway Labor Act.

16. Illustrative of such statutory interpretation and defining of law is the classic *Adair v. U.S.* (208 U.S. 161, 1908). Here the Supreme Court struck down Section 10 of the Erdman Act of 1898 (which replaced the Arbitration Act of 1888, regulating rail labor relations), thereby allowing a railroad to dismiss an employee for union activity. The Court held in *Adair* that labor was a commodity purchasable by the employer (208 U.S. 167, 1908). In 1930, however, the Court reversed itself and found that a railroad sponsoring a company union violated the Section 2, Third of the RLA, not allowing interference or influence in employees' choice of representatives (*T.&N.O.R.R. v. B.R.A.C.* 281 U.S. 548, 1930). Similarly, by the 1930s, as the courts interpreted seniority cases, especially on railroads, they gradually added to the strands of economic security of a worker under the web of federal acts for labor (Anon. 1937). Through the 1930s, almost all cases concerning seniority rules were from the railroads. Here, as in other matters, the web for rail labor pioneered for other workers.

17. Incidentally, it was the USRA additions to the web for railroaders that for the first time place work relations for American women specifically under the federal egis. These additions included equal pay for the same work. This principle of work relations was pioneered, as were so many others, in the railroad web, fire walled from the rest of the national economy. The USRA's General Order No. 27 of May 25, 1918 "ordered . . . the wages, hours, and other conditions of employment of the employees of the railroads. . . . " (USRA 1919:65). Its Article V. stipulated: "When women are employed, their working conditions must be healthful and fitted to their needs. The laws enacted for the government of their employment must be observed and their pay, when they do the same class of work as men, shall be the same as that of men" (USRA 1919:83).

18. Unlike the parallel federal web for work relations, the National Labor Relations Act of 1935, the RLA allows the organization of and collective negotiation for labor contracts (and seniority provisions) by first-line supervisors. For example, yardmasters, train dispatchers, and roundhouse

foremen obtain the same amount of job property right as rank-and-file employees.

19. Because under the web of the RLA, labor agreements are always continuously in effect, rail seniority cannot terminate from lapse of contract owing to passage of any amount of time.

20. The WJPA was the basis of the ICC's landmark *Oklahoma* conditions of 1944. Under the WJPA, a displacement allowance of 60 percent of compensation for up to 5 years, proportionate to years of service, was allowed an adversely affected railroader.

21. As actors in the web, railroads and unions may each act in concert with like organizations. For unions, this is done under the RLEA, an association of rail unions, usually more effective than one union acting alone. The railroads work through a number of their trade organizations, including the Association of American Railroads.

22. For a comprehensive review of the events discussed in this subsection, see Wilner 1991.

23. The defeats for rail labor included narrower issues as well. For example, the locomotive cab (control compartment) is the sole work site of the locomotive engineer who operates the locomotive and controls the movement of its trailing cars (Gamst 1975). During the national negotiation on wages and conditions of employment, in a 1986 arbitration under the aegis of the federal National Mediation Board, the Brotherhood of Locomotive Engineers was forced to accept the pattern settlement reached with another union mainly representing brakemen, switchmen, and conductors. This was so even for the engineers' request for improved industrial hygiene and safety in the locomotive cab (Gamst 1986b).

REFERENCES

N.B.: A number of complete standard citations to statutory, case, and administrative law are given in this chapter; thus, they are not repeated in these references.

Aalberts, Robert J., and Lorne Seidman
1992   The employment at will doctrine: Nevada's struggle demonstrates the need for reform. *Labor Law Journal* 43:651-62.

Ables, Robert J.
1962   *The History of and Experience under Railroad Employee Protection Plans.* Appendix Volume III. Report of the Presidential Railroad Commission. Washington, DC: U.S. Government Printing Office.

Abraham, Katherine G., and Susan H. Houseman
1993   *Job Security in America: Lessons from Germany.* Washington, DC: Brookings Institution.

Adams, Ray J.
1992   The role of the state in industrial relations. In *Research Frontiers in Industrial Relations and Human Resources.* David Lewin, Oliva S. Mitchell, and Peter D. Sherer, eds., pp. 489–523. Madison, WI: Industrial Relations Research Association.

Adelson, Andrea
1992   Judge grants waiver of notice law. *The New York Times* May 27:D1,D22.

Anonymous
1937   Seniority rights in labor relations. *Yale Law Journal* 47:73–98.

Applebaum, Herbert
1984   *Work in Non-Market and Transitional Societies.* Albany: State University of New York Press.

Barkin, Solomon
1954   Labor unions and workers' rights in jobs. In *Industrial Conflict.* Arthur W. Kornhauser, R. Dubin, and A. M. Ross, eds., pp. 121–31. New York: McGraw-Hill.

Beck, John C., and Martha N. Beck
1993   *The Change of a Lifetime: Employment Patterns among Japan's Managerial Elite.* Honolulu: University of Hawaii Press.

Bell, Daniel
1973   *The Coming of Post-Industrial Society.* New York: Basic Books.

Berg, Ivar
1979   *Industrial Sociology.* Englewood Cliffs, NJ: Prentice-Hall.

Black, Donald
1989   *Sociological Justice.* New York: Oxford University Press.

Bradsher, Keith
1992   Trade pact could cost up to 150,000 U.S. jobs. *The New York Times* Sept. 11:D1,D4.

Braverman, Harry
1974   *Labor and Monopoly Capital: The Degradation of Work in the Twentieth Century.* New York: Monthly Review Press.

CB&Q (Chicago, Burlington & Quincy Railroad)
1878   Schedule of Wages for Locomotive Firemen . . . in effect January 1, 1878.

Coleman, James S.
1990   *Foundations of Social Theory.* Cambridge, MA: Harvard University Press.

Commons, John R.
1957   [1924] *The Legal Foundations of Capitalism.* Madison: University of Wisconsin Press.

Conti Rossini, Carlo
1916   *Principi di diritto consuetudinario dell' Eritrea.* Rome: Unione Editrice.

Dalton, George
1967   *Tribal and Peasant Economies.* Garden City, NY: Natural History Press.

Daniel, W. W., and Elizabeth Stilgoe
1978   *The Impact of Labor Protection Laws.* London: Policy Studies Institute.

Dunlop, John T.
1970   [1958] *Industrial Relations Systems.* Carbondale: Southern Illinois University Press.

1988   Labor markets and wage determination: Then and now. In *How Labor Markets Work.* Bruce E. Kaufman, ed., pp. 47–87. Lexington, MA: Lexington Books.

1990   *The Management of Labor Unions: Decision Making with Historical Constraints.* Lexington, MA: Lexington Books.

1993   *Industrial Relations Systems,* rev. ed. Boston: Harvard Business School Press.

Dunlop, John T., et al.
1975   *Industrialism and Industrial Man Reconsidered: Some Perspectives on a Study over Two Decades of the Problems of Labor and Management in Economic Growth.* Princeton, NJ: Inter-University Study of Human Resources in National Development.

Durkheim, Emile
1947   [1893] *The Division of Labor in Society,* 2nd ed. Glencoe, Il: Free Press.

Ellingwood, A. R.
1928   The Railroad Labor Act of 1926. *Journal of Political Economy* 36:53–82.

Gamst, Frederick C.
1969   *The Qemant: A Pagan-Hebraic Peasantry of Ethiopia.* New York: Holt, Rinehart and Winston.

1970   Peasantries and elites without urbanism: The civilization of Ethiopia. *Comparative Studies in Society and History* 12:373–92.

1974   *Peasants in Complex Society.* New York: Holt, Rinehart and Winston.

1975   Human factors analysis of the diesel-electric locomotive cab. *Human Factors* 17:149–156.

1979   Wayto ways: Change from hunting to peasant life. In *Proceedings of the Fifth International Conference on Ethiopian Studies*. Robert L. Hess, ed., pp. 233-8. Chicago: University of Illinois.

1980   *The Hoghead: An Industrial Ethnology of the Locomotive Engineer*. New York: Holt, Rinehart and Winston.

1983   The development of operating rules. *Proceedings of the Railway Fuel and Operating Officers Association* 46:155-71.

1984a   Considerations for an anthropology of work. In *Work in Non-Market and Transitional Societies*. Herbert Applebaum, ed., pp. 56-61. Albany: State University of New York Press.

1984b   Beja. In *Muslim Peoples: A World Ethnographic Survey*, 2nd ed. Richard V. Weeks, ed., vol. 1, pp. 130-7. Westport, CT: Greenwood Press.

1984c   Wayto. In *Muslim Peoples: A World Ethnographic Survey*, 2nd ed., Richard V. Weeks, ed., vol. 2, pp. 852-6. Westport, CT: Greenwood Press.

1986a   The development of railroad discipline. *Proceedings of the Railway Fuel and Operating Officers Association*, 1985, 49:85-98.

1986b   A Presentation Advocating Certain Contractual Rules for Locomotive Standards and Practices in the National Agreement of the Brotherhood of Locomotive Engineers. Report BLE-FCG-86-1.

1987   The industrial relations of rail unions in Great Britain and West Germany: A review article in comparative industrial ethnology. *Anthropology of Work Review* 8:22-7.

1988a   Feudalism in Abyssinia? Further commentary in the on-going controversy. In *Proceedings of the Ninth International Conference on Ethiopian Studies, Moscow, 1986*, An. A. Gromyko, ed., vol. 4, pp. 70-80. Moscow: USSR Academy of Sciences.

1988b   The third seal opened and the black horseman emerged: An historic cultural ecology of Ethiopian poverty and famine. *Peasant Studies* 15:103-16.

1988c   The Qemant theocratic chiefdom in the Abyssinian feudal state. In *Proceedings of the Eighth International Conference of Ethiopian Studies, Addis Ababa, 1984*. Taddese Beyene, ed., vol. 1, pp. 793-8. Huntingdon, Cambs.: ELM Publications.

1989   The railroad apprentice and the 'rules': Historic roots and contemporary practices. In *Apprenticeship: From Theory to Method and Back Again*. Michael W. Coy, ed., pp. 65-86, 258-9, 274-7. Albany: State University of New York Press.

1990a Industrial organizational perspectives on the development and characteristics of the study of organizational cultures. In *Cross-Cultural Management and Organizational Culture*. Tomoko Hamada and Ann Jordan, eds., pp. 13–47. (William and Mary) Studies in Third World Societies No. 42.

1990b Highballing with flimsies: Working under train orders on the Espee's coast line. The railway history monograph: *Research Journal of American Railways* 19(1–2).

1991   Good peasants: Two transformations of traditional agriculture, in Ethiopia and Hispanic North America. *Reviews in Anthropology* 20:55–67.

1992a Zur Zufälligkeit der Entstehung nuer Kunststile Ergänzungen zum Aufsatz über die sogenannten "Fruchtbarkeitsidole" der Falascha von Abessinien. Zeitschrift für Ethnologie 117:117–8.

1992b The context and significance of America's first railroad, on Boston's Beacon Hill. *Technology and Culture* 33:1–36.

1993   What can be done to further standard operations and rules to raise the level of employee safety and efficiency? *Proceedings of the American Association of Railroad Superintendents, 1992* 96:108–17.

1994   The Qemant domestic cycle, ambilineality, and time. In *10 ème Conference Internationale des Etudes Ethiopiennes*, Paris, 1988, Palais de l'UNESCO. Organisée par la Société Franaise pour les Etudes Ethiopiennes.

Gamst, Frederick C., and Maximilian O. Baldia
1980   Über die sogenannten "Fruchtbarkeitsidole" der Falascha von Abessinien. Zeitschrift für Ethnologie 105:134–44.

Gersuny, Carl
1984   From contract to status: Perspectives on employment seniority. *Sociological Inquiry* 54:45–61.

Gibbs, Jack P.
1989   *Control: Sociology's Central Notion*. Urbana: University of Illinois Press.

Gomberg, William
1961   Featherbedding: An assertion of property rights. *Annals of the American Academy of Political and Social Science* 333:119–29.

1965   The work rule problem and property rights in the job. In *Labor*. Richard A. Lester, ed., pp. 365–8. New York: Random House.

Gould, Jay
1870   The Erie Railway Company. *Locomotive Engineers' Monthly Journal* 4:222.

Gross, Edward and Amitai Etzioni
1985 *Organizations in Society*. Englewood Cliffs, NJ: Prentice-Hall.

Guidi, Ignazio
1897– Il "Fetha Nagast" o "Legislazione dei re": Codice ecclesiastico e civile
1899 di Abissinia, 2 vols. Rome: Tip. della Casa Editrice Italiana.

Gutchess, Jocelyn
1985 *Employment Security in Action: Strategies that Work*. New York: Pergamon.

Harris, Marvin
1982 *America Now: The Anthropology of a Changing Culture*. New York: Simon and Schuster.

Herman, E. Edward, and Alfred Kuhn
1981 *Collective Bargaining and Labor Relations*. Englewood Cliffs, NJ: Prentice-Hall.

Hoebel, E. Adamson
1968 *The Law of Primitive Man: A Study in Comparative Legal Dynamics*. New York: Atheneum.

Hoebel, E. Adamson, and Everett L. Frost
1976 *Cultural and Social Anthropology*. New York: McGraw-Hill.

ICC (Interstate Commerce Commission)
1987 *1986 Annual Report*. Washington, DC: ICC.

Kalleberg, Arne L., and Ivar Berg
1987 *Work and Industry: Structures, Markets, and Processes*. New York: Plenum.

Kaufman, Bruce E.
1993 *The Origins and Evolution of the Field of Industrial Relations in the United States*. Ithaca, NY: ILR Press.

Kaufman, Herbert
1977 *Red Tape: Its Origins, Uses, and Abuses*. Washington, DC: Brookings Institution.

Keating, Edward
1953 *The Story of Labor: Thirty-three Years on Rail Workers' Fighting Front*. Washington, DC: Darby.

Kerr, Clark, and Abraham Siegel
1955 The structuring of the labor force in industrial society. *Industrial and Labor Relations Review* 8:151-68.

Kerr, Clark, John T. Dunlop, Frederick H. Harbison, and Charles A. Myers
1973 *Industrialism and Industrial Man*. London: Penguin Press.

Kerr, Clark, and Paul D. Staudohar, eds.
1986   *Industrial Relations in a New Age: Economic, Social, and Managerial Perspectives.* San Francisco: Jossey-Bass.

Kochan, Thomas A.
1993   Trade unionism and industrial relations: Notes on theory and practice for the 1990s. *IRRA Proceedings of the 45th Annual Meeting, 1993,* Anaheim, pp. 185–95.

Kochan, Thomas A., Harry Katz, and Robert B. McKersie
1986   *The Transformation of American Industrial Relations.* New York: Basic Books.

Kozak, Daniel J.
1989   Labor protection in the railroad industry. In *Government Protection of Employees Involved in Mergers and Acquisitions.* Herbert R. Northrup and P. A. Miscimarra, eds., pp. 499–554. Philadelphia: Wharton School.

Lavitan, Sar A., Peter E. Carlson, and Isaac Shapiro
1986   *Protecting American Workers: An Assessment of Government Programs.* Washington, DC: BNA.

Lowie, Robert H.
1947   [1920] *Primitive Society.* New York: Liveright.

MacGaughey, William
1992   *A U.S.-Mexico-Canada Free Trade Agreement.* Minneapolis: Thistlerose Publishers.

Marshall, Ray
1986   America and Japan: Industrial relations in a time of change. In *Unions in Transition.* Seymour M. Lipset, ed., pp. 133–49. San Francisco: ICS Press.

Meltz, Noah M.
         Dunlop's industrial relations systems after three decades. In *Comparative Industrial Relations: Contemporary Research and Theory.* Roy Adams, ed., pp. 10–20. London: Harper Collins.

Meyers, Frederic
1964   *Ownership of Jobs: A Comparative Study.* Los Angeles: University of California, Institute of Industrial Relations.

Nasar, Sylvia
1993   Layoff law is having slim effect. *The New York Times* August 3: D1–D2.

NYC&HR (New York Central and Hudson River Railroad)
1875   Labor Agreement with its Locomotive Engineers, signed by M. J. Rickett for the Brotherhood of Locomotive Engineers and by William H. Vanderbilt for the railroad.

Northrup, Herbert R., and Philip A. Miscimarra, eds.
1989 *Government Protection of Employees Involved in Mergers and Acquisitions.* Philadelphia: Wharton School.

Pankhurst, Richard
1968 *Economic History of Ethiopia, 1800–1935.* Addis Ababa: Haile Sellassie I University.

Perlman, Selig
1928 *A Theory of the Labor Movement.* New York: Macmillan.

Perrow, Charles
1986 *Complex Organizations: A Critical Essay,* 3rd ed. New York: Random House.

Plattner, Stuart
1989 *Economic Anthropology.* Stanford, CA: Stanford University Press.

Polyani, Karl, Conrad M. Arensberg, and Harry W. Pearson
1957 *Trade and Markets in the Early Empires: Economies in History and Theory.* Glencoe, IL: Free Press.

Reich, Charles
1964 *The New Property.* Yale Law Journal 73:733–87.

Sahlins, Marshall
1972 *Stone Age Economics.* New York: Aldine.

Sedler, Robert Allen
1965 *The Conflict of Laws in Ethiopia.* Addis Ababa: Haile Sellassie I University.

Shostak, Arthur B.
1991 *Robust Unionism: Innovations in the Labor Movement.* Ithaca, NY: ILR Press.

Schuster, Michael H.
1984 *Union-Management Cooperation: Structure, Process, Impact.* Kalamazoo, MI: W. E. Upjohn Institute for Employment Research.

Sjoberg, Gideon
1965 *The Preindustrial City: Past and Present.* New York: Free Press.

Trowbridge, Alexander B.
1986 A management look at labor relations. In *Unions in Transition.* Seymour M. Lipset, ed., pp. 405–18. San Francisco: ICS Press.

Udy, Stanley H., Jr.
1959 *Organization of Work: A Comparative Analysis of Production among Nonindustrial Peoples.* New Haven: HRAF Press.

USRA (United States Railroad Administration)
1919   *Public Acts Proclamations by the President Relating to the United States Railroad Administration and General Orders and Circulars Issued by the Director General of Railroads.* Washington, DC: U.S. Government Printing Office.

U.S. Senate
1973   *Senate Report 93–125.* 93rd Cong., 1st Sess. The Federal Paperwork Burden.

1974   *Legislative History of the Railway Labor Act, as Amended 1926 through 1966.* Washington, DC: U.S. Government Printing Office.

Wilner, Frank N.
1991   *The Railway Labor Act and the Dilemma of Labor Relations.* Omaha: Simmons-Boardman.

7

Post-Industrialism, Post-Fordism, and the Crisis in World Capitalism

Over two decades ago university students and professionals joined by some workers in the United States and France initiated an assault on the political establishment that challenged the boundaries between academia and the working populations of industrialized countries. The May uprising in France in 1968 and the Weathermen attack on the Democratic convention in Chicago in the same year seemed so unconnected with previous political processes related to class struggle in the workplace that social scientists began to invent a new set of labels for what was happening. In the 1970s "Post-Industrialism" theory posited a restructuring of society that removed the class struggle from center stage as a new hierarchy of technocrats defined the agenda for change. The awareness that hegemonic control was still exercised by capitalists relying on industrial revenues even with the growing importance of financial empires led to new categories of "Fordist Regimes" and "Post-Fordism," terms drawn from Gramsci's concept of welfare capitalism promoted by the Ford company in the early decades of the twentieth century.

Clearly the diminishing presence of an organized working class segment has changed the political arena in mature industrialized economies in fundamental ways that challenge the existing paradigms. The new social movements focusing on ethnic and gendered issues seem to transcend the categories of class conflict related to the workplace. But in order to understand the context in which they are generated, we have to go beyond the metropolitan-centered assumptions contained in both the Post-Industrial models of Touraine (1971) and Bell (1973) and the Fordist/Post-Fordist model as it has been set forth by Aglietta (1979, 1982) and Lipietz (1982, 1987). I shall critique the assumptions in each of these models and then suggest the emergent model of industrial restructuring related to both the decline of production in the old industrial centers and the newly industrializing countries. I shall argue that the most dynamic arenas for struggle and change lie outside the technocratic hierarchies of both industry and government that are identified by Post-Industrial and Post-Fordist theories as the leaders in structural change. They are found in the production sites of newly industrializing countries and in groups marginalized from the global economy, in the informal sector of Third World and declining industrial areas. These arenas lie beyond most theorizing of the postmodern condition, which refers to a relatively narrow sector of world cities serving as emergent global culture.[1]

POST-INDUSTRIAL MYTHS

In his book *The Post-Industrial Society, Tomorrow's Social History* (1971) Alain Touraine maintained that, in the emergent society programmed by technocrats, a radical departure in production methods has transformed economic organization to such an extent that the class struggle no longer has the same actors or stage. Rather, the conflict is between elites in decision-making roles and those among the technocrats who wish to transform their condition of dependent participation in the wider society as well as in the workplace. Responding to the same shifts, Daniel Bell published *The Coming of Post-Industrial Society: A Venture in Social Forecasting* (1973).

Both Touraine and Bell predicted the demise of organized labor as the redeemer of society and foresaw an enlargement of the power of the new technical elites. They argued their case on the basis of statistics showing shifts in employment from producing goods to service jobs and the implications of the new communications driven organization of production. However, they differed in their view of the future struggle. Touraine maintained that the May uprising in Paris, in which rebellious youths joined by elite technical workers and even professionals within advanced sectors of the economy were acting out the future struggle that revolved around social and cultural alienation rather than exploitation and economic wrongs. Rather than the formation of a newly constituted class struggle now led by alienated technicians envisioned by Touraine, Bell (1973:12) predicted a shift in the principles of stratification with tensions resulting from the bureaucratization of science, countered by increasingly specialized intellectual work.

In the decades following the publication of their books, the transformation of the economic base to service and financial "industries" brought a glimpse of the technocratic society envisioned by these social analysts. But it was limited to global cities like New York, London, and Tokyo[2] (Sassen 1992). At the same time that financial and information centers in global cities were taking shape in the 1970s and 1980s, indexes of world industrial production rose in both developed and developing market economies (Table 7.1a.). Although employment in industry decreased in the developed economies, it continued to increase in the developing economies (see Table 7.1b). Even in developed industrial countries, when we examine employment in industry differentiated by gender, we find that, although male employment fell in the decade between 1978 and 1987 in Canada and the United States, female employment actually increased (Table 7.2a). Furthermore, the strong industrial countries such as Germany and Japan gained employment, men in the former and both men and women in the latter country (Table 7.2a). The advancing frontier of industrialization prevalent when their theories of postindustrialism were projected can be seen in the employment increases of about 9 million for both men and women in China and an increase of 300,000 each for both men and women in Thailand (Table 7.2b).

At a time when global integration of industry was on the rise in the late 1960s and 1970s, theoreticians of Postindustrialism ignored the main dynamics of the industrial restructuring that began in the late 1960s. These were based on (1) the sourcing of production sites in formerly peripheral industrial areas and (2) the preferential employment of women in both old and newly industrializing countries that were giving shape to the new industrialization (Nash and Fernandez-Kelly 1983; Safa 1981). The relative invisibility of these new labor force participants meant that they were not considered to be significant actors in the central arenas of economic and political life. The prediction of the end of industrialization and the failure to foresee or even recognize such trends when they occur stem from the metropolitan and androcentric bias in theoretical constructs.

TABLE 7.1a. Industrial Production and Employment in Centrally Planned Developed and Developing Market Economies 1975-1987

	a. Industrial Production: World and Regions Index Based on 1980							
			Centrally Planned		*Market Developed*		*Market Developing*	
Year	*World*							
	Light	*Heavy*	*Light*	*Heavy*	*Light*	*Heavy*	*Light*	*Heavy*
1975	84	78	83	73	86	80	79	70
1978	96	95	95	91	98	96	93	89
1981	100	101	100	103	99	100	103	101
1982	100	98	102	107	97	95	105	102
1983	102	102	106	112	100	98	108	104
1984	107	110	109	119	104	107	116	113
1985	110	115	112	125	105	111	124	119
1986	114	118	116	132	108	112	140	132
J-J	106	105	103	105	103	104	122	110

TABLE 7.1b. Industrial Production and Employment in Centrally Planned Developed and Developing Market Economies 1975-1987

	b. Industrial Employment: World and Regions Index Based Year 1980							
			Centrally Planned		*Market Developed*		*Market Developing*	
Year	*World*							
	Light	*Heavy*	*Light*	*Heavy*	*Light*	*Heavy*	*Light*	*Heavy*
1975	91	93	97	93	102	98	80	80
1978	98	98	100	98	102	100	95	92
1981	98	99	101	101	95	97	100	102
1982	98	98	100	101	92	93	102	102
1983	98	97	100	102	91	91	105	104
1985	100	98	99	101	90	91	108	106
1986	—	—	100	102	90	90	—	—

Source: United Nations Statistical Yearbook 1985/6

FORDISM AND AFTER

In an attempt to address the issues of government intervention affecting capital labor relations that went beyond Marxist mode of production analyses, a new school of "Regulationists" (Aglietta 1979, 1982; Lipietz 1982, 1987; Mahane 1987) began to apply the label

of "Fordism," expanding it to include "peripheral Fordism" and "post-
TABLE 7.2a. Paid Employment in Manufacturing, Industrialized Countries
and Newly Industrialized Countries, 1978–1987

| | a. Industrialized Countries (Thousands) | | | | | |
| | Total | | Male | | Female | |
	1978	1987	1978	1987	1978	1987
Canada	1,933	2,017	1,594	1,449	495	568
France	5,368	4,393	3,701	3,045	1,667	1,349
Germany	3,466	3,534	1,953	2,083	1,512	1,450
Italy	4,698	3,986	3,228	2,673	1,470	1,312
Japan	11,090	12,150	7,270	7,880	3,820	4,280
United Kingdom	7,283	5,149	5,138	3,606	2,145	1,542
Unites States	20,505	19,065	14,268	12,801	6,237	6,264

TABLE 7.2b. Paid Employment in Manufacturing, Industrialized Countries
and Newly Industrialized Countries, 1978–1987

| | b. Newly Industrializing Countries | | | | | |
| | Total | | Male | | Female | |
	1978	1987	1978	1987	1978	1987
China	42,560	59,715	26,885	35,280	15,675	24,435
Hong Kong	816	868	402	438	414	430
India	5,677	6,271	5,105	5,700	572	571
Korea	2,409	3,675	1,519	2,188	889	1,487
Malaysia	†21,167	24,835	‡16,937	17,561	†8,503	7,274
Mexico	1,716	2,546	*1,628	1,762	437	609
Singapore	250	298	134	155	116	143
Thailand	1,613	2,300	953	1,261	661	1,039

*1980   †1981   ‡1982
Source: United Nations Yearbook of Labour Statistics 1988

Fordism" to take into consideration the restructuring of industry
in old centers and movement into newly industrializing areas on
the Asian and Latin American perimeter. The terms themselves
suggest that a kind of industrialization related to Gramsci's (1973)
view of corporate capitalism in the first quarter of the twentieth
century would evolve throughout the globe. Based on Aglietta's
(1982) model of an intensive regime of accumulation and a monopoly

mode of regulation that institutionalized the labor capital conflict, Lipietz (1987) expanded Gramsci's notion of Fordism to include the new institutional controls that emerged out of the labor struggles of the 1930s. While the state took over some of the activities identified with corporate welfare policies, Lipietz asserts that labor unions accepted the compromise inherent in Taylorite "scientific management" in return for high wages, stable employment, and a good benefits package. This "monopoly mode of regulation," tied to an "intensive regime of accumulation" made possible in large corporations and financial institutions, came into its own after World War II (Aglietta 1979; Lipietz 1987:29 et seq.; Mahane 1987; Murray 1988:8; Rustin 1989). The institutionalization of capital labor relations through the legalization of trade unions and the National Labor Relations Board, combined with Keynesian economic policies that stimulated or slowed down the economy through state spending, encouraged a vast expansion of mass consumer markets, which the Regulationists call Fordism.

It is worth restating Gramsci's view of Fordist hegemony in order to appreciate the distinction between the two phases of labor control, the one Gramsci refers to as Fordism in which "a new mechanism of accumulation and distribution of finance capital based directly on industrial production," and that which prevailed after the labor struggles of the 1930s opened the way for state intervention and the institutionalization of labor unions.

Hegemonic control operating within this earlier phase is according to Gramsci (1973:285), based on

> . . . a skillful combination of force, (destruction of working-class trade unionism on a territorial basis) and persuasion (high wages, various social benefits, extremely subtle ideological and political propaganda) and thus succeed in making the whole life of the nation revolve around production. Hegemony here is born in the factory and requires for its exercise only a minute quantity of professional political and ideological intermediaries.

The Ford Company epitomized the search for hegemonic control in the social welfare program for workers, combining a paternalistic interest in their home life, health and welfare with social science expertise (Gramsci 1973:223 et seq.; Meyer 1981). Yet Gramsci is very clear in stating that Fordism was anti-union in intent and independent of welfare state intervention.

This perspective on Fordism epitomizing corporate hegemony

(or "welfare capitalism" as some call it) in the production process reached its zenith between the two world wars. It incorporated workers' know-how in managerial practice, enhancing the process of technological innovation, with the assembly line setting the pace of production for the reduced numbers of workers in jobs that were not mechanized.

The debasement of labor through fragmentation of job, combined with the Babbage principle of maximizing the allocation of differently priced labor (Braverman 1974) led to worker absenteeism and resistance that was partially overcome by wage increases. This enabled workers to buy the cars they made and helped forestall cycles of overproduction and underconsumption in automobile and other industries within the monopoly sector.

The institutionalization of state intervention that the Regulationists identify with "monopoly regulation," or their version of Fordism, postdated the welfare capitalism that Gramsci identified with Fordism by two decades. "Welfare capitalism" offered only a tentative security and privileges associated with work in corporations integrated on a national basis, such as Ford and General Electric. The pensions and paid vacations that workers without a legal footing for their own unions wrested from capital in the early decades of the twentieth century were a pittance that did not allow them to expand their initiatives in a wider political field. Without the countervailing action of labor organized in nationally integrated trade unions in the 1930s that came of age in the post-World War II environment, capitalism might have led decades earlier to the crisis we now face.[3] By applying the term Fordism to the period that peaked after the introduction of state regulation, Lipietz conflates the corporate welfare period of the early twentieth century with New Deal regulation. This obscures the important transition in the labor process from corporate domination to trade union intervention following the legalization of trade unions. Although the Regulationists distinguish Fordism of the 1930s as a new "monopoly" mode of regulation, they extol Ford and Keynes as exemplars of the "great compromise" and the "virtuous world order" (Lipietz 1982:14), but it is grafted on to a Gramscian root that is contradictory to the governmental matrix that rescued the earlier phase of corporate welfarism from the depression. The defining characteristics of the compromise were worked out with government negotiators introducing the cost of living component during the wage freeze of the war years and the productivity ratios defining wage increases in the postwar period. The importance of the military industrial complex sustaining high rates of profits through growing demands for "defensive" armaments is reduced in a theory that focuses on enlightened action of a few opinion leaders in business and government.

CORPORATE HEGEMONY IN PITTSFIELD

The holistic analysis of an industrializing community in the United States gives us an insight into the multiple countervailing tendencies that influence the development of institutional controls adding up to a mode of regulation. I shall briefly assess the developments in the labor process in Pittsfield, Massachusetts, where I did fieldwork from 1982 to 1986[4] to show how the capital labor process developed in the period from 1903 when General Electric bought a thriving local plant producing power transformers, to the postwar era that is central to what the Regulationists call the Fordist regime.

In the period of oligopolistic control that began in the third quarter of the nineteenth century, the General Electric Corporation, formed in 1876, expanded with the purchase of several owner-operated plants including the Stanley Electric Company in Pittsfield.[5] Under the leadership of Gerard Swope during and after World War I, "Fordism" found a parallel in "General Electricalism" (Nash 1989). The company inaugurated a pension plan, credit operations for purchasing major appliances by the workers, and a wage almost double that earned in the textile mill that survived the first movement south in the latter part of the nineteenth century. Although the gains were not as dramatic as those won by auto workers in the Ford Plant, the workers at General Electric during the interwar years enjoyed slightly more security than those in competitive industries in the same community.

Despite monopolistic accumulation that Gordon, Edwards, and Rich identify with bureaucratic controls, the corporations persisted in exercising repressive controls over the work force. The General Electric Company resorted to Pinkerton detectives and special Metropolitan Police from Boston when the workers went out on strike in 1916 and 1918, and black and Portuguese "temporary" workers were hired in each of these conflicts. Any workers who were suspected of organizing a union were fired and blackmarked, preventing them from finding employment in most other factories. Management forestalled any direct negotiation with the multiple craft unions representing the skilled work force of machinists, machine tool makers, and winders, throughout the interwar period until 1940 when the United Electrical and Radio Workers with the backing of the newly formed National Labor Relations Board won a contract with General Electric representing the workers.

The wage-freeze and no-strike pledge during World War II imposed constraint on the newly won power of the unions. When the corporations refused to yield to the demand for wage increases after the war, massive labor strikes swept industry. The show of power by the unions alerted corporate leaders to the need to devise new strategies of control. The cold war and the anti-communist campaign endorsed by politicians as well as corporate leaders provided a pretext for dividing the unions and the rank and file. The United Electrical Workers lost over half its membership to the International Union of Electrical, Radio and Machine Workers, and the political agenda was lost along with many of the leaders.

The General Electric Company became a leader in managerial circles in the 1950s, and their labor relations were emulated throughout the industry and beyond. The labor relations director, Lemuel Boulware, who was promoted to vice president in the corporate hierarchy (possibly because of the newly recognized importance of labor relations) was able to undercut the role of negotiations by a technique in which management entered contract talks with a "firm, fair offer," incorporating the basic hopes and expectations of workers that were assessed by preliminary survey research techniques, and never deviating from this throughout the negotiations (Boulware 1969). The General Electric labor negotiations under Boulware were later censured by the National Labor Relations Board, but the failure of the corporation to bargain in good faith allowed them to keep trade unions on the defensive throughout the 1960s, weakened as they were by anti-communist campaigns that split the unions in the 1950s and 1960s. It was not until some of the union leaders, including Jim Matles (Matles and Higgins 1974) and Al Litano at the Pittsfield plant, achieved coordinated bargaining by the time of the 1969 strike were they able to achieve unity.

Gramsci's genius in developing the concept of Fordism was to emphasize the importance of public relations in creating the conditions for corporate hegemony to thrive, an issue that is neglected by the Regulationists. Throughout the 1950s and 1960s the corporations perfected their control over the media, whipping up anti-communist hysteria and successfully identifying any political behavior in the workplace as communist-inspired. Ronald Reagan gained his training in labor control during his years as public relations agent for the General Electric Company in the 1950s. A shop steward working in the plant at that time told me that when Reagan arrived in town he would get a briefing from labor relations men who would tell him what foremen were unpopular and what issues were bothering the workers before he went into the plant. In his pep talk to raise worker morale (and productivity), he targeted the unpopular supervisors in a joking manner that implied that he (and the corporation) were on their side. His promises of relief in these sessions often bore fruit in the firing of the unpopular foreman and reforms of at least the minor abuses in the system.

Even within the General Electric plant, distinct labor control systems coexisted. Bureaucratic control responding to the labor contract applied only to hourly workers while a large and growing force of exempt workers, what the General Electric Company called "individual contributors," did not punch in a time card and had greater latitude in their work schedules. The latest tactic in the labor control system is the threat of closure. This is explicitly outlawed by National Labor Relations Act, yet it was frequently played upon in the guise of briefing sessions on the state of the company. Workers were called together on company time throughout the decade of the 1980s to hear the divisional superintendent's report on the market, usually interlaced with promptings on the need for greater productivity to remain competitive. Workers accepted these reports in good faith, raising their levels of output and cooperating as far as possible in a setting where wage compression and the abolishing of incentive-piece rate systems had diminished the reward for effort. It was this tactic that played on the faith of the workers that they most resented when the Power Transformer Division was closed down in 1986 and General Electric formed a joint venture firm with Westinghouse in Canada to produce power transformers. In this case, the company was escaping antitrust regulations that forbade the linking of two companies in the same industry in the United States.

While I was doing fieldwork in Pittsfield the repressive management policies in a garment firm employing about a hundred people, principally female workers, was reminiscent of nineteenth-century firms. The owner-manager simply fired people when they attempted to organize the firm, then threatened the women physically, even driving his Cadillac into their picket line when they went out on strike. The paternalistic management in the Rice Silk Mill, which produces braid and specialty products, recruited their labor force from among women married to General Electric workers in a conscious effort to avoid the burden of health-care benefits that their husbands had, or the problems caused by laying off workers when production schedules slowed down. The individualized labor management relations of the Rice Company, for example, allowing each worker to take their birthday off and handing out turkeys at Thanksgiving and, most importantly, allowing the female-dominated labor force to have considerable flexibility in their working schedule, enabled them to successfully avoid trade union organization throughout the century that they had been in operation. Similar attention to individual workers' needs and interests in the 200-year-old Crane Paper Company to some extent made up for the lower paycheck than that received by General Electric employees. Women in the predominantly female work force at this firm considered themselves to be free of the sexual harassment that they claimed was endemic in the General Electric plant.

Spinoffs from the production units that were shut down by the General Electric Company spawned the twenty or so small plastic firms, each employing a dozen to over 100 workers, that exercised variations on the paternalistic model of management. The one larger firm that employed over a hundred workers was bought from an owner-managed company by Ethyl Corporation when the oil companies were trying to take advantage of their control over oil supplies in the 1970s by buying out petrochemical production sites that went out of business when their employees organized a union.

The coexistence of these small industrial firms with the single dominant corporation stabilized employment levels and provided alternative employment for family members of General Electric workers. The multiplicity of firms also provided scope for a variety of managerial practices that did not follow sequential, evolutionary developments in the labor control process but rather represented multiple strategies that, once initiated, remained in the repertoire of control mechanisms. The labor control system in the garment factory is reminiscent of what Regulationists would assign to the earlier age of the "competitive mode of regulation" than to the "monopoly mode of regulation." By ignoring such coexistent labor control systems, the Regulationists miss the supports for the system that lie beyond the purview of the hegemonic mode of regulation. The loss of these firms in the trend toward conglomerate buyouts in the 1970s and 1980s exacerbated the decline in the economy since they no longer acted as balancing mechanisms.

Hegemonic control throughout the period in which General Electric company dominated the economy of the city inhibited militant action by the labor force within its orbit. The only militant labor action that took place in the 1980s was carried out by a predominantly female-employed work force in a garment factory and the nurses in the Berkshire Medical Center. The exclusion of these workers from the agenda of union organization in preceding decades had left them outside the gains made by labor in the prosperous years up to the mid-1970s. As single heads of families, most of the garment workers were acutely conscious that their pay did not cover the costs of reproduction. The nurses' consciousness of exploitation came as the health "industry" abandoned the ethics of charitable morality in the rising commoditization of medical services. Aware of the enormous profits made in the medical center, they strove to increase their wage from $6.50 an hour to prevailing $10 hourly wages given to city garbage carriers and other service sector workers.

Pittsfield is becoming another ghost town, its working population only partially absorbed in the tourist and service sector that grew throughout the 1980s. Even this sector is in decline with the loss of an industrial base to maintain the restaurants, sports facilities, and redundant retail outlets that were the developers' answer to declining basic industries in the 1980s. The demise of the Power Transformer Division marks the decline of corporations and the Monopoly Mode of Regulation that went with it.

Despite the devastation already visible in the community as workers leave and real estate values decline, there is little overt expression of anger among the "primary" work force members formerly employed in the General Electric plant. In 1990 I returned to interview some of the workers in the random sample of 100 active and laid-off workers in 1982. None of my questions regarding blame or what should be done by the company or by government elicited any sense that the General Electric company had betrayed a trust. One worker laid off in 1986 who had accumulated a few shares of General Electric corporation in his decade at the plant stated that, as a shareholder, he understood the need to consider profits in determining whether to keep a plant open. The laid-off workers were more irritated at the union, which, up to the end, was fighting for seniority bumping rights at the same time that massive lay-offs were occurring. They supported the position that General Electric was in business for profits, sometimes reaffirming that they, as holders of GE stock, had the same vested rights in those goals and that they could not let any commitment to a community interfere with their decision to remain in production. These sentiments expressed by younger workers who entered the work force after World War II contrast with those of the older work force now retired who spoke more in terms of a social contract being undermined (Nash 1989).

Corporate hegemony was an effective means of "harmonizing" labor management relations in the plant and achieving an accord with the wider community through the 1980s. Research in a community-wide setting overcomes the unitary evolutionary scheme implied by terms such as repressive control, technical control (assembly line), bureaucratic control (collective bargaining and grievance procedures), and segmentation of the work force[6] or even more global concepts like Fordism that pose an evolutionary sequence from "competitive" to "monopoly" modes of regulation. With a holistic study we can perceive the distinct goals and strategies of firms that coexist in competitive labor markets and those in the monopoly sector. The very stability of the system depended upon an accommodation of the dominant company to smaller competitive firms within the same environment. This allowed some flexibility in the labor market, providing jobs for ancillary members of the family and alternative employment during changes in production schedules at the main plant. The hegemonic power of the corporation increasingly relied on the governmental mediation that was won by labor struggles first by giving unions bargaining power in the plant and then by providing welfare benefits and unemployment income when the corporation withdrew production. Fordism as a unified vision of the hegemonic process operating in nascent and late capitalism fails to capture distinct moments in the rise and decline of corporate hegemony and the variety of coexistent enterprises with distinct labor processes that facilitate the operation of the monopoly sector. The lack of correspondence between regimes of accumulation and modes of regulation that figure as the driving force in Regulation theory deprives the theory of predictive as well as analytical power (Brenner and Glick 1991).

NEWLY INDUSTRIALIZED COUNTRIES AND THE OLD INDUSTRIAL ORDER

By the 1960s the attempt to overcome a declining rate of profit in core industrial countries led to investment in overseas branches by large multinational corporations seeking a low-waged labor force. This move and the rationale for it were distinct from the strategies leading to the rise of corporate capitalism. It defeated the balance of forces between labor and capital that created the conditions for Fordism in the "core" countries as well as in the "periphery." In the old industrial centers it weakened the ability of labor to maintain the defenses they had constructed in the postwar period while in the developing areas it drew the most indefenseless sector of the labor force into production, participating in the patriarchal oppression of those societies to exploit young women in off-shore[7] operations that moved as soon as there was a hint of labor organization (Afshar 1985; Nash and Fernandez-Kelly 1983). Even in the newly industrialized countries[8] military force backed by international sanctions maintains the low wages that were their major advantage as a site of production.[9]

If Fordism is an inappropriate term for industrial core countries after World War II, "peripheral Fordism" is even more at variance in its overseas extension. "Peripheral Fordism" in Lipietz terms— mass production combined with a concern for underconsumption in the Third World—is a contradiction of the basic principles of Fordism. As Amsden (1990) points out, in the late industrialization of South Korea, Taiwan, India, Brazil, Mexico, and possibly Turkey, neither Taylorism nor intensive private capitalist accumulation characterize industrial development. The Asian industrialization from the early postwar Japanese development stressed learning on the shop floor of borrowed technologies that emphasized the participation of workers in the quality control at each step of production. Furthermore the state promoted industry through a variety of measures, including nationalized banks, export subsidies for textiles as production outstripped national demand, promotion of technological innovation and managerial skills, and manipulation of currency exchange.

A perspective that sees late industrialization as an extension of capitalist enterprises characteristic of mature economies misses the special dynamic not only of the Asian countries but also in Mexico and other Latin American countries. The import substitution program promoted by Raul Prebisch, Secretary of the Economic Commission for Latin America in the 1950s, relied upon government initiatives in capital formation, protective tariffs, and subsidies. While national industries enjoyed the kind of regulation of workers conditions paralleling the monopoly sector of the United States, the majority of workers were in the competitive sector or in self-generated enterprises in the informal economy. It is precisely the nationalized industries of the protected sector that are being undermined by the economic liberalization programs established as a condition for the repayment of debt in the crisis that peaked in the 1980s. The future of industrialization in Mexico will depend on the kinds of enterprises that will be generated by the North American Free Trade Agreement rather than a nationally based covenant between capital and labor.

In the new industrial frontiers, consumption in the developed centers has become the engine of production in the peripheral areas, giving ever-increasing importance to international servicing and information agents that coordinate demand and supply. Mahane (1987) uses Benneton as an example of the linkage from factory to market with computer transmitted information recorded in consumer outlets that allow the managers to determine new output. In this new age not only are technicians, technical draftsmen, and engineers eliminated, but the factory itself as a site of labor-management conflicts. The resulting decline in trade unions is accompanied by the decline in left political party support for welfare measures contained in the Monopoly Mode of Regulation.

CONCLUSION

The very unevenness in production processes within both highly industrialized countries and newly industrializing countries as well as that existing between such nations produces the contradictions that challenge at the same time that they support the existing hegemonic structures of monopoly capitalism. The super exploitation of marginalized workers within the advanced capitalist countries sustained the balance within communities and families that enabled the corporations to grant concessions to the core of organized workers in stable jobs. Pittsfield's competitive firms helped establish the stability that is often attributed to monopoly capitalist firms. By employing less-favored segments of the work force who are integrated oftentimes through kin and marriage to workers in the General Electric who enjoyed better benefits, these firms reinforced the stability of family and community that is not recognized either by Regulationists or by the sociology of work. Recognition of the wider range of relations affecting workers makes for greater success in trade union organization.[10]

This balance has been extended abroad in the overseas investments that enlarge the scope of multinational firms to exert control over the economy of entire nations. In the current period of global integration it is clear that what happens in the industrialized centers is tied to developments in what was called the periphery.

As nation states lose their control over their economies, workers cannot rely on government mediation to wage the battle. Nor can labor organizations continue to favor a select core of male or ethnic privileged workers when industries have the option of locating production sites in a world setting. The qualitative increase in concentration and centralization of capital brought about by the global integration of large corporations and financial institutions has reduced the power of the state to overcome the impact of a falling rate of profit on workers either in core or peripheral industrial sites (Mandel 1983:500).

The new dynamic of globalization clearly required a paradigmatic shift. As yet the alternative theories to classical Marxism have failed to meet the challenge. Postindustrial models failed to address the dynamic set in motion by the new international arena, and, in their attempt to address it, the peripheral-Fordist model ignores the cultural and social differences that affect the mode of regulation in newly industrial states. Regulationists also fail to capture the innovative tactics in the accumulation of capital through nationalized controls and the intensification of surplus value through participatory management on the shop floor in the newly industrializing countries.

Jameson (1989:44) sees in this diversity of coexisting modes of production the postmodern condition as a transition between two stages of capitalism as it becomes restructured on a global scale.[11] This vision of the postmodern condition comes from the pockets of global culture that now exist in cities that serve the new elites, but like Post-Industrial, Post-Fordist, and Regulationist concepts, Jameson includes in his postmodern perspective the arenas of regeneration. The shattering of the privileged position of unionized workers in large corporations in declining industrial areas may indeed provide a new basis for solidarity with discriminated segments of the working class in the newly industrializing countries. In the "new world order" with highly mobile and aggressively transnational business capital, unions are beginning to see that they too must go global. The United Electrical Workers, always a leading union, has begun to subsidize organizers at Mexican plants of the General Electric Company. Other examples of international action by unions cited by David Moberg (The *New York Times* December 19, 1993:F13) include the Farm Labor Organizing Committee helping its Mexican counterpart to win a stronger contract with the Campbell Soup Company when the company threatened to move south if they called a strike and the aid given by the International Association of

Machinists in getting South African workers who were locked out of the Crown Cork and Seal Company rehired by threatening to make their plight part of the American union's negotiation. After two decades of losing jobs to low-wage countries, the unions are becoming increasingly aware that they can only hold their own by expanding into the international labor arena.[12]

Just as Marx's vision of the vanguard of the revolutionary proletariat rising from the advanced frontiers of nineteenth-century industries caused him to ignore the marginalized proletariat of a backward Russian feudal society, so may a view focusing on core industrial centers ignore the frontiers of this future stage of capitalism. It is more likely that the new class struggle is emerging in the frontier economies where export-oriented investments are occurring in Asia, Latin America, and Africa. Jameson is one of the few prophets of the postmodern condition who envisions a new international proletariat rising in the convulsive upheaval we face. Even when these struggles are expressed in feminist demands of women in the new export processing zones or in neighborhood movements demanding basic services in the abandoned older industrial centers or the mushrooming barrios of the unemployed in cities of the South (considered globally), there is a potential basis for class-based action. In these areas the awareness of alternative social relations that fires rebellion may yet persist.[12]

As yet the common interests shared by workers in the North as well as South, in service as well as in assembly production, have rarely been articulated in international circuits. The World Federation of Trade Unions and International Confederation of Free Trade Unions, representing the interests of both First and Second World workers, underwrote an alliance with international corporations by accepting a wage differential in core and peripheral areas (Nash 1983:25). Now that the corporations have rejected their part of the bargain as they enter into an international labor pool to drive down wages in core industrial states, and now that the class interests of wage workers are no longer mediated in the cold war opposition of the communist and anticommunist camp, workers throughout the world may find the basis for common action. If this should happen, the explosive potential will exceed the expectations of theorists predicated on past models.

NOTES

1. The theory of Post-Industrialism encountered reactions ranging from enthusiastic responses to guarded skepticism. The binary ideal type

posed in the industrial/postindustrial model produced a spate of articles patterned on Redfield's (1941) folk urban model wherein Post-Industrialism is said to allow people to return to the communalistic values of a preindustrial period, finding self-realization and the overcoming of alienation (Trist 1976). The decline in the proportion of the labor force engaged in industry in the period from the turn of the century to 1972 was from 38 percent to 32 percent at the same time that the proportion of workers in agriculture dropped from 38 to 4 percent and in service rose from 24 to 64 percent.

2. Savitch (1989) included London, Paris, New York, and Tokyo as his postindustrial cities. While financial institutions and communication centers are best developed in those centers, the coexistence of these cities with Third World megalopolises changes the dynamic of how they relate to the world system.

3. Rustin (1989) coincides in the view that "Fordism" understates the importance of political and class factors in achieving a temporary settlement. Although Regulationists are careful to state that the gains were won by pressure from the working-class struggle, their focus on elite spokespersons, such as Ford and Keynes, relegate the masses to a behind-the-scenes pressure group, operating like a Greek chorus to affirm the words of the leaders.

4. Research carried out in 1982 and 1985 was supported by the National Science Foundation and National Endowment for the Humanities grants. Some of my findings are contained in *From Tank Town to High Tech; The Clash of Community and Corporate Cycles* (Nash 1989).

5. Passer (1953) shows how the major electrical machinery producing companies assisted each other in controlling the market by driving out of business or swallowing up companies that competed with them, bringing patent suits against innovating industrialists such as Stanley.

6. The implicit evolutionary sequence in these labor control systems in Gordon, Edwards, and Reich's (1982) *Segmented Work, Divided Labor* is also featured in the Regulationists. The tendency to equate the gains of labor in the 1930s with the compromise that came after the anticommunist movement launched by the Cold War in 1948, negates the significance of union autonomy. It was expressed earlier in the "end of ideology" viewpoint—Kerr, Dunlop, Harbison and Myers (1962) and Lipset (1964), with equally unproductive results. Based on extensive interviews with the leaders who built the unions in the 1930s in Pittsfield (Nash 1989), I feel that there was an important moment when labor realized its power in the late 1930s and then began to capitalize on it in the immediate post-World War II wave of strikes. It was not until 1948 with Truman's endorsement of the Cold War politics that the divisiveness of the anticommunist crusade broke the political role.

7. Off-shore implies the evasion of government regulation that inspires these operations. It is the antithesis of Keynesian controls assumed to be

the companion of Fordist regimes.

8. Newly industrialized countries as used by United Nations data sources include Hong Kong, Singapore, Taiwan, South Korea, India, Argentina, Brazil, Mexico, Spain, Portugal, Greece, and Yugoslavia. Some include Iran, Malaysisa, Pakistan, Philippines, and Thailand. These are sometimes referred to as semi-industrialized countries (Rhys 1985:59).

9. Kim (1990) details the means by which Korean workers are intimidated in their attempts to organize workers in national and multinational branches of electronic firms. Enloe (1989) reviews the militarization accompanying industrialization in the Pacific.

10. Lipsig-Mumme (1989) shows that Canadian labor unions maintained membership and even grew somewhat during the decline of U.S. trade union membership in the 1970s and 1980s. She attributes this to the inclusion of a wider range of objectives in organized labor.

11. Frederick Jameson (1989) comments on Mandel's rescuing the analysis of the current stage of capitalism from the "colonization" by the right-wing theorists of postindustrialism with his book, *Late Capitalism*. He attributes his own theorizing on postmodernism to the influence this book had on him.

12. Based on studies of the work force in the 1970s, Mann (1973: 32 et seq.) found the most active awareness of alternative social relations in production among workers in Italy and France. He attributes their greater class consciousness to the "reinforcing effects of traditional and idiosyncratic contradictions" (Mann 1978:67). With the intersection of archaic and advanced technological industries in Italy and France, the coexistence of class conflict with individual alienation bringing about revolutionary consciousness is more likely to be found than in working-class movements of the United States and Great Britain where the reformist solutions are sought.

REFERENCES

Aglietta, Michael
1979   *A Theory of Capitalist Revelation: The U.S. Experience.* London: Verso.

1982   World capitalism in the 80's. *New Left Review* 136 (Nov.-Dec.)

Afshar, Haleh, ed.
1985   *Women, Work, and Ideology in the Third World.* London: Tavistock.

Amsden, Alice
1990   Third world industrialization: "Global Fordism" or a new model? *New Left Review* 182:5-32.

Bell, Daniel
1973   *The Coming of Post-Industrial Society; A Venture in Social Forecasting.* New York: Basic Books.

Boulware, Lemuel R.
1969   *The Truth about Boulwarism: Trying to Do Right Voluntarily.* Washington, D.C.: Bureau of National Affairs.

Braverman, Harry
1974   *Labor and Monopoly Capital.* New York: Monthly Review Press.

Brenner, Robert, and Mark Glick
1991   The Regulation School and the West's economic impasse. *New Left Review* 188:45–121.

Burawoy, Michael
1979   *Manufacturing Consent; Changes in the Labor Process under Monopoly Capitalism.* Chicago: University of Chicago Press.

Enloe, Cynthia H.
1990   *Bananas, Beaches, and Bases: Making Feminist Sense of International Politics.* Berkeley: University of California Press.

Ferlerger, Lou, and Jay R. Mandle
1987   Democracy and productivity in the future American economy. *Review of Radical Political Economy,* 19(4):1–15.

Gordon, D., R. C. Edwards, and M. Reich
1982   *Segmented Work, Divided Workers; The Historical Transformation of Labor in the United States.* Cambridge: Cambridge University Press.

Gramsci, Antonio
1973   Americanism and Fordism. In *Prison Notes.* New York: International Publishers, pp. 277–320.

Habermas, Jurgen
1979   Legitimation problems in the modern state. In *Communication and the Evolution of Society,* Translation of talk given in 1974. Boston: Beacon Press.

Hall Stuart
1988   Brave new world. *Marxism Today* :24–9.

Howe, Carolyn
1986   The politics of class compromise in an international context: Considerations for a new strategy for labor. *Review of Radical Political Economy* 18(3):1–22.

Jameson, Frederic
1989   Marxism and postmodernism. *New Left Review* 176 (July/Aug): 31–46.

Jessup, Bob
1987   Regulation theory, Post-Fordism and the state: More than a reply to Werner Benefield. *Capital and Class* 147:147–68.

Kerr, C., J. T. Dunlop, F. H. Harbison, and C. A. Myers
1962   *Industrialism and Industrial Man.* London: Heinemann.

Kim, Seung Keung
1990   Capitalism, patriarchy and autonomy: Women factory workers in the Korean economy. Ph.D. thesis, Cuny Graduate Center.

Krasner, Stephen
1985   *Structural Conflict; The Third World against Global Liberalism.* Berkeley: University of California Press.

Lipietz, Alain
1982   Towards global Fordism. *New Left Review* 132.

1987   *Mirages and Miracles; The Crisis of Global Fordism.* Translated by David Macey. London: Verso.

Lipset, S. M.
1964   The changing class structure and contemporary European politics. *Daedelus* 93.

Lipsig-Mumme, Carla
1989   Canadian and American unions respond to economic crisis. *Journal of Industrial Relations* 31(2):229–56.

Mahane, Riahine
1987   From Fordism to ?; new technology, labour markets and unions. *Economic and Industrial Democracy* 8(1):5–60.

Mandel, Ernest
1983   *Late Capitalism.* London: Verso.

Mann, Michael
1973   *Consciousness and Action Among the Western Working Class.* New York: Macmillan.

Matles, James, and James Higgins
1974   *Them and Us: Struggles of a Rank and File Union.* Englewood Cliffs, NJ: Prentice-Hall.

Meyer, Stephen III
1981   *The Five Dollar Day; Labor Management at Ford Motor Company 1908–1921.* Albany: State University of New York Press.

Murray, Robin
1988   Life after Henry (Ford). *Marxism Today.* (Oct) :24–29.

Nash, June

1983   The impact of the changing international division of labor on different sectors of the labor force. In J. Nash and M. P. Fernandez-Kelly, eds., *Women, Men, and the International Division of Labor.* Albany: State University of New York Press, pp. 3–38.

1989   *From Tank Town to High-Tech; The Clash of Community and Industrial Cycles.* Albany: State University of New York Press.

Nash, June and M. Patricia Fernandez-Kelly

1983   *Women, Men, and the International Division of Labor.* Albany: State University of New York Press.

Passer, Harold

1953   *The Electrical Manufacturers 1875–1900; A Study in Competition, Entrepreneurship, Technical Change, and Economic Growth.* Cambridge: Harvard University Press.

Prebisch, Raul

1959   Commercial policy in the underdeveloped countries. *American Economic Review,* (49):251–73.

Redfield, Robert

1941   *The Folk Culture of Yucatan.* Chicago: University of Chicago Press.

Rhys, Jenkins

1985   Internationalization of capital and the semi-industrialized countries: The case of the motor industry. *Review of Radical Political Economy* 17 (1/2):59–81.

Rustin, Michael

1989   The politics of post-Fordism, or the trouble with new times. *New Left Review* 175 (May-June).

Safa, Helen I.

1981   Runaway shops and female employment: The search for cheap labor. *Signs* 7(2):418–33.

Sassen, Saskia

1992   *The Global Cities: Tokyo London and New York.* Princeton, NJ: Princeton University Press.

Savitch, W.

1989   *The Post-Industrial City.* Baltimore: Johns Hopkins University Press.

Touraine, Alain

1971   *The Post-Industrial Society; Tomorrow's Social History: Classes, Conflicts and Culture in the Programmed Society.* New York: Random House.

Trist, Eric
1976   Toward a postindustrial culture. In R. Dubin, ed. *Handbook of Work, Organization, and Society*. Chicago: Rand McNally, pp. 1011–31.

Williams, Gwynn A.
1960   Gramsci's concept of hegemony. *Journal of the History of Ideas*. 21:5786–99.

8

The Contingent Character of the American Middle Class

Contending as I do that the middle class is a category that can be treated as a group—albeit, a dynamic one—first requires justification as it flies in the face of conventional social science wisdom. Not only do we as social scientists tend to consider that class and status intersect, so that an individual's own standing is not bound by class boundaries, but that the stratification system itself is a continuum and maintained so by both intragenerational and intergenerational mobility. This is still not inconsistent with studying the elite and the poor as groups because the former does act in terms of group interest on occasion and the latter should even when they cannot. In contrast, the middle class has not entered the political arena mobilized around class interests per se. On particular economic issues, it is often divided; many issues, such as generational or urban rural differences, matter far more than class identity.

The concept of a middle class, Lockwood (1992) argues, enters into classical social science debate either as a contradictory class that is on the verge of collapse (Marx) or as a product and instrument of industrialization (Weber) or as a proxy for moral classification that offsets the unstable conditions of modernity (Durkheim).

The idea that the middle class is important for social control and stabilization—for good or for bad—is not new. It was Aristotle who probably first recognized the existence of the urban middle class when he drew attention to its buffering role in a stratified society. His claim was that it protected the poor from the exploitation by the rich and powerful and, at the same time, protected the rich and powerful from the plots and intrigues of the aggrieved lower classes. "For where some possess much, and the others nothing, there may arise an extreme—either out of the most rampant democracy, or out of an oligarchy" (1943:191). Tocqueville in describing preindustrial conditions in America shared Aristotle's concerns, specifically, that in the absence of an articulated middle class, the very conditions of political and economic equality may make it difficult for citizens to "preserve their independence against the aggressions of power" (Tocqueville 1945, vol. 1:56).

CLASS AND STRATA

In the absence of any evidence that members of the middle class have forged bonds with the working class, as Marx and Engels predicted, and without a clear statement by Durkheim on the social and economic nature of social class, the more complex Weberian conception of the independence of status and class prevailed in American social science. Indeed, the decades following World War II brought considerable optimism. The middle class was expanding due to affluence and increasing opportunities for white-collar workers in the service sector (Dahrendorf 1959). Systematic, empirical work focused on the gradations of social class, which itself was conceptualized as a composite of occupational prestige, income, and education, and also on the dynamics of social mobility.

This is not to say that categorical classes have been ignored in the social sciences, but the focus has been on those groups who have masterfully—or luckily—secured their economic fortunes, notably the very rich (Domhoff 1974, Veblen [1899] 1953), and also on those groups whose economic well-being is imperilled, notably the inner-city blacks (Wilson 1987) and the homeless (Rossi 1989). One suspects the middle class has been ignored because its members were doing so well. They neither needed to be unmasked nor did they need advocates. Also, it was said, they are just too boring. As anthropologist John Gulick (1973:234) wrote, "I think that middle class American culture is probably the last culture in the world that most American anthropologists would want to study." But about fifteen years later, an important book on the middle class was published by anthropologist, Katherine Newman (1988). It is called, *Falling From Grace: The Experience of Downward Mobility in the American*

Middle Class, and Newman was one of the first to recognize the precarious economic conditions of white-collar workers.

JUSTICE UNDERPINNINGS OF CLASS

As I have noted, social scientists abandoned the idea of group-based classifications, arguing that class is a reification or deflects attention from the empirical observation that income, prestige, and education are resources that are located on a continuum. However, there are two compelling reasons why class remains a useful concept. The first is empirical and relates to people's perceptions of class differences, and the second is related to issues in moral philosophy. At the core, these are closely connected.

When people are asked about the society in which they live and where they locate themselves, they describe a class structure of different distinguishable segments and situate themselves in one of these segments. In research on capitalist Australia and post-communist Hungary, Evans, Kelley, and Kolosi (1993) report that individuals describe the past and the present in terms of class divisions. In other words, people perceive their societies not in terms of gradations of socioeconomic strata but in essentialist class terms, and they will "read" their nation's history in terms of the shifts in the relative sizes of classes. Evans et al. (1992) report that when Hungarians and Australians were asked what type of society they preferred, 80 percent of the individuals in each of the two samples said they preferred a equalitarian class system, while only 24 percent of the Australians described their country in these terms and only 40 percent of the Hungarians did. One inference I draw from this research is that when individuals are asked to stand apart from the stakes they have in their occupational attainments, earnings, and lifestyle—the bread and butter of self interest—they articulate class differences in frameworks of justice.

Historically, reform has been more effective when it is linked with the articulation of group inequalities, not that of individual inequalities. The former is more likely to lead to fundamental change; the latter usually results only in minor tinkering—adjustments in income-tax brackets, unemployment benefits, or in tax deductions. Notwithstanding the notable lack of persuasiveness of Marx in reform-minded circles, Himmelfarb (1991) traces the success of Charles Booth and Seebohm Rowntree in persuading Victorians of the shocking conditions of the English urban poor, which led to a series of ameliorative acts aimed at improved housing, working conditions, wages, and child welfare. Booth, though no socialist himself, was praised by Marxists and socialists alike for bringing about fundamental reform. Of Booth's eight social classes, four comprised the poor and the very poor, and together added up to 30.7 percent of the population of London. Rowntree's contributions shed further light on the meager diets of the poor. By focusing on the conditions that affected the lives of a substantial proportion of the London population, rather than on class polarization, and also in terms of groups rather than individuals, Booth and Rowntree stirred the conscience of Victorians—not only the rich but the shopkeepers and craftsworkers as well (whose support, it might be speculatively added, Marx and Engels would have had difficulty mustering).

Again, some contemporary economists are emphasizing that class is a set of categories, not a continuum. For example, Sen (1992), for reasons of public policy, distinguishes his own earlier work on distributional measures on economic inequality from his more recent analysis of groups in order to focus on intergroup variation. The argument is complex, but it essentially draws attention to systematic disparities that can be traced to sources of inequality due to class as well as to other differences, notably race, gender, region, age, and disability. Criticizing Rawls's conception that economic justice is procedural and deals with redress only in individual and noncontingent terms, Sen argues instead that justice involves intergroup comparisons—notably, interclass comparisons—and not individual ones. Moreover, other group differences are confounded with class. That is, justice evaluations and public policy then must take into account the empirical confounding of class with race and other group differences. Sen, thus, removes the blindfolds that constrain Rawls's judges, with the justification that class differences are systematically rooted in other group differences. Inequalities, in other words, are confounded.

It is owing to these considerations that I emphasize the categorical character of class. Somewhat perversely, however, I focus on the middle class, not the poor. I do so for three reasons. First, to understand the social and economic context of poverty in contemporary America, it is important to acknowledge the historical origins of the middle class and the more recent blurring of the lines between the poor and the middle class. Second, I contend that class formation is both economic and cultural. This is important for it sheds light on the origins of legitimacy and the codes of class boundaries and also clarifies how class differences can be pernicious. Third, I think we have missed the analytical point Marx made about the working class. Namely, if the emergence and the trajectory of the industrial proletariat was based on changing relations between workers and the mode of production and the owners of capital (of which there can be little doubt) so can the current changing situation of the middle class be understood in similar terms.

I have not lost sight of Sen's point but build upon it by contextualizing group differences. The middle class is embedded in relations with other classes, and the fact that the upper class is predominantly white and that the poor includes disproportionate numbers of minorities is an important consideration. Moreover, class relations cannot be understood outside of history—that is, to say, cohort differences within a class, the collective traditions of interclass relations, and the expectations that the members of a class have for their progeny. A moral philosophy of class must take into account the empirically based understandings of the social sciences.

EMBEDDEDNESS OF CLASS

The conventional wisdom in mid-twentieth century social science was that a modern industrial economy is the fail-safe generator of a national middle class, just as this national middle class is the lubricant of the industrial urban economy. The political institutions and economic arrangements that the middle class helped to create and greatly strengthened, it is widely believed, cannot fall prey to oligarches or give way to anarchy. This is because American democracy is synonymous with the market economy that rests on postulates of individual freedom and enterprise, which are, after all, what fashioned the American middle class.

But, ironically, just as social historians have mustered convincing evidence that the American middle class is relatively new, taking shape only after the Civil War, there are indications that the American middle class might unravel. I intend to briefly summarize the argument that the American middle class originated in the Gilded Age, flourished through the initial decades of the twentieth century, survived the worst of the Depression, and then rebounded after World War II. I will argue that the historical conditions that supported the economic foundations of the middle class are now fundamentally altered.

These considerations cannot resolve the paradox stated by Tocqueville, because Tocqueville's portrait of American society was drawn at a time when "wealth circulates with inconceivable rapidity" (Tocqueville 1945, vol. 1: 53) and (excluding the "Negroes and the

Indians"), Anglo-Americans were united by common opinions, a feeling of pride in a common government, and equality of fortune (vol. 1, esp. 405–19). Tocqueville could not have predicted the consequences of industrial growth for the differentiation of classes, for his comparison was between the vestiges of European aristocracy and its accompanying class lines and preindustrial America that had all of the earmarks of an equalitarian society.

The thesis of this chapter is that the once-robust American middle class is in jeopardy. This poses the Tocquevillian paradox in a new way. If it truly were to unravel and thereby create an increasingly large lower-middle class, with a gap between it and the professional and monied elite, questions about political stability would be raised anew. The conditions in America are very different from those in the early nineteenth century when Tocqueville wrote; there is greater ethnic and racial diversity, and this diversity is confounded with differences in economic resources.

To lay out the broad framework for my analysis, I treat class as a social category that is contingent on a set of economic conditions and cultural conventions. The social science conception that developed in the 1950s and 1960s cast the middle class as a diffuse and large segment of the population, including middle to high wage earners, salaried workers, and retirees and indeed, in cultural terms, conceived of the rich as embracing middle-class values that related to work and achievement. These rich were just more exuberant in the way they lived and played.

The distinctions that earlier helped to define the internal make up of the middle class—such as the white collar/blue collar line and the difference between salaried and wage earners—became increasingly less significant in the post-World War II era. So did the internal distinctions within the old middle class, such as between professionals and nonprofessionals or those between entrepreneurs and employees. However, in our postindustrial service economy, the dividing line between the middle class and the disadvantaged is perhaps becoming less distinct empirically, but as it defines a boundary of social and cultural distinction, it is becoming increasingly salient. The contradiction here is that the perceptions of those still economically secure are that the historical conditions of the success of the middle class—an expanding economy—is less the issue than the achievements of individuals. The increasingly weakening line between the middle class and the poor breeds competition for scarce resources. It also breeds myth-making; the rhetoric of individual achievement helps to create a rigid moral boundary between the have's and the have-not's.

It is because middle-class culture so successfully and insidiously engulfed the entire society, that as a social stratum it can now make no claims for itself except in the terms of its own historical prodigiousness. That is, as an economic and social entity it has sown the seeds of its own crisis of authenticity precisely because an ethos of cultural democracy that relates to the idea of work-hard-and-you-can-make-it is not at all contradictory to economic inequalities, undemocratic work organizations, and hierarchical social institutions. A full-scale depression would reveal the implications of this contradiction.

ECONOMY OR CULTURE?

The extent to which class is rooted in cultural or economic factors remains a powerful debate in the social sciences long after Marx's and Engels's work on class in the last century and Weber's response early in this century. In American social sciences, a rich tradition developed in community studies, in large part with the objective of disentangling economic from cultural components of class. While the Lynds (1937) elaborated the economic factors that defined and perpetuated class lines, Warner (Warner, Meeker and Eell (1960 [1949]) contended that the real differences were not so much economic as linked to the cultural significance of differences in lifestyle and occupations.

More currently, researchers working within this tradition, including Gans (1962) and Halle (1984), tend to be more sensitive to the interplay between economic and cultural factors, and the historical tradition that builds on the work of E. P. Thompson (1963) is also based on the premise that the cultural and political context has as much influence upon shaping consciousness and institutions of a social class as do economy and industrial development, but Thompson urges us to consider the historical conditions under which either economic or cultural factors predominate in the creation of class.

The lifestyle and institutions that provided the vital cultural identity of the American middle class in its early origins were contingent on a set of unique historical conditions. Paradoxically, these conditions involved both great initial economic inequalities followed by rapidly increasing affluence. In the first place, it can be argued that economic disparities are particularly important for the development of class awareness, but increasing affluence provided the wherewithal for creating a distinctive lifestyle that reflected class membership. Rules about class membership gave way as the cultural codes of the middle class became widely shared. The conditions that make this possible included the following: Many semiskilled and skilled blue-collar jobs paid more than white-collar jobs in the service sector; dual incomes helped to make family status ambiguous; family members were often extremely diverse in terms of income, education, and occupation; and, lifestyle differences were increasingly eroded as a result of the wide abundance of consumer products and broad participation in cultural and recreational activities.

It is useful to briefly summarize the importance of inequalities and affluence for the acquisition of class consciousness among the growing numbers of the assorted "middling folks" about 1870—the institutionally unorganized that included the self-employed, shopkeepers, store clerks, professionals, and petty merchants. The acquisition of a solid middle-class identify for such a miscellany was not fully appreciated by Marx, but nevertheless it was difficult to dismiss on the basis of historical scholarship.

One premise of my argument is that culture must be sufficiently articulated for it to be salient for marking class lines. However, under conditions of rapid social change, the cultural meanings become flaccid and barely relate to social categories. As Elias (1978) contends, when everyone eats with their hands, table manners do not play a role in distinguishing the rich from the poor. But under conditions of social rigidity, manners, accoutrement, demeanor, and lifestyle generally are powerful mechanisms of distinction. The process is a dialectical one because manners are invidiously destructive of class differences too; the acquisition of manners—Elias's metaphor for etiquette, dress, leisure preferences, accent, and a whole lot more— permits "passing" and thus increases social mobility. Herein lies a clue for understanding the expansion of the middle class and, at least as important, the widespread belief that the middle class has no fixed lower boundary.

A specific example is provided by Mukerji's (1983). In her carefully documented history of the role of calico in eighteenth-century England she explains how such a seemingly trivial item helped to fortify and then to destroy class differences. Calico, an expensive material imported from India, was a mark of rank and distinction for the wealthy and elite women in eighteenth-century England. Yet with the introduction of Arkwright's waterframe machine and new advances in bleaching and chemical dying, the mass production of calico expanded its availability to encompass a far larger segment of the population.

Thus, cultural capital interacts with economic opportunities and abets in the making and the unmaking of class. Under conditions of stagnation and scarcity, it creates and reifies class lines. Yet, under conditions of growth and expansion, cultural capital is highly fluid and it helps to undermine class differences.

HISTORICAL CONTEXT

The origins of the American middle class have been relatively ignored whereas scholarship has focused more on understanding the disparities between the very rich and the very poor in the nineteenth century. Social scientists (as well as novelists and journalists) have quite correctly deplored the hubris and social irresponsibility of the nineteenth-century wealthy and romanticized and decried the misfortunes of the nineteenth-century poor. There is no question that the economic conditions created by industrial wage labor, high rates of immigration, and the collapse of the southern economy after the Civil War, combined with the growing wealth of private capitalists, created glaring discrepancies between the rich and the poor. Estimates of wealth distribution for northern American cities around 1870 suggest that the top one-tenth of 1 percent had 15 percent of the wealth, and slightly over 50 percent of the population had no real or personal wealth (Soltow 1975; Gallman 1969).

Great inequalities were a fact of postbellum America, but it is also the case that there was unprecedented economic growth that affected the prospects of very large numbers of wage earners. While inequalities persisted, wages (in real dollars) increased about 50 percent between 1860 and 1890 (Long 1960). Increasing prosperity and industrial development generated a need for services—retailers, wholesalers, proprietors, shopkeepers, professionals, and clerks—that were distinct both from the class composed of industrialists and bankers and from the large class of wage earners and casual workers. In the midst of prevailing inequalities that were generated by industrialization but directly benefiting from growing affluence (also a product of industrialization) urban white-collar workers emerged as a distinct social class.

The work of Stuart Blumin (1989) provides a benchmark for research on nineteenth-century urban classes. What Blumin terms the "elusive Middle Class" emerged in the late nineteenth century out of the congeries of what were called "the middling sorts" in the late eighteenth and early nineteenth centuries. The growth of the middle class was possible owing to exactly the same economic conditions that created the wage-earning manufacturing class, specifically, technological developments, industrial growth, and improved overall economic conditions. What distinguished the white-collar middle class from the blue-collar working class were differences in occupational niches, family configurations, and these were reinforced by residential segregation and differences in household economy (see Archer 1991; Archer and Blau 1993; Thernstrom 1973).

According to Blumin (1989: 136), what was critical for the emergent identity of the middle class was the slow disappearance of the artisan class, which formed the fragile boundary between white-collar jobs and manual work. The shrinking numbers of artisans and skilled craftsmen helped to fortify the lines between white-collar and blue-collar workers and between nonmanual and manual labor.

Extending this argument I contend that these are the very structural conditions under which cultural factors became increasingly salient in the development of class identity. The very fact of glaring inequalities between, on the one hand, workers in sweatshops, slaughterhouses, and factories and, on the other hand, wealthy industrialists and bankers enabled the "middling folk" to extract and overprice the cultural codes of a white-collar lifestyle.

Lifestyle, Institutions, and Ecology

Partly because members of the urban working class—comprised of native and foreign-born manual workers—were residentially segregated and partly because of blue-collar attire, white-collar workers could forge a lifestyle that drew on upper-class models. But the middle class was not entirely aping the rich, as it was also creating its own social institutions, such as public universities (many sons and daughters of the rich went abroad to study), newspapers, voluntary associations, department stores, and libraries.

Class membership is not simply rooted in institutions and economic comfort, however, and in periods of high mobility, cultural edgework is serious business. Edgeworking class lines was rooted in moral self-righteousness, and the intolerance of working-class habits and behavior as well as contempt of conspicuous ethnic minorities—blacks, Orthodox Jews, Orientals—motivated zealous efforts to reform beer halls, vaudeville houses, public theaters, and common coquetry.

Late nineteenth-century culture was strongly rooted in urban ecology. Housing segregation and, therefore, access to amenities, helped to fortify differences in lifestyle. Writing about such differences, Trachtenberg (1982: 128) describes how housing reinforced the barriers between social classes. Sanitation—now trivial as a result of the universality of indoor plumbing—decisively divided houses and neighborhoods, establishing insidious social distinctions.

Yet if access to such amenities established conspicuous class differences, these, in turn, could be elaborated by subtle nuances in cultural expression and lifestyle. If there was one key symbol of the middle class in the decades following the Civil War, Gwendolyn Wright (1981) stresses it was the neighborhood and the fledgling suburb. In these decades neighborhoods took on a new meaning and form of social organization, and those who could afford a house away from crowded tenements bought into neighborhoods that were clearly segregated by ethnic, racial, and collar lines. The home, "how it was furnished, and the family life the housewife oversaw, contributed to the definition of the 'middle class,' at least as much as did the husband's income" (Wright 1981: 99). Historian J. M. Burns (1985: 119–26) describes in detail the household routines that as a composite distinguished the middle-class nineteenth-century family from its upper and working class counterparts. Education for the boys and proper training for the girls, a maid servant, small families, well-appointed parlors, and a modest carriage were important symbols that delineated middle-class from both upper-class and working-class lifestyles.

Trachtenberg (1982: 129) also draws attention to the cult of domesticity that emerged in the American city in the nineteenth century. "With the rise of food and clothing industries, domestic labor came to consist chiefly of budgeting and shopping rather than making. From the place of labor for self-support, the home had become the place of consumption. How to be a 'lady who does her own work' came very quickly after the Civil War to mean how to be a lady who shops; indeed who sustains herself as a 'lady' by wise and efficient shopping."

Edgeworking class lines also expressed itself in the most trivial pursuits. The link between social class formation and trivialities of daily life is described in the recent work of cultural historians, most notably in the book by John F. Kasson (1990). Established codes of behavior, he observes, were most highly evolving in the late nineteenth century as self-conscious assertions of bourgeois respectability. Symptomatic of an age with rapidly declining economic inequalities were great symbolic differences in social decorum and behavior. Yet, many of the daily routines of middle-class households rested on fine points of manners and household management that could be learned very easily from manuals of etiquette and guidebooks for home management. Emotional control, self-discipline, proper public deportment—the moral codes of the middle class—could more readily be cultivated than could wealth, a prominent lineage, or inherited prestige be acquired. Easy acquisition of these behaviors, as Norbert Elias (1978) has written, provides a mechanism for social leveling that strengthens the egalitarian character of a society.

But Kasson (1990) also suggests that these established codes of behavior often serve as a check against a fully democratic order and in support of special interests, institutions of privilege, and structures of domination. The reason is that the codes become increasingly subtle and rarefied, and, moreover, by their nuances and cost, generally had a slight lead over working-class aspirations. Yet, it must be noted that most members of the urban middle class were themselves parvenu, and in a booming economy class membership is not a zero-sum game. The subtleties of status distinction may be important in daily routines, but we might argue, along the lines of Goffman (1959), that daily routines can be staged so that in meaningful social realms many nuances can be finessed.

Declining Economic Equalities

Continued economic prosperity between 1900 and 1930 fostered sufficient opportunities for the expansion of a middle-class lifestyle more broadly than ever before in history. New technologies of the late nineteenth century and early twentieth century brought bicycles, plumbing, electricity, the phonograph, sewing machines, and radio into virtually all urban households. Once gentrified, middle-class institutions, such as baseball, the penny press, the department store, national celebrations, and parades fostered democratic participation as they cut across class and ethnic lines (Barth 1980; see also Ryan 1989). Even national private organizations that were administered by wealthy elites, were, according to Hall (1982), remarkably interconnected with the diverse public through dependence on common personnel and institutions.

The decades between 1900 and 1930 were critical for the consolidation of the American middle class. Abundant consumer goods, improved conditions of work, and declines in unemployment led to genuine change in the lives of all Americans (Jacoby 1985). Mass credit meant that houses and a little later, automobiles, were within reach of millions of working families (Lebergott 1984: 436), and the restriction of immigration undoubtedly contributed to the sense of security for a largely white, white-collar class. Except for the very rich—who could draw on reserves—and the very poor—notably the blacks, who were the last hired and the first fired—the Depression had a random effect on all groups in the middle, and, furthermore, the common hostility against wealthy business leaders probably helped to strengthen the idea of the middle class.

The end of the Depression also meant the beginning of the gradual decline in economic inequalities. The expansion of white-collar and salaried workers was made possible by high rates of college attendance and the ever-increasing demand for skilled workers. And, the prosperity that followed World War II accelerated both these trends.

The federated middle class of the mid-twentieth century was built on the bedrock of expanding economic and educational opportunities. High rates of mobility permitted the vast diffusion of manners, lifestyle, home decor, and leisure patterns. Nationalism that grew out of the Second World War probably helped as much to promote feelings of a common destiny as did the virtual universality of Sears and Roebuck catalogs, Victory Gardens, and the war-time switch from butter to margarine. Moreover, the national media were impervious to differences in geography, language, accent, and race. The same media that advertised the products that would assemble a middle-class household helped to clarify and diffuse a morality that dictated standards of child rearing, church attendance, sexuality, and appropriate gender roles. Although the American middle class had an initial monopoly on forms of cultural capital in the early part of the century, by mid-century the rules whereby they could be acquired were widely known and readily accepted.

Whereas in nineteenth-century America, the initial economic distinction between manual and nonmanual workers could be expressed in symbolic and cultural terms and fortified in urban institutions, residence, and lifestyle, in the 1940s and 1950s, claims to middle-class respectability and success became increasingly easy to make, and, in the presence of sufficient opportunities for upward mobility, they were so authentically.

My own analyses (Blau 1989) suggests that the great importance of the middle class—not the rich elites—is the adoption of cultural practices and the creation of cultural tastes. The main explanation for the diffusion of opera and radio, chamber music and television, theater and rock concerts is the relative size of the middle class in an urban place. And, regardless of their own education and income, individuals who live in predominantly middle-class communities are likely to be consumers of culture (Blau and Quets, 1989). That is, it is concluded that cultural tastes and habits are more a function of opportunities rather than a matter of appropriation, as Bourdieu (1984) contends.

Decline of the Middle Class

Beginning in the 1960s to the present, the cultural legitimacy of the middle class has been called into question by political and intellectual currents. While dissenters of the 1960s did not quite undermine the cultural foundations of the American middle class, they anticipated the broader appeal in the 1970s for less ostentatiousness. More importantly, the 1960s was a decade of rights-setting agenda that addressed the needs of those who were not the beneficiaries of the economic growth of the first half of the century: African-Americans, women, Hispanics, Native Americans. Many of these issues rested squarely on marketplace demands, notably, equal pay and equal opportunities. Such claims are completely consonant with middle-class notions that impersonal economic, bureaucratic, and educational institutions must be precisely that—impartial and impersonal. There were, after all, hazy notions that members of the middle class had made it on these very grounds. Hard work had paid off, should pay off, and the ground rules were perceived as having been fair and square.

Paradoxically, the self-justification of the middle class is rooted in libertarian ideas about individual achievement that can be reconciled with the norms of the marketplace, whereas alternative lifestyles of African-Americans, Hispanics, and homosexuals are less easily accommodated. In private, domestic, and neighborhood matters the American middle class is notably unbending.

In spite of this, the rock bed of middle-class lifestyle—the suburb and, more specifically, traditional domestic life—is giving way. Increasingly in large cities, white-collar suburbs are populated by commuters—dual-income-earning families; single, unmarried adults; and cohabiting adults—while institutional child care is increasingly prevalent. Class claims, David Harvey (1989: 229) argues, are based on two conditions. First, they rest on place-bound identity, but place-bound identity gives way to high rates of geographical mobility, increasingly smaller families, and neighborhoods of commuting individuals. Second, these claims must rely on the motivational power of tradition, but, as I have argued, this tradition has been seriously undermined by economic realities. As Bellah et al. (1985: 153) describe the plight of the middle class, it is merely a "community of memory, a nostalgic recollection of past accomplishments, history, and exemplary individuals."

Gans (1988) eschews the idea of a white-collar class completely, lumping together upper working class with lower white-collar workers, a result of the routinization of office work and the improved wages of blue-collar workers. As early as the mid-1970s Bell (1976) described the members of the middle class as tenaciously clinging to their traditional lifestyle as their economic well-being was being threatened.

The long postwar boom from 1945 to the recession of 1973 was built on a certain stable set of labor control practices, consumption patterns, and forms of political economic domination that were especially favorable to the middle class. While economists describe the economic rigidities of this period, the only manifest problem that affected the daily lives of Americans was sustained inflation. However, the 1973 recession, followed by the 1975 oil shortage, and a new phenomena—high inflation and high unemployment—altered the rules of economic life and wrecked havoc with major Northeast metropolises (Harrison and Bluestone 1988). Real productivity declined from a long time average of 3.0 percent to .9 percent and it remains there; in the middle of that decade unemployment reached 8 percent and the percentage of uninsured Americans grew to 43; the index of hourly earnings declined by 12 percent in the short period between 1978 to 1983; and, in the same period the lowest quintile of the population lost 17 percent in transfer payments. During the 1980s and early 1990s there has been a steady increase in economic inequalities, as a result of gains among the rich, deterioration of the economic conditions of the poor, and declines in the income of the middle class (Duncan, Smeeding, and Rodgers 1992; Sobel 1989; also see Lichter and Eggebeen 1993). This was due in part to the economic conditions already summarized and also to a steady decline of full-time workers in core labor sectors accompanied by an increase in contract workers and in part-time workers in peripheral or secondary labor sectors.

Over a decade ago, Lester Thurow (1980: 40) warned that the economy is in a "morass from which we cannot escape." Since then, economists have documented the secular trend of increasing economic inequalities, the growing numbers of unemployed and working poor, and the high rates of underemployment (for example, Butler and McDonald 1986). For the first time since the end of the Depression, the gap between the rich and poor is widening while the proportion in the middle declines. In the context here that means declining opportunities for upward mobility and increases in downward mobility. College graduates compete with high school graduates for jobs and high school graduates compete with high school dropouts. Young, married, dual-career breadwinners cannot afford the down payment on a mortgage, there is an increase in the numbers holding two jobs, and the numbers defaulting on private credit loans and giving up private health insurance are reaching new highs each year.

Yet we must take note of the cultural context of economic decline. There are glaring contradictions between, on the one hand, a national middle-class culture that successfully spawned democratic institutions, egalitarian patterns of lifestyle and consumption, and an ethos that linked hard work with success and achievement and a capricious economy and faltering economic institutions on the other.

A good case can be made that a severe economic depression would affect the middle class far more than the Depression of the 1930s did. There are three reasons for this. The middle class of the 1990s, as I have characterized it, includes congeries of occupations that lack a place-bound and work-place identity but share a memory of economic success. To the extent that hard work and achievement were core cultural values, the collapse of economic institutions could very well entail a major reevaluation and overhaul of these core values, which themselves are already contradictory. Moreover, the economy of today is greatly different from the one that spawned job security for millions of workers. Contemporary investment practices and foreign competition are taking a large toll in major corporations just as massive layoffs are affecting huge numbers of factory workers and employees of state and local governments. In short, in a severe depression under the conditions of what is described as the postindustrial economy, high-paid executives, professionals, and engineers share risks of unemployment along with factory and office workers.

While it is evident that the middle class may share economic interests with the poor and working class, the middle class has little or no experience in class politics (Schattschneider 1960). Nevertheless members of the middle class possess great political savvy in social movements such as ecology, civic and school issues, civil rights, and election reform. This perhaps bodes well for forging bonds with those who remain in the working class, who have, after all, superior traditions in the politics of economy.

CONCLUSIONS

The American middle class is contingent on equality of opportunities. The decades between the end of the Great Depression and the mid-1970s fostered the conditions that led to its tremendous growth and its cultural and social consolidation. If the economy fails, the middle class could not provide the buffer between the elite and the poor, not because, as conventional wisdom suggests, it is distinct but rather because middle-class values and culture have been so widely embraced that the class has become expansive. Paradoxically, its economic values—namely, those that deal with the efficacy of individual achievement—now appear increasingly contradictory. As Michael Kammen (1991) suggests, the American myth that mobility and success is a matter of individual striving rests uneasily in a democratic society in which there is little economic growth.

The 1990s has been a decade of self-reflection in the academy. I have mentioned the significance of Amartya Sen's work, and there are others who have redirected their technical expertise to writing about economic justice. Yet, still, in the tradition of Charles Booth and Seebohm Rowntree, whose meticulous ennumerations greatly sobered the Victorians, public policy, one hopes, will be informed by our contemporaries who count: the homeless (Rossi 1989), African-Americans who live in poverty (Massey and Denton 1993), and the children of the poor (Lichter and Eggebeen 1993).

ACKNOWLEDGMENT

An early version of this chapter was presented at the annual meetings of the American Anthropological Association, 1990, and the historical arguments are drawn from a portion of a chapter in my book, *Social Contracts and Economic Markets*. I am indebted to the National Science Foundation for support for empirical research on nineteenth-century cultural organizations (SES-9108923, SES-8907665), which is collaborative with Kenneth C. Land. For criticisms and suggestions, I thank Melanie Archer, Peter M. Blau, Herbert J. Gans, Arne Kalleberg, and Rachel Rosenfeld.

REFERENCES

Archer, Melanie
1991 Self-employment and occupational structure in an industrializing city. *Social Forces* 69: 999–1025.

Archer, Melanie, and Judith R. Blau
1993 Class formation in nineteenth-century America. *Annual Review of Sociology* 19: 17–41.

Aristotle
1943 *Politics*. Translated by Benjamin Jowett. New York: Modern Library.

Barth, Gunther
1980 *City People: The Rise of Modern City Culture in Nineteenth-Century America*. Oxford: Oxford University Press.

Bell, Daniel
1976 *The Cultural Contradictions of Capitalism*. New York: Basic Books.

Bellah, Robert N., Richard Madsen, William M. Sullivan, Ann Swidler, and Steven M. Tipton
1985 *Habits of the Heart*. New York: Harper & Row.
Blau, Judith R.

1989 *The Shape of Culture*. Cambridge: Cambridge University Press.

1993 *Social Contracts and Economic Markets*. New York: Plenum.

Blau, Judith R., and Gail Quets
1989 *Cultural Life in City and Region*. Akron, OH: Center for Urban Studies, University of Akron.

Blumin, Stuart M.
1989 *The Emergence of the Middle Class*. Cambridge: Cambridge University Press.

Bourdieu, Pierre
1984 *Distinction*. Cambridge, MA: Harvard University Press.

Burns, James MacGregor
1985 *The Workshop of Democracy*. New York: Vintage Press.

Butler, Richard, and James B. McDonald
1986 Income inequality in the United States. In *Research in Labor Economics*, vol. 8, part A, pp. 85–140. Greenwich, CT: JAI Press.

Dahrendorf, Ralf
1959 *Class and Class Conflict in Industrial Society*. Stanford, CA: Stanford University Press.

Domhoff, G. William
1974   *The Bohemian Grove and Other Retreats.* New York: Harper & Row.

Duncan, Greg J., Timothy M. Smeeding, and Willard Rodgers
1992   W(h)ither the Middle Class? A Dynamic View. Policy Studies Paper no. 1. Syracuse, NY: The Maxwell School of Citizenship and Public Affairs, Syracuse University.

Elias, Norbert
1978   *The History of Manners. The Civilizing Process,* vol. 1. Translated by Edmund Jephcott. New York: Pantheon.

Evans, M. D. R., Jonathan Kelley, and Tamas Kolosi
1992   Images of class. *American Sociological Review* 57: 461–82.

Gallman, Robert E.
1969   Trends in the Size Distribution of Wealth in the Nineteenth Century. In *Six Papers on the Size Distribution of Wealth and Income.* ed., Lee Soltow, pp. 1–24. New York: National Bureau of Economic Research.

Gans, Herbert J.
1962   *The Urban Villagers.* New York: Free Press.

1988   *Middle American Individualism.* New York: Free Press.

Goffman, Erving
1959   *The Presentation of Self in Everyday Life.* Garden City, NY: Anchor.

Gulick, John
1973   Urban anthropology. In *Handbook of Social and Cultural Anthropology,* ed. J. Honigmann, pp. 979–1029. Chicago: Rand McNally.

Hall, Peter Dobkin
1982   *The Organization of American Culture, 1700-1900.* New York: New York University Press.

Halle, David
1984   *America's Working Man.* Chicago: University of Chicago Press.

Harrison, Bennett, and Harrison Bluestone
1988   *The Great U-Turn.* New York: Basic Books.

Harvey, David
1989   *The Condition of Postmodernity.* Oxford: Basil Blackwood.

Himmelfarb, Gertrude
1991   *Poverty and Compassion.* New York: Knopf.

Jacoby, Sanford M.
1985   *Employing Bureaucracy: Managers, Unions, and the Transformation of Work in American Industry, 1900-1945.* New York: Columbia University Press.

Kammen, Michael
1991   *Mystic Chords of Memory*. New York: Knopf.

Kasson, John F.
1990   *Rudeness and Civility: Manners in Nineteenth Century Urban America*. New York: Hill and Wang.

Lebergott, Stanley
1984   *The Americans: An Economic Record*. New York: W. W. Norton.

Lichter, Daniel T. and David J. Eggebeen
1993   Rich kids, poor kids: Changing income inequality among American children. *Social Forces* 71: 761–80.

Lockwood, David
1992   *Solidarity and Schism*. Oxford: Oxford University Press.

Long, Clarence D.
1960   *Wages and Earnings in the United States, 1860-1890*. Princeton, NJ: Princeton University Press and the National Bureau of Economic Research.

Lynd, Robert S., and Helen Merrell Lynd
1937   *Middletown in Transition*. New York: Harcourt, Brace & World.

Massey, Douglas S., and Nancy A. Denton
1993   *American Apartheid*. Cambridge, MA: Harvard University Press.

Mukerji, Chandra
1983   *From Graven Images*. New York: Columbia University Press.

Newman, Katherine S.
1988   *Falling From Grace: The Experience of Downward Mobility in the American Middle Class*. New York: Free Press.

Rossi, Peter H.
1989   *Down and Out in America*. Chicago: University of Chicago Press.

Ryan, Mary
1989   The American parade. In *The New Cultural History*. Lynn Hunt, ed., pp. 131–53. Berkeley: University of California Press.

Schattschneider, E. E.
1960   *The Semi-Sovereign People*. New York: Holt, Rinehart and Winston.

Sen, Amartya
1992   *Inequality Reexamined*. Cambridge, MA: Harvard University Press.

Sobel, Richard
1989   *The White Working Class*. New York: Praeger.

Soltow, Lee
1975   The Wealth, Income, and Social Class in Large Northern Cities of the United States in 1860. In James D. Smith (ed.) *The Personal Distribution of Income and Wealth. Studies in Income and Wealth*, vol. 39, pp. 233–76. New York: National Bureau of Economic Research.

Thernstrom, Stephan
1973   *The Other Bostonians*. Cambridge, MA: Harvard University Press.

Thompson, E. P.
1963   *The Making of the English Working Class*. New York: Pantheon.

Thurow, Lester C.
1980   *The Zero-Sum Society*. New York: Basic Books.

Tocqueville, Alexis de
[1836] 1945 *Democracy in America*. Translated by George Lawrence, edited by J. P. Mayer. New York: Doubleday.

Trachtenberg, Alan
1982   *The Incorporation of America*. New York: Hill and Wang.

Veblen, Thorstein B.
[1899] 1953 *The Theory of the Leisure Class*. New York: New American Library.

Warner, W. Lloyd, Marchia Meeker, and Kenneth Eell
[1949] 1960 *Social Class in America*. New York: Harper.

Wilson, William Julius
1987   *The Truly Disadvantaged*. Chicago: University of Chicago Press.

Wright, Gwendowlyn
1981   *Building the Dream: A Social History of Housing in America*. Cambridge, MA: The MIT Press.

9

Processes of Retirement

Quite obviously what they were trying to do was to get rid of the older, higher priced, people, so they could save money. So there was a slight feeling that we've been turfed out, as a money saving proposition. It sort of got me a little angry, even though it was done in a kindly fashion.
—Engineer, bought out of his job by an early retirement program.

You had to get managerial permission to do this [take early retirement]. And there was the fine print which said if you're essential to the enterprise you can't do it. So there was some fair amount of bitterness among people who were not allowed to go.
—Same respondent, later in the interview.

Retirement, like a layoff, and like resigning a position, separates someone from the community of work. The retired person is no longer counted on to fill a position, perform a task, or simply show up. It is regularly the experience of the retired who return to their former workplace that they no longer matter in the same way to those who continue to do the work of the world. Yet retirement has its compensations: the retired person no longer need struggle with morning and evening commutes nor do battle with work's deadlines and bosses and frustrating colleagues. The problem of retirement is that its negatives and its positives are so closely linked. As one retired former manager said, when the time came around for his yearly performance report, even while it was a wonderful relief to no longer have to produce a brag sheet, but it was dismaying to realize that now no one cared.

Because retirement is both freedom and marginality, it is apt to be regarded ambivalently. A mixed view of retirement is especially likely among those men and women who had valued their work highly and had been valued highly by others because of it. As one expression of this, at every age those who earn more are less likely to retire (Ruhm 1989). The explanation seems to be not so much a matter of lost income, since the retirement wealth and income of high earners should be more nearly adequate than that of those who earned less, but rather the increased emotional importance of the job.

Given the mixed nature of the retirement experience for those for whom work was emotionally or socially sustaining and given the illegality of mandatory retirement rules, how does it happen that people for whom work had value nevertheless retire? This paper explores this issue. The paper is based on interviews with forty-nine men and twenty-eight women, all either recently retired from managerial or professional positions or within a year of retirement from such positions. Most were interviewed once before their retirement and again within six months afterwards.

All but about a dozen of the men were recruited from four upper-income suburbs by use of street lists that give the names, ages, and occupations of all residents at every address. Men who were at least age sixty-two and in upper-middle-class occupations were telephoned and asked if they intended to retire within the next year; those who said they did were asked if they would be willing to be interviewed about their retirement plans. About 80 percent of those asked agreed to be interviewed. The remaining men were recruited through personnel managers of three large firms who asked retiring employees if they would be willing to be interviewed about their retirement.

Finding women who were retiring from managerial and professional positions was more difficult. Most of the women in the sample volunteered to be interviewed in response to a story about the study that appeared in the local newspaper. Other women came to the study through the cooperative personnel managers.

EXPECTATIONS REGARDING RETIREMENT

The movement to establish a retirement age was promoted from the first by people not themselves of retirement age. Actually, the expectation that retirement will occur sooner or later in most people's later years, though now well-established, is of recent origin.

Graebner (1980) writes that in 1890 about 70 percent of white males over 65 were gainfully employed. Nor did support for a program for the retirement of older workers, an idea that was being promoted at the turn of the century, come from the older workers themselves. Rather, support for the idea came from business owners who hoped that the result would be greater efficiency and from younger workers who hoped they would inherit the jobs of the aged workers. Support for introduction of retirement programs came, too, from leaders of labor unions, who represented mostly the younger workers.

The Social Security Act of 1935 did much to make sixty-five the age of retirement by stipulating that full benefits could be obtained only then. By the time men who had grown up with the Social Security Act were themselves in their sixties, retirement at age sixty-five was accepted as a normal life transition. By 1981, about 90 percent of men whose ages were in the sixty-five to seventy-five bracket defined themselves as retired (Parnes and Less 1985).

Still, surveys of the retired conducted forty and fifty years ago uniformly found that retirement was imposed rather than freely chosen. Reasons for retirement were largely layoffs and illnesses. But more recent surveys find many more among the retired reporting that they had voluntarily chosen to retire. Labor economists believe the change to be due to the increased proportion of workers who can look forward to adequate retirement income (Quinn and Burkhauser 1990). Indeed, since postponing retirement means postponing receipt of income from Social Security and private pensions, motivation for retirement can be based on workers' desire to maximize some combination of wages and pensions (Quinn and Burkhauser 1990:315).

Yet detailed interviews with respondents who had been in managerial and administrative positions suggest a decision process in which of most importance is the emotional meaning of work and the job. In this process the expectation of retirement income plays a facilitative role, making retirement appear to be a practical alternative. Even so, many among the managerial and professional respondents with whom we spoke described their work as having been important for their well-being. Although they retired, they did not do so because they desired retirement. For others, developments in their work or their relationships with colleagues had made their work situations so disagreeable that they wanted to leave their work. Knowing that they could manage financially facilitated the retirement.

There seem to be four classes of motivations for retirement.

First are the motivations of ill health or physical decline. Then are those having to do with desire to escape from work. And then there are motivations within the workplace and not at all in the retiring person, which result in people being forced into retirement. The fourth class of motivation for retirement is attraction to the possible uses of a life in which time would not be commanded by work.

By and large, respondents reported that they had retired because illness or aging made it impossible for them to continue with their work, because they wanted to escape their work, or because they had been pushed out. There were only a few among our managerial and professional respondents who reported that they had left their work because they wanted to enjoy retirement's promise of leisure or opportunity for new activity. Only one of our respondents seemed to have left his work because he wanted to pursue another activity and only four seemed to have left their work to enjoy leisure.

Inability to Continue

Illness. Poor health is regularly seen by labor economists as the most important noneconomic determinant of retirement (Quinn and Burkhauser, 1990). There is, however, uncertainty regarding how the quality of health should be measured and, on occasion, suspicion that health problems often merely are a socially acceptable explanation for the decision to retire.

Several in our sample of managers and professionals reported that they had been forced to relinquish work because of ill health or diminished physical capacity. None seemed to exaggerate the role that health had played in their retirement. Several reported actively resisting departure from work for as long as they could. One man, disabled by a wasting disease, hoped he could continue to contribute to his firm by working at home.

The initial reaction of the respondents who had discovered in their early sixties that physical problems were interfering with their ability to work was to hope that the condition would prove temporary. Especially where they felt identified with programs or with services, as was the case, for example, with a head of an academic department and a physician, they strongly resisted accepting that health problems necessitated their retirement.

A woman who was a college professor, approaching sixty-five, living alone, was head of her academic department. She had suffered from a wasting illness for three or four years.

I was slowing down in certain ways that only I could determine. First of all were my eyes. They were getting worse. It took me two years to find a doctor that could handle my eye problems, because they're different. Then, I was falling down. I went to a doctor and he told me that I should use a cane.

Despite these infirmities, the respondent insisted on continuing at work. She told her dean that her health was failing and obtained his reassurance that it was all right for her to stay on. She arranged for cabs to take her to and from work. She hired a young man to shovel her walk in winter and devised stratagems for ensuring that cab drivers would help her from sidewalk to cab and from cab to sidewalk. And she hired assistants who could help her prepare classes and papers and also bring her lunch.

The respondent's health continued to deteriorate. She noticed that increasingly she was leaving work undone and that her energy had begun flagging. Against her wishes, her relatives became engaged. A sister took her to visit a nursing home. The respondent was outraged. But then a trusted graduate student told her that she was endangering herself by refusing to retire. She said to us, about that conversation, "I was hearing the truth. And the truth was, it was time to go." Later that week she arranged for her retirement and for her entrance into the nursing home.

Another respondent, an engineer, not quite sixty-five at the time of our first interview, had been diagnosed with cancer a month earlier. He could have retired on a full pension had he wanted to. Instead he took a leave from his work. He believed he would soon be able to return. When we saw him a second time, about a year later, his illness had forced him to leave work, and he was beginning to relinquish hope that he would return to work. He still had not taken retirement. He said, about the way his bout with illness had begun:

I had been in for pneumonia, had taken some antibiotics and seemed to be improving, but not enough. So they sent me in for x-rays. And they spotted a place in the lung that, finally, with a needle biopsy, was diagnosed as malignant. I can't say that I was surprised, because I've been a smoker all my life. The tests indicated that it was probably still just in that one spot. And that meant that the odds of cure were extremely high. However, when they removed it they removed lymph nodes from three other locations and there was a metastasis to them. I [still] thought that I'd probably be back to work within a month. But between arthritis acting up and just not getting my strength back, I haven't. I'm beginning to wonder whether I will.

In a similar fashion, a self-employed consultant in his late sixties, despite having been seriously injured in an auto accident, planned to return to work. He described himself as staying home only temporarily, so that he could look after the sister who had been injured in the same accident. Actually, his own injuries made it unlikely he could ever resume a strenuous schedule. Nevertheless he postponed acceptance of himself as already retired.

A sales manager had a heart attack when in his early sixties. On leaving the hospital he was told by his physician that to continue on his job would risk his life. He nevertheless continued with the job, although determined to be more relaxed in its performance. He finally retired, not because of his health, but because the conditions of his work became unacceptable. (His retirement is discussed further below.)

In general, respondents found acceptance of retirement for reasons of health to be a kind of giving up to a superior force. They struggled against it until they were finally convinced they were not to win. (See Howell 1992, for a similar report by an airline pilot of reluctance to accept "medical retirement.")

But if retirement was regularly resisted, despite illness, nevertheless it seemed to be the case that once accepted, illness could serve as a kind of justification for the retirement. Those who had retired for reasons of illness were noteworthy in their absence of resentment toward the workplace. Illness permitted retirements in which relationships with the community of work remained unspoiled.

Aging. Infirmities associated with aging—diminished energy or diminished steadiness of hand or eye—though their recognition might be resisted just as were infirmities produced by illness, were different in one respect. Infirmities due to aging, once acknowledged, required acceptance as irreversible. If a surgeon's hand had become unsteady as a result of aging, he could not image that time would bring improvement. However, full acceptance that aging had brought about diminished skills or energies might require a good deal of self-observation.

One respondent reported that he had been led to retire after witnessing his reduced ability to handle foreign assignments. He was an engineer whose firm's contracts were largely in foreign settings. In his mid-sixties, he was given an Asian assignment not much different from assignments he had been given throughout his career. But this time he found the physical wear of the flight, followed by three weeks hard work in a primitive setting, harder to manage than it had been before. In addition, while on the job a younger assistant had seemed to him more competent than he was himself. The return home was again exhausting. After his return he became ill, an illness he blamed on the stresses of the assignment. He notified his company that he was retiring.

Several other respondents also felt that aging had left them less able to do their work. One former surgeon had experienced pressure at his hospital to retire from surgery. Exactly what the pressure was he left unclear, but he seemed himself to have become worried about his vulnerability to malpractice suit. He retained a part-time medical practice but stopped doing surgery. A former general practitioner said that he no longer had the energy to work the hours required to rent an office and pay a staff. He too retired in a partial way; he now worked two days a week as an organization's house physician.

Obsolescence of skills or inability to learn new skills the job required might be seen as another expression of aging. An accountant decided to retire on trying, and failing, to learn computer skills. His firm would have retained him, but he had begun to feel himself unable to keep up with his younger colleagues.

Repudiating Work

Some respondents reported that they had long wanted to leave their jobs or their firms. Retirement, for them, was, like divorce, a way to escape an unsatisfactory social situation.

One respondent, a minor executive in a large firm, had long been angry with her superiors who, she believed, had repeatedly passed her over for promotion. Her firm required an advanced degree for the next level up but she had learned her profession on the job, not in business school.

> I got up to the plateau where I didn't get anywhere. They stopped promoting me. And they started promoting people that I trained, that learned their jobs from me. These were younger people coming out of business schools and coming with a financial degree, or a Master's Degree in Business Administration, which I didn't have. It hurt, seeing them get ahead of me.

This respondent retired as soon as she became old enough to obtain a full pension. Her husband had already retired and she wanted to join him in travel, but most important in her retirement was her anger at having been treated so shabbily by her firm. She had some hope that the firm would have difficulty in replacing her.

There were many ways in which work could be disagreeable enough to lead to retirement. One man complained that his colleagues isolated him because his values were more liberal than theirs. Another man reported that his contributions, though they had proven valuable to the firm, had been inadequately recognized. In several cases reorganization of their firms changed conditions of work in ways respondents found unacceptable: a woman was required to transfer to a branch office distant from her home; a man was demoted and given work of marginal importance; another man was demoted while being retained in the same department. One respondent, a technician, was asked to follow procedures in his work that he thought unnecessarily awkward. His objections were discounted, and so he asked for a transfer to another department. The transfer was refused. The respondent retired.

In all these instances retirement was a form of resignation from work. Earlier in their careers these men and women would not have been able to quit. But now, with the possibility of a pension adequate to their needs and the status of "retired" to explain their leisure, they could choose not to do work they found disagreeable. In the words of several of the respondents, they didn't have to put up with it.

Nevertheless, some respondents seemed to feel that they needed to argue that their departure from their firms had been justified. Consider the following account. The respondent began with two reasons for retiring: wanting to escape a job that had become disagreeable and wanting to enjoy property that had been left him:

> When I reached age sixty-four, pressures where I was employed had increased. I was a senior engineer and they were piling the work on me. And I began to feel tired. My father had passed away two years earlier and left me a small property in the South. And at that point I decided to retire and spend some time there.

These reasons might seem sufficient to justify retirement. Nevertheless, the respondent went on to offer still another justification: his had been a life of hard work and dedication, its only reward the success of his children. All this dutifulness, the respondent implied, justified a retirement in which he and his wife could attend to their own needs.

> I was born and brought up on a farm and I put in many years of hard work. I worked a good forty or forty-five years. I had four children, all of whom have gone through college and gone on to bigger and better things. And I have a daughter who has earned a doctorate and a son who has earned a law degree. And my youngest son has a master's and a very responsible job. And, of course, financial resources were strained throughout that period. And my wife and I have both worked a good long time to get these kids through college. I thought of retirement quite a few years prior to retirement.

Here, as elsewhere in our materials, men and women who had retired voluntarily seemed to feel the need to justify having left the world of work. One kind of justification was that the work world had provided little recognition of their service. Another was that their jobs had been disagreeable or that they had been treated badly. And still another was that they had already given the world of work all it could reasonably ask for, and they now had the right to attend to themselves.

Some respondents said that they were retiring because they were tired of working and wanted the freedom not to work. One, a successful lawyer, said that he had lost the drive he once had had. He noticed that he no longer could get himself up for court appearances. Now, he said, he looked after the needs of long-time clients but refused new work. Soon he might send his long-time clients to someone else. A few other respondents also said, essentially that they had worked long enough. They had no particular desire for the life of the retired, except as it represented freedom from continuing work. Retirement was for them escape rather than opportunity.

Pushed Out

Despite the absence of mandatory retirement rules and the presence of legal bars to age-based dismissals, some of our respondents were pressed to leave their jobs by their firms. In one instance, a new group took over a woman's firm and almost immediately abolished the woman's job. The woman said that she was too shocked and hurt to retire—she had to demonstrate, at least to herself, that her competencies remained. She found another job in her field, worked another two years, and then, with her self-esteem restored, retired.

> It took me that length of time to adjust and to get over the terrible hurt I was feeling. And then I just discovered that I was really ready to retire.

Most often pressures on a respondent had been subtler than abolishing the respondent's job. One respondent reported being asked, at his yearly evaluation, "What are your retirement plans?" Several respondents described being excluded from important work activities. With no explanation given, important assignments went to others, committees formed and the respondent wasn't asked to join. A management consultant to whom this was currently happening described the experience:

> I've been not really feeling like I wanted to set the date of my retirement. And now I have the feeling that I'm probably having it set for me, in a sense, even though it hasn't been set. Just reading the tea leaves. When the Senior VP of Personnel says you've got to find something to do that makes you worth [your salary], which is the way it was put to me, that tells me that if you don't find something to do that's worth [the salary], that they're going to do something about it.
>
> And there have been a number of committees that have been formed in this new section where it would have been a logical place to put somebody where they really do want to have experience, and that they could have placed me in, they didn't. I've gone from being involved in almost every important place in the company to being involved almost in none of them, really. Zero. It's kind of gone from all to nothing.
>
> I'll be sixty-four next month. Most people think of sixty-five as the retirement age. It's not, really, legally, any more. I probably would not think about retirement if it hadn't been for all this. And for having the ability to retire very comfortably.

Some respondents who felt pressed to retire were able to negotiate arrangements with representatives of their work communities that permitted them to retain membership in their communities of work, albeit in a more limited role. If they could feel that they continued to have a valued place in the world of work, their feelings about retirement might be not at all bitter. A woman who had been a faculty member of a medium-sized university described accomplishing just such a feat.

> The administration likes you to retire because financially they don't have to pay such high salaries. They can get a faculty member with a lower salary. I could, legally, have put a very heavy insistence on continuing to teach until I'm seventy, full-time. I think there is a law or something, you don't have to retire. But I found it wasn't wise, in order to be on good terms with my dean, with the institution. And they offered me half-time teaching plus benefits: health and other benefits.
>
> Of course at half time I get only half salary. But I get the full benefits, both pension and health insurance, which makes it worthwhile. The health insurance is very expensive, and they pay the full health insurance.
>
> I could have insisted on my legal rights and said I want to go on teaching, but I think all around it's better this way. I weighed it both ways.

This respondent's negotiations with her dean had been protracted, with offers and counteroffers. The respondent had on her side the law prohibiting forced retirement. But the dean had on his side the ability to make continuation of fringe benefits contingent on a timely retirement and to threaten, if retirement should be resisted, a poisoned relationship.

As was the case with respondents who had volunteered for retirement, this respondent, too—perhaps because her retirement had required her agreement—brought in additional justifications. There were other things to do. And, also, she could recognize that she was aging.

> I have grandchildren and I want to leave a memory for them, also to have a little time with them. And so now I have more time for doing other things. And, physically, you're not as alert, you tire a little. Sometimes age tells. I'm not as physically strong as I was ten years ago, although I'm in good shape and good health. So I don't want to push it to the limit that the students say, well, she's no longer a good teacher, or she's slowing down in her reflexes.

Next to retirements for reasons of health, pressures from the workplace were the second most frequent of the reasons for retirement in our sample. These pressures included a few in which retirement was produced by a layoff or firing. More often, the workplace marginalized the person by excluding the person from important tasks, sometimes by assigning the person work that was of little importance. Marginalization might be accompanied by explicit statements about the person's expected retirement. In a few instances pressures to retire led to negotiations, and these, sometimes, went well enough to permit such continued relationships as consultancies and part-time employment.

Several respondents had been bought out of their jobs by an offer of early retirement. A few described offers they could not refuse; they were told that should they refuse the offers their jobs would probably be abolished. They later were angry with their firms. But even when no such pressure was applied, and when the early retirement programs provided generous benefits, those who had been bought out had resentments: after all the years they had given to their firms, they were so little respected that the firm would pay handsomely to be rid of them.

In general, if those who voluntarily left their firms felt they needed adequate justifications for having done so, those who were pushed out (or bought out) by their firms resented what they interpreted as betrayal. They had been loyal to their firms; their firms, in response, had shown them indifference.

Some women reported pushes to retire emanating from their spouses. Husbands who had themselves retired tended to want their wives to retire along with them. The women might have their own reasons for retiring, but the pressures from their husbands could not but play a role in their thinking. One woman, about sixty, said:

> I'm thinking of retiring when I'm sixty-two because I think that's a good time as far as Social Security is concerned, which is two and a half years from now. I'm just tired of working, frankly, And it's hard with Phil retired. There are things that he would like to do, trips that he would like to make. And I can't do them.

In our sample the women whose husbands had retired and who were themselves in their late fifties or early sixties seemed mostly to want to work a bit longer, perhaps until something closer to their own mid-sixties. They weren't yet ready to leave the world of work. The woman just quoted went on to say:

> If I work until sixty-two, Social Security benefits are vastly improved. Actually, it hadn't occurred to me to retire. I'm not ready yet. I'm tired, but not that tired. I figure I've got another couple of years left. And I think that it's probably better for Phil that I'm not around all the time. Give him his chance to make his transition.

For many women, as well as for many men, work is where the action is. Leaving work for retirement, even with a retired spouse, requires giving up a lot. The few who had acceded to a spouse's wishes that they retire seemed to have done so largely from feelings of obligation rather than from attraction to whatever might be the benefits of leisure.

Schizmogenic Interaction Leading to Retirement

In several cases it appeared that retirement had resulted from a process in which the respondent and those with whom he or she worked withdrew from each other in a process of interaction that might be called schizmogenic. Three respondents reported a scenario that began with the entrance of a new boss into a work situation in which the respondent had become a trusted and relatively autonomous figure. The new boss wanted control over the respondent's department. The respondent resented the new boss's intrusion into the respondent's domain. In two of the instances the new boss asked for a statement of objectives against which the respondent's performance could be evaluated. In the third instance the boss began his first conversation with the respondent with a question about the respondent's plans for retirement.

The respondents felt their worth to be questioned. They resisted the new boss's efforts to supervise them more closely than they had been supervised in the past. In retaliation the new boss made them aware of his or her irritation. In one instance the new boss required a respondent who had reported directly to the previous boss to report to someone of lower status—in effect, demoting the respondent. At some point in this process of escalating tension, respondents gave up and retired.

One of the respondents who went through this was sales manager of a printing firm. About a year before the interview he had suffered a serious heart attack. On his return to work he was greeted by a new head of the firm—the previous head had retired. Whereas he had been permitted by the previous head to run the sales department his way, he was asked to provide his new boss with a statement of objectives. He tried to be cooperative and avoid conflict with the new boss, but he soon became convinced that the new boss's policies would be disastrous for his department. For a time he tried to protect his department from policies he thought misguided, but he finally gave up.

> This new person came in as the general manager. A very diligent, hard-working young person who did things his way. He would do things without really consulting with me that affected my department and affected the management of the company. Where, heretofore, it would always be, "We're going to do this, what do you think about this?"
>
> Changes were going on as far as the sales department were concerned that I was not supportive of. One was changing the compensation for the sales person. And I could see the sales slipping because of the parameters that they were instituting in the company about credit and margins of profit, and things like that. They'd say, we've got to retrench. So that was a determining factor [in the retirement decision].

Most important in this respondent's decision to retire was his inability to protect his salespeople's incomes. He felt that unless he could make good on his commitments to his staff he could not command their loyalty, and then his own job would be impossible. He told his new boss that he was retiring; the new boss did nothing to dissuade him.

One manager, not yet retired, gave desire to avoid this scenario as a reason for taking retirement. Having an adequate pension made this sort of preventive action possible.

> In the corporate field there's always a change in policy and managerial directions. And when you've spent thirty-four years in a particular line and you think you know the way it should be handled and maybe a new president comes in— I'm not saying this will happen here, but I've seen it happen elsewhere—there's a conflict of emotions between the old fire dog and the new top dog. Why go through an emotional upheaval at your age?

Respondents who had been caught up in schizmogenic processes that had ended in their retirement seemed regularly to have become embittered toward their workplace. They had systematically been frustrated in their efforts to make their situations tolerable. By the time they moved to retirement, they were nursing a backlog of hurt.

In another form of schizmogenic process, a respondent who had been an executive in a family business retired in a way that estranged him from the relative who headed the business. The respondent was a department head within the business, and there had long been tension between him and the relative. The respondent said that for years he had been treated badly. And then, a last straw, a woman who had worked for the respondent, someone whom he had trained and had, indeed, sponsored within the firm, was made his superior. In a fury the respondent went to the relative and said this was intolerable. He also said that he would like the firm to buy his interest in the firm so that he would have enough money for his retirement. He added that he did not want to hurt the firm by his departure and would be willing to continue on a part-time basis. The relative reacted by arranging for the respondent's interest to be bought and by requiring the respondent to leave the firm immediately. The respondent, a few months after his retirement, was filled with anger. We talked with him again a year later, and his anger had abated only slightly.

Attracted by Retirement

Only five respondents in our sample had retired because of the attractions of retirement. Four of the five said that they wanted to enjoy the freedoms of leisure. Although they had plans for travel or work around the house or visits with children and grandchildren, it was the leisure to do what they wanted that attracted them. And although two or three of the respondents did in fact spend much of their first year of retirement working on their homes, none had retired to do this. Working on their homes was a rewarding way for them to use their free time, but it was not the reason they had retired.

Only one among our respondents had retired to take up an activity about which he cared a great deal. This respondent had long wanted to become a craftsman in wood. He left his business so that he might realize this dream. At sixty-three, with enough money in investments to assure him of an income for the rest of his life, he sold his business to his employees for its cash on hand and went to school to learn woodworking. Two years later he had his own woodworking shop. He was busy and described himself as fulfilled. He had no trouble selling his products; indeed, he had a waiting list of clients.

THE ROLE OF RETIREMENT INCOME

In what has been presented to this point regarding the processes leading to retirement, little attention has been given to the availability of a pension. What role do pensions play in retirement? Economists and public policy analysts alike assume that an individual's retirement date is responsive, at least in part, to the amount of pension income he can expect and to its scheduling. Among economists' models of retirement behavior, attempts to maximize the present value of lifetime income are central elements, along with, in some models, the value of leisure and of opportunities to consume. (See Mitchell and Fields 1982, Gohmann 1990). Empirical study suggests that simply being eligible for a pension has little effect on the timing of retirement, but that retirement is hastened by being eligible for a pension whose benefits would be high relative to one's salary or wages. It isn't the pension, it's the pension's size compared to income, that matters (Mitchell and Fields 1982).

Yet few respondents in this study timed their retirements so as to maximize a combination of their pension and earnings incomes. The exceptions were a few respondents who had accepted attractive early retirement offers. However, the size and perceived adequacy of the pension that could be expected did play a role in many respondents' retirement decisions. Having an adequate pension— or at least being able to anticipate maintaining an adequate living standard on pension plus income from savings—made retirement a plausible alternative to continuing to work. It did not necessarily make retirement attractive, but it did make retirement seem available if there was an other reason to want it. In particular, it made it possible for someone who felt burdened or misused at work to say, "I don't have to put up with this."

At the same time, one of the frightening aspects of permanent departure from work is the recognition that no more money will be earned, that living standard (and independence) is now entirely dependent on what has already been put aside. Yet most respondents, no matter how well they had prepared financially, felt vulnerable to doctors' and hospitals' bills, and many were fearful of inflation's erosion of the value of their pensions and savings. No matter how much had been saved, nor how large the pension that would be received, it might not be enough. For many among the retired, careful husbandry of investments was a matter of some importance.

Some respondents did seek to maximize their pension incomes, because of awareness that no matter how much they received, it might conceivably not be enough. They might work an additional year or two, despite an unsatisfying job situation, to obtain the increased security a larger pension could bring.

Many early retirement programs give workers who elect them additional pension benefits as well as an immediate bonus for signing. By doing this the plans reduce two incentives for continuing to work: the wish to add to the size of the eventual pension and the attraction of an employment income significantly greater than potential retirement income. But early retirement programs seem to be effective by suggesting to people not only that they would be foolish to pass up so good an offer but also that the firm sees them as dispensable.

In sum, it does not seem that retirement pensions produce retirement so much as they make retirement seem a practical alternative, given other reasons for considering retirement.

CONCLUSION

Retirements of managerial and professional people are consequences of decision processes expressive of a mix, different from case to case, of individual motives, pressures from representatives of the firm, and developments in the interaction of individual and firm. Only rarely is the dominant motive for retirement an individual's attraction to the opportunities of retirement. Rather, individuals retire because their work has become difficult or impossible for reasons of health or aging, or has become distressing because of workplace conflict, or boring because they have withdrawn investment in it. Or, sometimes, retirement has been imposed, or results from an interactive process in which individual and firm progressively distance themselves, ending with their separation.

Few retirements seem to be produced by aging alone, although the aging process may give rise to infirmity that leads to retirement. Most retirements are the result of developments in the relationship of individual and firm that would have led the individual to leave the firm whenever they occurred, before retirement age as well as after, had that been financially and socially possible. Retirement provides the aging worker with an alternative to continuing on the job. Whether that option is used depends on other factors.

ACKNOWLEDGMENT

Work reported here was supported by a grant from the National Institute of Aging, 1-R01 AG07363-01.

REFERENCES

Gohmann, Stephan F.
1990 Retirement differences among the respondents to the retirement history survey. *Journal of Gerontology*, 45(3):S120–7.

Graebner, William
1980 *A History of Retirement: The Meaning and Function of an American Institution, 1885–1978*. New Haven, CT: Yale University Press.

Howell, Grant
1992 The wrong stuff. *Air Line Pilot*. (August), pp. 38–40.

Mitchell, Olivia, and Gary S. Fields
1982 The effects of pensions and earnings on retirement: a review essay. *Research in Labor Economics*, 5, pp. 115–55.

Parnes, Herbert S., and Lawrence J. Less
1985 The volume and pattern of retirements, 1966–1981. In *Retirement among American Men*. Herbert S. Parnes et al., eds., pp. 57–77. Lexington, MA: Lexington Books.

Quinn, Joseph F., and Richard V. Burkhauser
1990 Work and retirement. In *Aging and the Social Sciences*. Robert H. Binstock and Linda K. George, eds., pp. 307–27. New York: Academic Press.

Ruhm, Christopher
1989 Why older Americans stop working. *The Gerontologist*, 19 (June): 294–9.

10

The Socio-Economics of Work

Socioeconomics is a discipline that combines the perspectives of neoclassical economics with those of sociology, anthropology, psychology, and political science. The synthesis proceeds along three major axes: instead of assuming that people are maximizing one overarching utility, their satisfaction, it is assumed that they respond to two or more irreducible sources of valuation: their satisfaction and their moral values. (Both are subject to cultural interpretations, socialization, peer pressures, and leadership influences).

Second, instead of assuming that people choose their means rationally, it is assumed that much of their decision making is affected by emotions and values and that their ability to deliberate and process information (to act rationally) is rather limited. Finally, instead of assuming that the individual is the center of the social universe, it assumes individuals act as members of groups and hence many variations in their behavior are to be explained on the collective level. Further details and the ethical implications of the change in perspectives are spelled out elsewhere. (Etzioni 1988; Etzioni and Lawrence 1990; Coughlin 1991; see also the new *Journal of Socio-Economics*).

As the preceding very terse statements suggest, socioeconomics is concerned with evolving a constructive paradigm rather than adding to the voluminous literature critical of neoclassical economics. Indeed, it seems that one of the main reasons neoclassical economics continues to reign, despite some very telling criticisms of its assumptions, findings, and policy conclusions (Thurow 1983), is that one cannot replace a paradigm with nothing. Critics of neoclassical economics have been able to come up with numerous observations, case studies, and statistical findings, based on a rich variety of assumptions and premises but only recently have those begun to accumulate into one overarching, explanatory, and predictive paradigm, which we refer to as socioeconomics. (It follows that socioeconomists have not given up on the "science thing" and are reluctant to replace neoclassical economics only with narratives, interpretive writings, and other humanistic but not "hard" scientific approaches.)

This essay seeks to launch a systematic overview of work applying the socioeconomic perspective to explicate assumptions and point to lacuna rather than present new findings or new theorems. First, it examines the nature of work, noting that the reasons people work derive from a multitude of rewards, which are psychic, social, and cultural, as well as economic. Next, it asks why neoclassical economists continue to advise organizations to offer money as the only work incentive. Socioeconomics seeks to codify an alternative theory of incentives. In particular, the value of work is often deeply rooted in one's culture. The final portions of this essay examine the normative and culturally based meanings of work and the division of work within the family.

WORK VERSUS LABOR

Arendt (1958) captured the difference between work that is sheer drudgery and work that contains intrinsic rewards, is enjoyable, and builds identity by using the term "labor" to refer to the first kind and "work" to the second. Most neoclassical economists view work implicitly or explicitly as labor. Because their paradigm is built around the pleasure principle, they typically assume that work is pain and that people must be provided with *external* rewards in order for them to put up with the travail of labor. (The same narrow view of the psyche is reflected in most of the labor economics literature wherein only external rewards are discussed, no other rewards are recognized, and, we shall see, pay-for-performance is preferred over salaries and wages.)

Socioeconomics assumes that much work, albeit not all, contains an important (though varying) amount of intrinsic rewards. One need not travel far to meet such workers. Quite a few academicians, especially among those who already command tenure, could reduce their work hours significantly with no, or only little, loss of income. They work, often long and hard, because of social rewards (e.g., prestige), because they are part of a social group that appreciates dedicated and extensive work, and because academics build their self-identity around their work and find inherent pleasures in an essay well written, new findings, a table analyzed, and so on. Many other professions and occupations provide, to varying degrees, similar rewards. Many "blue-collar" workers are motivated in part by intrinsic rewards of work. In the past, many locomotive engineers and conductors were reluctant to leave their positions when they reach the mandatory retirement age of seventy. Today, some engineers enjoy their craft, its tasks, and their responsibilities so much that aspects of their work are a constant topic of conversation, they seldom miss a run, and on days off they operate, gratis, steam and other locomotives for small "rail buff" carriers (Private communication with Gamst).

Juster (1986) finds that the average American worker prefers work with some leisure over full-time leisure (although most would like more leisure). He suggests that there are internal rewards (e.g. personal satisfaction) associated with all activities, as well as external rewards and cites data to suggest "that the intrinsic satisfaction from work, which represents an addition to the extrinsic reward in the form of income, is generally *higher* than the intrinsic satisfaction from leisure" (Ibid. 16). As Juster points out, this finding is completely incompatible with the neoclassical approach that assumes not only that leisure is pleasurable and work painful but that leisure is the reward a person obtains by working.

Gamst (1984: 58) shows the correlation between work and culture. Anglo-Saxons often view work as both a moral necessity and a curse. Other societies, such as the Amhara and Qemant of Ethiopia, shun all manual labor. He also challenges the notion that work is limited to gainful toil. There is also what is called "volitional work," work that receives no payment, but is beneficial to society. He concludes

> Work gradates into activities marginal to or of no direct relation to earning a living. Work satisfies not just material need, but social aspiration for status and organization of community. It satisfies psychological maintenance of self-image and provides a label for easing interpersonal relations (59).

All said and done, it seems productive to assume that (a) people work for a variety of motives; (b) profiles of job motivations differ among individuals (some are more pecuniarily oriented and some are more attracted by opportunities to express themselves, etc.); (c) jobs differ in the satisfaction they can provide (some provide more opportunities for developing social relations on the job than others); and (d) it is unproductive, costly, and unappealing from a humanitarian viewpoint to treat all people in all jobs as if they are laborers rather than workers. (This approach is of course in line with the multiutility idea, a core principle of socioeconomics.) It is in this paradigm ideas, such as providing opportunities for workers to self-actualize, to identify with their work, and so on, find their systematic theoretical home.

Once one begins building from the preceding paradigm, one recognizes the special significance of matching people to jobs rather than trying either to change people—in order to make them more responsive to the preexisting rewards jobs offer or to change jobs— to enhance the rewards jobs offer to particular profiles of motivations. Improved matching requires neither changing personalities nor jobs, and hence is much more efficient. Baker, Etzioni, Hanse, and Sontag (1973: 777–8) showed that "either because of some basic needs, or because they are formed early in life and are not easily altered, personalities cannot easily adjust to fulfill any and all organizational role requirements without substantial strain." The authors then develop a measure of personality dimensions that influence peoples' responses to key aspects of work; these, in turn, allow for better matching of persons and roles, hence making more of labor into work. It may be argued, quite appropriately, that such a procedure would lead to discrimination because of various disadvantages suffered by many minority groups. This may be corrected, at least in part, by changing the job specifications so they become race and gender neutral. As a result, the suggested approach will cease to be a pure matching operation.

INCENTIVES

Neoclassical economists advocate performance-based pay over promotion or other compensation systems and express surprise that virtually no organizations use pay-on-performance systems, such as paying people for each yard of fabric they weave or ton of coal they dig. "The potential benefits of tying pay to performance are obvious, and it is surprising to economists that firms apparently resist introducing bonus-based compensation plans with enough financial 'action' to have a major motivational effect" (Baker, Jensen, and Murphy 1988:596). The evidence they cite from research by Medoff and Abraham "indicates that explicit financial rewards in the form of transitory performance-based bonuses seldom account for an important part of a worker's compensation" (Ibid. 595). Lawler also finds that "pay is not very closely related to performance in many organizations that claim to have merit increase salary systems" (Ibid.). For neoclassical economists, top management in particular "is an occupation where incentive pay is expected to play an important role, but Baker, Jensen, and Murphy point out that actual executive-compensation contracts look very different from those predicted by economic theory" (Ibid. 610). The data shows that there is little pay difference within firms between those with low or high performance ratings (Ibid. 595), and most organizations use promotion incentive systems rather than pay-for-performance (Ibid. 600). While neoclassical economists suppose that promotion systems lack incentives for those who have been passed over and fail to provide optimum job matching by moving good people up to higher managerial levels, merit-pay critics note that "while financial incentive schemes improve productivity in principle, in practice they induce significant adverse side effects that are costly to employee morale and productivity" (Ibid.).

Baker, Jensen, and Murphy conclude that, "there may be more efficient ways to increase the level of pay, such as introducing bonuses based on individual performance, but managers and personnel executives [particularly because they are not principals and do not directly bear the cost of unwarranted salary increases-A.E.] have little incentive to adopt these economically efficient alternatives" (Ibid. 614).

During a faculty seminar I conducted on socioeconomics at the Harvard Business School, Jensen presented the findings summed up above. At that point I turned to the more than a dozen other non-neoclassical social scientists present to ask if we had any other systematic explanation of the amounts of incentives people are given for their work.

Several interesting observations were offered. Some suggested that old-fashioned workers largely sought monetary compensation while the new ones were more preoccupied with self-expression. Some suggested that we pay more for power (hence the system of greater pay for higher rank, for more control). One colleague proposed that we pay people to reduce their anxiety so they can focus on their work (hence the benefit of working mostly for fixed incomes rather than pay-for-performance). Among the studies cited in the seminar discussion was that by Herzberg, Mausner, and Snyderman (1959). However, all said and done, it seems fair to say that a systematic socioeconomic explanation of compensation for work remains to be worked out. There are findings, insights, and suggestions but so far no cumulative, predictive account.

WORK AND SOCIETY: A MATTER OF MORAL EVALUATIONS

Socioeconomics does not hesitate to recognize the moral issues raised by social analysis, a pivotal issue in the study of work. That is, moral issues are not a segregated matter, another division like a Sunday religion. They are an integral part of social life and hence central to the study of human conduct and institutions.

The point was first driven home to me when, as a poor fifteen-year-old kid, I worked as a part-time plumber's assistant. The work was hard (largely carrying metal pipes) and the plumber's demeanor was not loving, to put it mildly. At the time I had read *The Razor's Edge* by Somerset Maugham, about Larry, the son of an affluent family and a World War I pilot. Shocked by the war, he lingered somewhere between a nervous breakdown and psychosis, finding himself lost in peace time. His family was increasingly dismayed that he did not go out and find a job. I had a hard time understanding why the rich were so anxious for him to go to work.

Socioeconomics provides answers to this question—work is, in part, a moral undertaking. Different societies and cultures put different moral valuations on work. To draw on well-known examples, in ancient Greece and Rome and during the Middle Ages, Larry would not have been troubled. Work, especially manual work, was a matter for slaves and serfs and peasants. Free persons, not to mention privileged citizens, were engaged in different pursuits, at least if they sought the moral acceptance of their peers and community. These pursuits ranged from an active civic life to cultural activities, from making war to courtship.

With the onset of modernity in the West, the moral standing of work has changed,though unevenly. Not all classes, ethnic groups and subcultures evaluate work in the same way. As Max Weber already established, some cultures accord work a much higher moral value than others. Weber attributed the differences in secular moral evaluations of work and with it achievement, self-discipline, saving, and wealth to differences in religion. This conclusion generated an enormous debate that remains unsettled. The most recent version of it is found in efforts to explain differences among various immigrant groups and minorities, especially black Americans, regarding work (and welfare) (Steele 1990; Williams 1990; Applebome 1990: Nicholson 1990). Progress in socioeconomics will require clearer answers to these questions; what causes differences in work orientation and achievements—subculture, a psychology of victimization, or lack of opportunities—and what are the effects of past and present discrimination on work habits and attitudes?

THE DIVISION OF WORK WITHIN THE FAMILY

Neoclassical economists long treated the family as a unitary structure, making decisions unanimously (e.g., what to purchase) and in effect reflecting the decisions of the breadwinner, who was, historically in the modern West, simply assumed to be the male. As a result, male preferences and family choices were often treated as one and the same.

To the extent that neoclassical economics turned to study the family internally, under the influence of Becker (1974) and others, it has treated the family as a marketplace in which two autonomous individuals exchanged income for services (typically, the husband's income for the wife's services). Becker writes that "the time of different family members is their primary scarce resource", (317) and the sexual division of the labor force can therefore be described as the efficient allocation of each family member's time. Men, particularly white married men, earn more than married women in the labor force and "through the usual substitution effects, [this would] induce a family to use less of the first member's [the husband's] time in home production and more of the second member's [the wife's] time"(318). According to Becker, married people would not seek to trade roles because as each accumulates "human capital" in his or her respective sector, he or she becomes increasingly productive in that sector and it is in the family's interest to maximize productivity.

In recent years a significant body of literature on this topic arose under the influence of the feminist movement and women's studies. No attempt is being made here to review this literature, but I wish to flag the importance of some of its conclusions for the issues at hand. First, the literature highlighted a major general socioeconomic thesis: *there are no transactions among equals* (Etzioni 1988: 82). Husbands did not simply trade some of their income for their wives services but did so in terms that reflected the husbands' superior power, as established in law and the marketplace well into the 1950s and 1960s and in some ways still today. Husbands had more control of the use of assets, credits, and ownership than did their wives. The exchange was on terms highly favorable to the husbands (as indicated by the costs of the same services outside the household). Virginia Woolf wrote in 1938, which remained true for years, that the wife's "spiritual right to a share of half her husband's income peters out in practice to an actual right to board, lodging and a small annual allowance for pocket money and dress" (56). Today feminist theorists claim that the concept of "the family" masks inequities and antagonistic interests including the relative poverty of the wives (since they still are often dependent on their husbands' wages), the contribution of domestic labor in maintaining the work force, and the unequal distribution of occupations and goods within the family (Hartmann 1981; Hochschild 1989). And, when the family broke up, the husbands used to—and still do, although to a lesser extent—receive a disproportional share of the family assets. Finally, to the extent that work outside the household provided more power, prestige, and opportunities for self-expression than in the household, husbands did, and to some extent still do, have a strong advantage. This picture of structured exchange among the powerful and the weak, rather than unstructured, open, and among equals, should be kept in mind because it is found in all other parts of the economy. Whether it is in the relations among oil companies and the owners of gas stations, auto manufacturers and car dealers, large versus small manufacturers and supermarkets (which are forced to keep shelf space for the larger producers), and so on.

Second, studies of the family hint at the merit of recognizing "I" and "We" zones. That is, families are not well-conceived as bundles of individuals transacting, as equals or not. Families are best viewed as having a zone of shared identities, commitments, and interests, "We" zones, as well as those of two or more individuals. Thus, while some purchases are clearly designated for the husband (say, his ties) and for the wife (say, her makeup), others are shared (purchases for infants). Families differ significantly in the extent of the We vs. I zones. If the We zone is meager, the family may be on the verge of disintegrating. If the We-ness zone is very extensive, the needs of the weaker members are likely to be neglected. It is here that the two ideas combine: the We zone as well as the relations among the I zones is structured, reflecting the relative power of the members as well as the values they hold and share.

To reiterate: the preceding discussion provides only an outline of ideas and agents for a socioeconomics of work; most of the work in this area remains to be done.

ACKNOWLEDGMENT

The author is indebted to Suzanne Goldstein, Cathy Milton, and Sharon Pressner for research assistance.

REFERENCES

Applebome, Peter
1990   At the heart of anguish on getting past racism. The *New York Times*, April 30, 1990. pp. A18.

Arent, Hannah
1958   *The Human Condition*. Chicago: The University of Chicago Press.

Baker, George P., Jensen, Michael C., and Kevin J. Murphy
1988   Compensation and incentives: practice vs. theory. *Journal of Finance*. 43(3): pp. 593–616.

Baker, Sally Hillsman, Amitai Etzioni, Richard A. Hanson, and Marvin Sontag
1973   Tolerance for bureaucratic structure: Theory and measurement. *Human Relations*. 26(6): 775–86.

Becker, Gary
1974   Is economics theory with it?: On the relevance of the new economics of the family. *American Economic Association*. 64(2): 317–9.

Coughlin, Richard M. (ed.)
1991   *Morality, Rationality, and Efficiency: New Perspectives on Socio-Economics 1990*. New York: M. E. Sharpe.

Etzioni, Amitai
1988   *The Moral Dimension*. New York: Free Press.

Etzioni, Amitai, and Paul Lawrence (eds.)
1990   *Socio-Economics: Toward A New Synthesis*. New York: M. E. Sharpe.

Gamst, Frederick C.
1984   Considerations for an anthropology of work. In *Work in Non-Market and Transitional Societies*, Herbert Applebaum, ed., Albany: State University of New York Press, pp. 56–61.

Hartmann, Heidi I.
1981   The family as the locus of gender, class, and political struggle: The example of housework. *Signs: A Journal of Women in Culture and Society*, (6) spring: 366–94.

Herzberg, F., B. Mausner, and B. B. Snyderman
1959   *The Motivation to Work*. New York: John Wiley & Sons.

Hochschild, Arlie Russell
1989   *The Second Shift: Working Parents and the Revolution at Home.* New York: Viking Press.

Juster, F. Thomas
1986   Preferences for work and leisure. *Economic Outlook USA.* First Quarter, pp. 15–17.

Nicholson, David
1990   The American dilemma at century's end. *Washington Post Book World.* September 9, 1990. p. 1.

Steele, Shelby
1990   *The Content of Our Character: A New Vision of Race in America.* New York: St. Martin's Press.

Thurow, Lester C.
1983   *Dangerous Currents.* New York: Random House.

Williams, Patricia J.
1990   A kind of race fatigue. *New York Times Magazine.* September 16.

Woolf, Virginia
1938   *Three Guineas.* New York: Harcourt, Brace, and World Inc.

Contributors

HERBERT APPLEBAUM is the Director of Construction for Hartz Mountain Industries in New Jersey. Awarded the doctorate in anthropology from the State University of New York at Buffalo, he is the former editor of *Anthropology of Work Review*, the publication of the Society for the Anthropology of Work. His previous publications include *Royal Blue: The Culture of Construction Workers*; *Work in Non-Market Societies*; *Work in Market Societies*; and *Perspectives in Cultural Anthropology*. His latest book, published by SUNY Press, is *The Concept of Work, Ancient, Medieval, and Modern*.

MARIETTA L. BABA is Professor of Anthropology and Acting Chair of the Department of Anthropology at Wayne State University in Detroit, Michigan. She is a business and industrial anthropologist with research interests in the areas of technological innovation and organizational culture. Dr. Baba received her Ph.D. in physical anthropology in 1975 from Wayne State University. Her background includes nearly a decade of research in the field of molecular evolution (as an associate of Professor Morris Goodman, School of Medicine at Wayne State) and studies in primate ethology at the Yerkes Regional Primate Center. Dr. Baba's career is highlighted by funded research from the National Science Foundation, the state of Michigan (through the IPPRI program), and several industrial organizations. She also has served as consultant and advisor to major manufacturing and service corporations, labor unions, federal agencies, and state economic development organizations. Dr. Baba is past president of the National Association for the Practice of Anthropology (a unit of the American Anthropological Association, the AAA), and she has served as a member of the Executive Committee of the AAA's Board of Directors. Recently Dr. Baba was appointed Advisory Editor for Organizational Anthropology by the *American Anthropologist*. She also has been appointed to serve as one of two AAA delegates to the International Union of Anthropological and Ethnological Sciences.

IVAR BERG received his Ph.D. in sociology from Harvard University in 1960. He has served on the faculties of Columbia University, where he was Dean of the Faculties, 1969–71 and Vanderbilt University and is now Professor of Sociology at the University of Pennsylvania. One of his dozen books, *Education and Jobs: The Great Training Robbery* (1970) figured prominently in *Griggs vs. Duke Power Co.*, a landmark civil rights decision, handed down by the Supreme Court in 1972, and has continued to be an influential volume in the areas of human resources and labor economics.

JUDITH R. BLAU is Professor of Sociology at the University of North Carolina at Chapel Hill. She received her Ph.D. at Northwestern University. During the recent past she has published articles and monographs on the organization and ecology of contemporary culture. Her current research with Kenneth C. Land deals with historical analyses of religion and higher education, and she is completing a book on complex organizations.

AMITAI ETZIONI is a University Professor at the George Washington University, Washington, D.C. He received his doctorate in sociology from the University of California, Berkeley. He is currently the editor of *The Responsive Community*, a new journal that explores the balance between individual rights and community responsibilities. He is also the founder of the Society for the Advancement of Socio-Economics and the author of *The Moral Dimension* (New York: Free Press, 1988).

FREDERICK C. GAMST is Professor of Anthropology at the University of Massachusetts, Boston. He has thirty-nine years experience with the railroad industry (railroads, rail labor unions, and governmental agencies) as an operating employee, academic researcher, and professional consultant. He has researched railroads in Great Britain, Ethiopia, Eritrea, Germany, Canada, the Czech Republic, and the United States and has studied agrarians and foragers in the Horn of Africa (Ethiopia, Eritrea, Somalia, and Djibouti). Gamst has written over ninety articles, chapters, and notes; more than a hundred consulting reports and technical papers on the railroad industry; and numerous reviews and has been an expert witness or researcher for some thirty cases on the industry. His books and monographs include *Travel and Research in Northwestern Ethiopia* (1965), *The Qemant: A Pagan-Hebraic Peasantry of Ethiopia* (1969), *Peasants in Complex Society* (1974), *Studies in Cultural Anthropology* (1975), *Ideas of Culture: Sources and Uses* (1976), *The Hoghead: An Industrial Ethnology of the Locomotive Engineer* (1980), *Highballing with Flimsies: Working under Train Orders* (1990), and *The Internal Communications of the United States of North America by Franz Anton Ritter von Gerstner*, 2 vols. (in press).

WALTER GOLDSCHMIDT is Professor Emeritus of Anthropology at the University of California, Los Angeles, where he has taught since 1946. He has also held appointments in the Departments of Sociology and Psychiatry. He received his doctorate from the University of California, Berkeley, in 1942, after study at the University of Texas. Prior to coming to UCLA he was Social Science Analyst with the U.S. Department of Agriculture, for which he did rural research in California. His major ethnographic research has been on the Sebei of Uganda and as director of a multisociety study, the Culture and Ecology in East Africa Project. He has also studied the Nomlaki and Hupa Indians of California and the Tlingit of Southeastern Alaska.

Goldschmidt is a past president of the American Anthropological Association and the American Ethnological Society, was editor of the *American Anthropologist* and founding editor of *Ethos*. He is author of three theoretical treatises, *Man's Way, Comparative Functionalism*, and his recent *The Human Career*, which lies at the base of his contribution to this volume.

JUNE NASH is Distinguished Professor of Anthropology at the City College of the City University of New York. She has done fieldwork in a declining industrial city of Massachusetts and is now working in Chiapas, Mexico, where she undertook her first fieldwork in 1957. Her publications include *From Tank Town to High Tech: the Clash of Community and Industrial Cycles; Women, Men and the International Division of Labor* with M. Patricia Fernandez-Kelly; and *Crafts in the Global Market: the Impact of International Exchange on Middle American Artisans*.

ROBERT S. WEISS is Research Professor at the University of Massachusetts, Boston. He was awarded the doctorate in sociology at the University of Michigan. He has been concerned with issues of work and organizational behavior for three decades, beginning with his Ph.D. thesis, *Processes of Organization*. (Ann Arbor, MI: Survey Research Center, 1955.) His present study of retirement continues the examination of the careers of managers and professionals reported in *Staying the Course: The Emotional Life and Social Situation of Men who Do Well at Work*. (New York: Free Press, 1990.)

Index

A

Y

Z